INVISIBLE RAYS

THE HISTORY OF RADIOACTIVITY

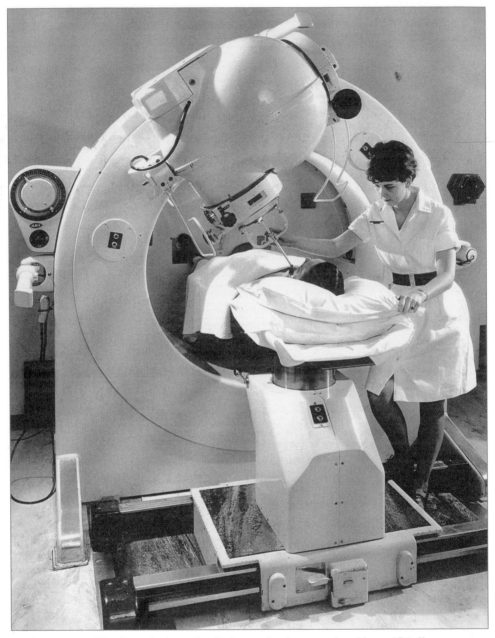

Radium was used in the early days of radiotherapy but it was replaced by artificially radioactive isotopes in the 1950s. This illustration shows a patient being treated by a cobalt-60 machine in 1968. (Nycomed–Amersham)

INVISIBLE RAYS
THE HISTORY OF RADIOACTIVITY
G. I. BROWN

SUTTON PUBLISHING

First published in the United Kingdom in 2002 by
Sutton Publishing Limited
Phoenix Mill · Thrupp · Stroud · Gloucestershire · GL5 2BU

British Library Cataloguing in Publication Data
A catalogue record for this book is available from the British Library

ISBN 0 7509 2667 8

Typeset in 11/15pt Ehrhardt.
Typesetting and origination by
Sutton Publishing Limited.
Printed and bound in England by
J.H. Haynes & Co. Ltd., Sparkford.

Contents

Preface		vii
Acknowledgements		viii
1	Cathode Rays	1
2	X-Rays, Radioactivity and the Electron	8
3	Pierre and Marie Curie	19
4	Lord Rutherford	39
5	Inside the Atom	51
6	Ten Sorts of Tin	61
7	Artificial Radioactivity	69
8	Early Uses	85
9	The Fission of Uranium	96
10	Hiroshima and Nagasaki	110
11	Aftermath	125
12	Atoms for Peace	139
13	Living with Radiation	152
14	Modern Uses	161
15	Nuclear Accidents	174
16	Problem Areas	193
17	What Next?	213
Appendices		
I	The Uranium and Actinium Decay Series	221
II	Einstein's Letter to President Roosevelt	222
III	World Nuclear Reactors	224
IV	Enriching Uranium	226
Notes		229
Bibliography		235
Selected Websites		237
Index		239

Preface

Few discoveries have had such a shattering effect on long-established scientific theories, and on all our lives, as those of X-rays, and the alpha-, beta- and gamma-rays associated with radioactive elements such as radium, towards the end of the nineteenth century. They were mysterious because they were invisible; they ushered in a new era in medicine; they paved the way for the elucidation of the structure of atoms; and they made possible the building of atomic bombs and nuclear power stations. But when it was found that exposure to them could severely damage human cells they came to be regarded by many as very sinister. A high dose could be immediately fatal, while lower doses could cause radiation sickness (with a possible lingering death being preceded by unpleasant symptoms such as nausea, diarrhoea, headache, hair loss, bleeding or anaemia); the onset of a variety of cancers; possible sterility; and genetic mutations that could lead to birth defects in future generations.

The human race has always been exposed to some degree of naturally occurring, invisible radiation, but increasing the amount by making more, as a consequence of building nuclear bombs and power stations, has caused much concern and a strong, international anti-nuclear lobby has contributed to much passionate controversy around the world. Many people have an instinctive fear of radiation, which they can neither see nor feel, yet which they know to be inherently harmful, and the slow political progress made in controlling the proliferation of nuclear weapons, together with a series of disastrous accidents in nuclear power plants, has done little to increase their confidence.

This book traces the history of invisible rays from 1789 to the present day; it explains the major discoveries and concepts involved, and highlights the lives of the remarkable band of scientists who did the pioneering work; it also describes the many beneficial uses, and draws attention to some of the associated hazards and problems.

Vital decisions will soon have to be taken, particularly in countries such as Britain and the United States where no nuclear plants have been built in recent years, about the future of nuclear power and the disposal of radioactive waste. This book will help the reader to judge the background against which such decisions have to be made.

Acknowledgements

I would like to thank the following organisations and individuals for their help in providing information and/or illustrations:

Association Curie et Joliot-Curie; ADAC Laboratories Ltd; AMEC Border Wind; Amersham Pharmacia Biotech UK Limited; Argonne National Laboratories; The Association for Science Education; BNFL; The British Institute of Radiology; The Cavendish Laboratory, Cambridge (Keith Papworth); Clarks; CND; The College of Arms; DETR; Deutsches Röntgen-Museum; Dicon Safety Products (UK) Ltd; Elekta Oncology Systems Ltd; Ernest Orlando Lawrence Berkeley National Laboratory; Food Standards Agency; Ford Motor Company; Glasgow University; ICI; Isotron plc; Los Alamos National Laboratory; Nucletron UK Ltd; Nycomed-Amersham plc (Ed Lorch); Peter Harper; The Pugwash Conferences on Science and World Affairs; Scottish Environment Protection Agency; Swiss Association for Atomic Energy; United Kingdom Atomic Energy Association (Nick Hance); United Kingdom Nirex Ltd (Dr Ian Crossland).

I am also grateful, once again, to my wife for her patience and constant encouragement and help.

CHAPTER 1
Cathode Rays

The history of radioactivity began, peacefully enough, in 1789, when a mineral called pitchblende was analysed by Martin Heinrich Klaproth. He was born at Wernigerode, in Germany, on 1 December 1743, and wanted to study theology but the family could ill-afford the expense because they had lost all their possessions in a great fire when Martin was only 8 years old. So he decided, when he was 15, to take up an apprenticeship with an apothecary and this led him into a distinguished career during which he founded, almost single-handed, the new science of analytical chemistry. When he began his life's work almost nothing was known about the true composition of any single mineral; by the time of his death, he had himself analysed over 200 different samples, working out the methods of doing it as he went along. His collected works, *Contributions to the Chemical Knowledge of Mineral Bodies*, ran to six volumes and many of the techniques that he pioneered and described are still in use today.

His achievements were rewarded when he was appointed as the first Professor of Chemistry at the newly founded University of Berlin in 1810. A year later he received the Order of the Red Eagle from the King of Prussia. He died on 1 January 1817.

One of the many minerals he studied came from a mine at Jáchymov in the Joachimsthal

Martin Heinrich Klaproth.

Eugène Peligot.

district of Bohemia and was called pitchblende. The mine had been opened in 1518 to provide silver for making local coins called Joachimsthalers, which had become the unit of currency – the Thaler – all over central Europe by the seventeenth century. Pitchblende was at first thought to contain ores of zinc and iron, but Klaproth disproved that and extracted a black powder from it, which he took to be a new element. 'Up till now', he wrote in 1789, 'seventeen individual metals have been recognised. I now propose to increase this number by adding a new one.'[1] William Herschel had discovered the planet Uranus in 1781 and Klaproth chose the name Uranium for his supposed new element.

No one doubted his discovery until fifty years later, in 1841, when the Frenchman Eugène-Melchior Peligot, who was Professor of Analytical Chemistry at the Central School of Arts and Manufactures for thirty-five years, proved that Klaproth's black powder was, in fact, not uranium but uranium oxide. It was therefore Peligot who actually first made pure uranium, though he tends, somewhat unfairly, to get less credit than Klaproth. Perhaps the latter's write-up by some contemporary historians as a paragon of all virtues has something to do with it. One such described Klaproth as 'incorruptible, true, honourable, good, modest, benevolent and pleasant . . . he was neither selfish, ambitious, avaricious, slighting, contemptuous, vainglorious or boasting . . . and to all that may be added a true religious feeling, so uncommon among men of science of his day'.[2] Poor Peligot. His life, 'always calm and methodical, was entirely consecrated to the science that he loved with passion and to his family that he cherished no less'.[3]

In accordance with the accepted views of the day, the new element was thought to be made up of atoms of uranium, which, like those of any other element, were regarded as indestructible, indivisible, minute particles. Next to nothing was known about any atoms, but John Dalton, the originator of the atomic theory in

1808, had laid great stress on the supposition that different elements had atoms of different mass. At the time it was not possible to ascertain the actual mass of anything so small as a single atom but, by using much chemical ingenuity, it did become possible to measure their *relative* masses. This was done on the arbitrary basis of allotting the smallest atom, that of hydrogen, a relative atomic mass of 1.

The value of the relative atomic mass of uranium eventually turned out to be 238. That is, one atom of uranium was 238 times heavier than one atom of hydrogen. The value was of some significance because it showed that the uranium atom was the heaviest atom yet discovered, but that revelation did not cause any great excitement because the element seemed to be of only theoretical interest. The only known use for one of its compounds was in colouring glass, and almost a hundred years had to pass before uranium hit the headlines.

There was, however, one contemporary research project associated with uranium that did, later, prove to be very important. In 1838 a Chair of Physics had been established in association with the Natural History Museum in Paris, and the first professor was Antoine-César Becquerel, who had already built up a good reputation for his work on a number of varied electrical topics. A year after taking up his new office he turned his attention to the phenomena of fluorescence and phosphorescence. When he retired in 1878, he was succeeded by his son Edmond, who continued in the family tradition by spending much of his time in preparing and studying new fluorescent and phosphorescent materials. Some crystals of potassium uranium sulphate that he made were of particular importance because they played a central role in the discovery of radioactivity by his own son Henri in 1896.

While Edmond Becquerel was busy making his crystals, a number of other scientists were investigating the effects of passing electricity through gases at low pressures. Such a line of research became possible because improvements in the design of suction pumps, notably by the German glass-blower Heinrich Geissler in 1855, had made it relatively easy to keep gases in a container under very low pressures. The experiments were carried out in glass tubes sealed at both ends. The pressure of the air, or any other gas, inside the tube could be lowered by attaching a suction pump to a side-arm leading out of the middle of the tube, and an electric current could be led through the gas via metal conductors fitted into the tube at both ends. The conductors were

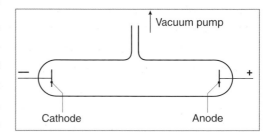

A discharge or Geissler tube.

called electrodes. That through which the current entered the tube was called the cathode; the other was the anode. The tube was referred to as a vacuum or discharge tube or, sometimes, a Geissler tube. A modified and modernised version can be seen in any strip-lighting tube.

Even with an electricity supply as high as 10,000 volts the current that passes through air in the tube is very small so long as the air is at normal atmospheric pressure. But, as the air is gradually pumped out of the tube, the current increases. At first a rather furry-looking spark appears, and this is followed, as the air pressure is reduced still further, by a beautiful glow that fills all the tube apart from two dark regions towards the cathode end. With a further lowering of the pressure, the whole tube becomes filled with a dark space and the glass of the tube fluoresces in a colour that depends on the type of glass. Very much the same series of changes takes place with gases other than air in the tube but a range of different colours is involved. The phenomena were first described by William Watson in 1748. 'It was', he wrote, 'a most delightful spectacle when the room was darkened, to see the electricity in its passage: to be able to observe not, as in the open air, its brushes or pencils or rays an inch or two in length, but here the coruscations were of the whole length of the tube between the electrodes, that is to say, 80cm.'[4] And in 1882 one of the early experimenters, the German physicist Heinrich Hertz, who was the Professor of Physics at Karslruhe Technical College and who discovered radio waves in 1888, wrote that 'the gases perform the maddest antics under the influence of discharges and produce the strangest, most varied, and most colourful phenomena. My place now really looks very much like a witch's kitchen.'[5]

An explanation of these mysterious and odd phenomena only came about very slowly, between 1858 and 1900, as a result of experiments carried out in Germany by Julius Plücker and his student Wilhelm Hittorf, and some ten years later by Sir William Crookes in England. First Plücker observed, in 1858, that the glow in a discharge tube could be deflected by a strong magnetic field. Then Hittorf took over. Born in Bonn in 1824, the son of a merchant, he was educated in his native town and in Berlin. His main interest at first was mathematics but he soon turned his attention to physics and chemistry and began to teach and do research at Bonn University and, later, at the Academy in Münster. His paper 'On the Conduction of Electricity by Gases' was published in 1869. In it he reported that placing a thick metallic shape between the cathode and the anode within a discharge tube caused a shadow of the shape to be cast when a current was passed through the tube with the gas at low pressure. The position of the shadow suggested that some kind of rays, which travelled in straight lines, must be coming out of the cathode. As there was no fluorescence in the glass within the area of the shadow, he concluded that the rays must be causing the fluorescence.

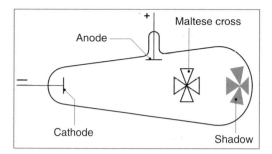

Cathode rays casting a shadow in a Crookes tube.

These were, at the time, quite remarkable revelations but they were not received with widespread acclaim and did not have any great impact on contemporary scientists. Perhaps that was because no one had any idea what the rays might be; perhaps Hittorf was 'ahead of the times' and too few were prepared to follow him into unknown territory; perhaps he was too unfashionable and too little of a publicist. He was certainly a very thorough and careful experimenter but he was a reserved and shy bachelor, lacking any obvious signs of enthusiasm, imagination or ambition. He spent almost all his working life at Münster without receiving any offers of promotion, and he was old by the time some belated honours did come his way. He retired at the age of 65 and lived out the rest of his life being looked after by his younger sister. He died in 1914, aged 90.

William Crookes, eight years older than Hittorf, was an entirely different sort of person. He was born in London in 1832, the son of a Regent Street tailor who had twenty-one children, five by his first wife and sixteen by his second. Crookes was educated first at the Grammar School in Chippenham, Wiltshire, and later at the Royal College of Chemistry. The latter institution had been founded in 1845 on the recommendation of a committee appointed with the purpose of trying to improve chemical education in England. It was chaired by Prince Albert and its first director was the famous German chemist and educationalist A.W. Hofmann. On completing his studies, Crookes acted as an assistant to Hofmann before going on to work in the meteorological department of the Radcliffe Observatory in Oxford and later as a lecturer in the Chester College of Science. He returned to London in 1856, and three years later founded *The Chemical News*, of which he was the proprietor and editor for almost half a century.

Crookes was like Hittorf in as much as he was a meticulous and skilful experimenter, but he had a much wider vision, many more interests and a far greater influence on contemporary scientific thought. One commentator describes him as 'a savant, who ornaments any company and whose life work is an inspiration for the present generation and the generations of men of science to come'.[6] He discovered a new element, thallium, in 1861, and measured its relative atomic mass in 1873; he

A drawing of Sir William Crookes by Robert Austin RA. (ICI)

also applied his scientific mind to electric lighting, beet sugar, diamonds, safety glass, sanitation and world food problems; he wrote many books; and following the death from yellow fever of a younger brother in 1867, he developed a passionate interest in psychic phenomena and spiritualism. The high offices he held included the Presidencies of the Society for Psychical Research, the British Association for the Advancement of Science and the Royal Society. He was knighted in 1897, became a member of the Order of Merit in 1910, and died on 4 April 1919.

Crookes used some extremely well-designed, pear-shaped discharge tubes, made by his laboratory assistant Charles H. Gimingham and widely known as Crookes tubes, to confirm and extend Hittorf's observations. In particular, he found that a miniature paddle-wheel, freely suspended between the electrodes within a discharge tube, rotated when a current was passed through the tube. This suggested that the rays emanating from the cathode – christened 'cathode rays' by Eugen Goldstein in 1876 – must consist of some sort of particle and could not be like rays of light. But another German, Heinrich Hertz, had shown that the rays would pass through thin metal foils so that, if they did consist of particles, they must be extremely small ones.

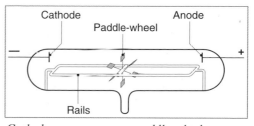

Cathode rays can rotate a paddle-wheel.

It was all very mysterious, with the particulate nature of the rays being strongly supported in Great Britain and the wave nature preferred in Germany. Crookes summarised his own rather vague conclusions in 1879 in a paper entitled 'Radiant matter; or the fourth state of aggregation'. In outline, he concluded that the cathode rays consisted of a beam of molecules. The beam had peculiar characteristics, he thought, because the space within a Crookes tube was occupied by a fourth state of matter, which was neither solid, liquid nor gas. 'The phenomena in these exhausted tubes', he wrote, 'reveal to physical science a new world . . . where we can never enter, and with which we must be content to observe and experiment from the outside.'[7]

It was a bold and imaginative hypothesis but it was too vague to carry much authority or to do much to answer the basic questions about the nature of the cathode rays. That answer only came some twenty years later, towards the end of the nineteenth century, when the secrets of Crookes's 'new world' were revealed through Wilhelm Röntgen's discovery of X-rays, Henri Becquerel's discovery of radioactivity and Sir J.J. Thomson's extension of the investigations begun by Hittorf and Crookes, which led to the discovery of the electron.

CHAPTER 2

X-rays, Radioactivity and the Electron

A number of scientists had noticed that unused packets of photographic plates, still in their original wrappers, were liable to become fogged if they were in the vicinity of a Crookes tube when it was switched on. It is said, in fact, that Crookes himself had complained to the Ilford company which supplied his photographic material that they had sold him faulty plates. With hindsight, it is easy to suggest that any of these scientists could have discovered X-rays if they had considered more carefully what might be causing the fogging. As it was, the discovery was left to a not very well-known German professor, Wilhelm Conrad Röntgen. It was perhaps a matter of better luck rather than greater perspicacity.

Röntgen turned his attention to the study of cathode rays in 1894 and he made his first major discovery on 8 November the following year. In order to obtain a narrow beam of cathode rays he was working with a Crookes tube that was almost completely surrounded by thick, black cardboard. He was also using pieces of paper coated with a strongly

Röntgen demonstrating the use of X-rays. (Published in The Windsor Magazine, *April 1896)*

fluorescent substance, barium platinocyanide, to detect the position of the beam. By chance, one of the pieces of coated paper had been left on the bench alongside the Crookes tube and, when Rontgen came to use the tube in the dark, he was surprised to see some fluorescence on the paper. It disappeared when the tube was switched off. He knew that cathode rays could not penetrate through air to any great extent, and as there were no light rays in the darkened room he concluded that some new type of emanation must somehow be coming from the tube. 'For brevity's sake,' he wrote, 'I shall use the expression "rays"; and to distinguish them from others of this name I shall call them X-rays.'[1]

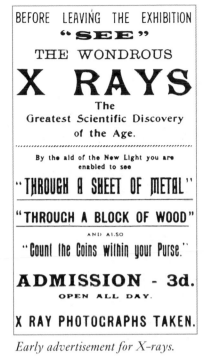

Early advertisement for X-rays.

His discovery seemed so astonishing that he could scarcely believe it, so he spent the next few weeks in a thorough re-examination of what he had done before publishing his findings on 28 December 1885 in a paper entitled 'On a New Kind of Rays'. His unexpected and sensational revelations were greeted with immense excitement all over the world, and in 1896 there were almost a thousand papers on X-rays and nearly fifty books. Röntgen wrote to a friend that 'All hell broke loose'[2] and when he was asked 'What did you think about it all?', he replied 'I didn't think, I investigated.'[3]

He had found that X-rays travelled in straight lines and could produce shadows; that they fogged unwrapped photographic plates; that they could not be deflected by a magnet; and that a gas through which the rays were passed would conduct electricity. But most surprisingly he had found that they were extremely penetrating, though the extent of the penetration depended on the nature of the material used and its thickness. The fact that the X-rays would pass through human flesh more readily than through human bones had enabled him to take the world's first X-ray photograph on 22 December 1895. It showed the skeleton of his wife's hand and, also, that she was wearing two rings on one of her fingers.

Röntgen suggested that the X-rays were produced by the bombardment of the glass in the Crookes tube by the cathode rays, and he found that they were produced even more effectively when cathode rays bombarded the surface of a metal rather than glass. This is how the rays are produced nowadays in commercial X-ray machines. Röntgen was not, however, sure about the nature of the X-rays and it was not until 1912 that they were shown to be like ultra-violet rays but with a very, very much smaller wave-length.

Röntgen was born in Lennep, near Düsselfdorf in Germany on 27 March 1845. As his mother was Dutch, he spent much of his youth in Holland and had his early education in Utrecht. Later he went to the Federal Institute of Technology in Zurich, Switzerland, where he graduated in mechanical engineering in 1866 and was granted a doctorate for research into gases in 1869. This led to a variety of university posts culminating in professorships in Physics first at Würzburg University (1888–1900) and then at Munich University (1900–20). He did research in many areas of physics and the three papers he published on X-rays, in his early fifties, are greatly outnumbered by the fifty-three he published in other fields.

His main non-scientific interests were in country pursuits such as hunting, shooting, climbing and walking, and these suited his generally introvert nature, which stemmed from an extreme shyness. He shunned the world-wide publicity that his discovery generated, and he never tried to patent anything to do with X-rays or to seek any financial gain from their commercial development. When he was granted the first-ever Nobel Prize for Physics, in 1901, he gave the money attached to it to Würzburg University to be used for the advancement of science.

Unfortunately, the latter years of his life were not very happy. In common with others he suffered some ill-health as a result of over-exposure to X-rays, a danger that was not recognised in the early days. Moreover, the value of his savings was greatly diminished by the currency inflation that struck Germany after the First World War, and his wife, to whom he had been married for forty-seven years, died in 1919 after a long illness. A life-long friend wrote: 'His outstanding character was his absolute integrity. He was in every sense the embodiment of the ideals of the nineteenth century; strong, honest and powerful, devoted to his science and never doubting its value; in spite of self-criticism and great humour, perhaps endowed with some unconscious pathos; of a really rare faithfulness and sense of sacrifice for people, memories and ideals . . . but open-minded in his acceptance of new ideas.'[4] He died on 10 February 1923.

* * *

Antoine Henri Becquerel, the son of Alexander Edmond and the grandson of Antoine-César, was born in Paris on 15 December 1852. He received his secondary education, in science and engineering, at the École Polytechnique and the École des Ponts et Chaussées. In 1876, at the age of 23, he began to teach and do research at the École Polytechnique, moving in 1878 to the Natural History

Henri Becquerel in his laboratory. (Archives Curie and Joliot-Curie)

Museum of Paris, where he eventually succeeded his father as professor. His original research projects were in the field of optics, but he maintained an interest in the work begun by his father and grandfather on fluorescence and phosphorescence, and this came to the fore when he learnt of Röntgen's discovery of X-rays. The source of the X-rays from a Crookes tube appeared to be the fluorescent glass of the tube, and this led Becquerel, and others, to think that other fluorescent sources might produce X-rays. A fellow Frenchman, Henri Poincaré, wrote: 'It may not be very probable, but it is possible, and doubtless easy enough to verify.'[5] So Becquerel set out to do just that.

His method was simple. He placed a fluorescent or phosphorescent substance on top of a photographic plate wrapped in black paper, and caused the substance to fluoresce or phosphoresce by exposure to ultra-violet light or by some other means. If the substance did emit any X-rays under these conditions the plate would be affected. At first, using a number of different substances, there were no unusual signs on the plates when they were developed. But everything changed, quite dramatically, when he decided to use some crystals of potassium uranium sulphate that his father had made some years previously. At the start of the last week in

February 1896, he put two of these crystals on top of a photographic plate and placed a silver coin underneath one of them. He then exposed the whole assembly to strong sunlight for some hours. When he developed the plate he saw the silhouette of the crystals and the shadow of the coin, and he thought that the fluorescent crystals must have emitted X-rays. But within a week he had to change his mind.

On 26 and 27 February he made up some more similar assemblies of potassium uranium sulphate crystals and photographic plates, but poor weather meant they could only be exposed to very little sunlight so he put them on one side in a dark drawer in a cabinet. The sun did not shine for the next two days and the assemblies remained in the dark until Becquerel, tired of waiting, developed the plates on 1 March. He expected to find only very feeble images because the crystals had been exposed to very little sunlight, but much to his surprise he found that the silhouettes were extremely clear. And in next to no time he had found that they were just as clear if the crystals were not exposed to any sun at all or even if he used different uranium compounds that were not fluorescent. The idea that fluorescence and X-rays were connected had to be abandoned. The uranium compounds must be emitting some penetrating radiation from within themselves. Henri did not know what the radiation was (that only became clear at the start of the next century) but he did discover that a gas through which it was passed would conduct electricity, so it had something in common with X-rays.

Becquerel received world-wide acclaim for his discovery of what came to be known as radioactivity. He became a foreign member of the Royal Society of Great Britain, and of the Academies of Science in Berlin, Rome and Washington, and he shared the Nobel Prize for Physics in 1903. In his own country, he was appointed President of the Académie des Sciences in 1908, but he did not enjoy that honour for long because he died very suddenly of a heart attack, at the age of 55, on 25 August that year. He always played down his role in the discoveries he had made, claiming that it was more of a family affair. 'These discoveries', he wrote, 'are only the lineal descendants of those of my father and grandfather on phosphorescence and without them my own discoveries would have been impossible.'[6] The family continued to do him proud when his own son, Jean, followed him as professor at the Natural History Museum. Can there be any other example of the same family holding the same important, scientific and academic post for four generations?

* * *

The discoveries of X-rays and radioactivity were both remarkable and unexpected but at the time they were not fully understood, so they joined cathode rays in the category of 'unsolved mysteries of science'. Unravelling the mysteries was a lengthy process, but an important step forward came in 1895, when the Frenchman Jean Perrin, who won the Nobel Prize for Physics in 1925, built a Crookes tube with an electric charge collector inside it which was connected to an external electrometer. When he directed a beam of cathode rays into the collector he found that the electrometer recorded a negative electric charge, but when he deflected the rays away from the collector, using a magnetic field, the electrometer recorded no charge. This was followed in 1897 by one of the all-time great experiments in physics, carried out by Sir J.J. Thomson in the old Cavendish Laboratory at Cambridge University, which led him to conclude that cathode rays consisted of a stream of minute, negatively charged particles.

Thomson was able to measure the velocity of the particles, and the ratio of their charge to their mass, which is written symbolically as e/m, by using a specially designed discharge tube in which the cathode rays could be concentrated into a narrow beam by passing them through two parallel slits. The position of the beam could be picked up by the fluorescence it caused at the end of the tube, and the beam could be deflected by passing it through either a magnetic or an electrical field. Alternatively, the two fields could be applied together. The electrical field was provided by applying a voltage between two parallel, metallic plates positioned within the tube; the magnetic field came from an electromagnet which consisted of two coils of wire outside the tube, in the vicinity of the parallel plates, through which a current could be passed. By having the electric and magnetic fields at right angles to each other the deflections they caused were in opposite directions.

The extent of the deflection depended on the velocity of the particles and on their mass (m) and their electrical charge (e). Application of the electrical field moved the fluorescent spot at the end of the tube away from its central position but it could be restored to that position by applying the magnetic field. By measuring the strengths of the two fields which were required to cancel each other out, it was possible to calculate the velocity of the particles and, once this was known, the e/m ratio for the particles could be obtained by measuring the deflection caused by either the electrical

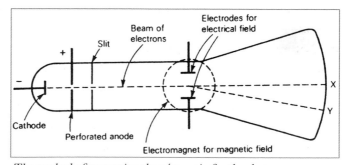

The method of measuring the e/m *ratio for the electron.*

The frontage of the old Cavendish Laboratory in Cambridge. (Cavendish Laboratory)

or magnetic field alone. Thomson found that this ratio was always the same irrespective of the type of gas within the discharge tube or the type of metal from which the electrodes were made. He concluded, in 1897, that cathode rays consisted of 'negatively charged electricity carried by particles of matter' and

Thomson's apparatus for measuring the e/m *ratio. (Cavendish Laboratory)*

that 'this matter was the substance from which all the chemical elements are made up'.[7] These particles came to be known as electrons, though the word had been used in a rather different sense as early as 1881.

The next step was to measure the electrical charge on an individual electron. Thomson did this, somewhat inaccurately, in 1898, but a much more accurate value was obtained in a classical experiment carried out by Professor Robert Millikan at the University of Chicago in 1909. Taking the charge value and the charge-to-mass ratio value together, it transpired, surprisingly, that the mass of the electron was only about 0.000,000,000,000,000,000,000,000,000,09 kg. It was almost two thousand times lighter than the hydrogen atom, which had previously been regarded as the lightest known particle.

Nothing so small could ever have had a bigger future. The electron has been at the centre of many scientific developments and many aspects of everyday life ever since it was discovered. Thomson had suggested in 1897 that it was probably a component part of all matter and he was right, even though some of his contemporaries thought he was pulling their legs. It also soon became clear that an electric current was simply a movement of electrons. When a 100 watt electric light-bulb is switched on, the current that passes represents a flow of approximately 2,800,000,000,000,000,000 electrons per second. And a television picture is built up by the organised bombardment of the screen by a beam of electrons.

* * *

Joseph John Thomson was born in Manchester on 18 December 1856. His father was a publisher and antiquarian bookseller and it was his original intention to pay for his son to serve an apprenticeship with a local firm of locomotive

Extract from a draft account of the discovery of the electron, written by J.J. Thomson.
(Cavendish Laboratory)

manufacturers when he left school at the age of 14. As there was no immediate vacancy available, the young Thomson went to Owens College, which later became Manchester University, to pass the time. When his father died, aged 38, in 1872, the family realised that they would be unable to pay for any apprenticeship, so he decided to continue his studies. The railway's loss was to be science's gain, because while at Owens College he was advised to try for an Open Scholarship at Cambridge University. It must give hope to all aspiring candidates that he failed at his first attempt but he was in the end successful and he entered Trinity College in 1876 when he was nearly 20.

He arrived only two years after the completion of a new physics laboratory at Cambridge, built at a cost of £8,450 and paid for by the generosity of the Duke of Devonshire, who was Chancellor of the University. It was called the Cavendish Laboratory after Henry Cavendish, a kinsman of the duke, who had been a successful if somewhat eccentric experimental scientist in the eighteenth century. At the tender age of 28, Thomson found himself in charge of this laboratory, having succeeded to the Cavendish Professorship of Experimental Physics, following in the footsteps of the great Clerk Maxwell and Lord Rayleigh. 'I felt', he wrote, 'like a fisherman with light tackle who had casually cast a line in an unlikely spot and hooked a fish much too heavy for him to land.'[8] At the time it was probably the most distinguished post of its kind in the world and Thomson made it even more so by building up an internationally renowned school of physics, working mainly in the field of atomic structure.

Thomson was of medium stature and with his droopy, scraggy moustache and shuffling gait he was, to all outward appearances, the epitome of an absent-minded professor. His son George saw him as 'a much loved but inscrutable Jove, mostly in the Olympian clouds of his own thoughts'.[9] But beneath that caricature there was an outstanding personality, a great

Drawing of Sir J.J. Thomson by Tom Purvis. (ICI)

intellect and a brilliant expositor. Yet he was very friendly and human. He had plenty of shrewd common sense, a boyish sense of humour, a passion for sporting activities (one friend referred to him as a walking Wisden), a love of flowers and a lively interest in other people which was greatly enhanced by his wife's strong support. He was affectionately known, throughout his time at Cambridge, as 'The Professor' or simply 'J.J.'

He was not renowned for his manipulative skill and it is said that his faithful assistant Ebenezer Everett used to like to keep him at a safe distance from any fragile apparatus. Yet one of his associates wrote: 'When a hitch occurred in a piece of apparatus, he would jot down a few figures and formulae in his tidy, tiny handwriting, on the back of someone's fellowship thesis, or an old envelope, or even the laboratory cheque book, and produce a luminous suggestion, like a rabbit out of a hat, not only revealing the cause of the trouble, but also the means of a cure.'[10] Such intuitive skills were certainly needed, because much of the apparatus used in the early days in the Cavendish Laboratory was not highly sophisticated. Indeed, one contemporary worker said that much of it was held together by 'string and sealing-wax', and that 'the theory of atomic structure was born in a tin can'.[11]

The midwives were a host of research students who streamed in to the Cavendish, attracted by Thomson's reputation, from all over the world; remarkably, seventy-five of them moved on to professorships in fifty-five different universities world-wide. Without exception, they found in 'J.J.' an inspiring father-figure for whom they came to have the greatest respect and affection. When he died, on 30 August 1940, his Nobel Prize, his knighthood and his Order of Merit went with him, but the loyalty and memories of those who had worked with him remained. They all paid their fulsome tributes. 'I cannot think of any other man who, in such measure, did so much intellectual good to so many others in his lifetime'[12] was typical.

He himself attributed whatever success he may have had to 'good parents, good teachers, good colleagues, good pupils, good friends, great opportunities, good luck and good health'.[13] His ashes were laid to rest in Westminster Abbey near the tombs of Isaac Newton, Charles Darwin, John Herschel, Lord Kelvin and Ernest Rutherford.

CHAPTER 3
Pierre and Marie Curie

When Pierre Curie married Marie Sklodowska on 26 July 1895 he said that he had found a wife 'made expressly for me to share all my preoccupations'.[1] And so it was to be. Pierre, aged 36 and regarded by most of his friends as a confirmed bachelor, worked at l'École de Physique et de Chimie in Paris, lecturing, supervising some thirty students, and trying to find time to do his own research. The school had been set up after the Franco-Prussian war as the French sought to improve their industrial and scientific standards. It was not a prestigious establishment and Pierre's pay was not much better than that of a factory worker. Nor were the facilities for research at all good. There was an ill-equipped laboratory but it had to be used mainly for teaching purposes so Pierre did most of his work in a narrow passageway. Later he moved into a glassed-in, lean-to room which also served as a store and a machine shop.

Pierre was not, however, ungrateful. He made the most of it and had already built up a very good reputation through his research on crystals and magnetism. In 1880, when he was only 21, he had discovered, in collaboration with his older brother Paul-Jacques, that flat plates cut with the proper orientation from some naturally occurring crystals, such as quartz, tourmaline and Rochelle salt, exhibited a small voltage across them when they were stressed by elongation or compression. Similarly, the plates underwent minute expansion or contraction in size when

Cartoon of Pierre and Marie Curie, originally published in Vanity Fair, and Marie's signature.

an external voltage was applied to them. The phenomenon came to be known as piezoelectricity and it is applied today, using specially synthesised ceramic materials based mainly on barium titanate, in making watches, microphones, gramophone pick-ups, gas lighters and other devices. The Curie brothers also used the piezoelectric effect to measure very small currents of the order of 50×10^{-12} amperes. They did this by opposing (bucking) the current to be measured by setting it against the voltage from a quartz crystal stressed by hanging a weight from it. The voltage was proportional to the weight, so that the weight needed to counterbalance the unknown current gave a measure of the current. This method played a central role in Marie's experiments fifteen years later.

Pierre's work was 'the dominant preoccupation' of his life and he attacked it with 'persevering effort and incessant labour'.[2] So relative poverty and cramped quarters were some of the things he could offer to share with Marie, along with his high ideals and a burning passion for scientific research. She was not put off. 'It would', she wrote to him, 'be a beautiful thing, in which I dare hardly believe, to pass through life together hypnotised in our dreams; your dream for your country; our dream for humanity and for science.'[3] Fortunately, Marie was no stranger to hardship. Born in Warsaw on 7 November 1867, the youngest of five children, she was christened Marya but was generally called Manya by her family. Her father was a teacher of physics and mathematics at a local school and her mother ran a private school for young girls. Her parents were proud, cultivated and intelligent, and they organised their family life on the basis of 'plain living and high thinking' but it was never easy because the people of Poland were dominated, even oppressed, by Russia. This provided an atmosphere of conflict which was particularly marked in the educational field.

The family began by living in the mother's school but when Manya was only a year old her father Vladislav accepted another teaching post, which at the time seemed a good idea. He became a deputy headmaster so he was entitled to be known as Professor Sklodowski and he was provided with an official flat into which he moved his family. This enabled his wife to give up her school which, as the family had grown, had become too much of a burden for her. Alas, everything began to go wrong. Manya's mother was stricken with tuberculosis and in 1873 her father was demoted by the Russian head of his school for supposed lack of cooperation in implementing Russian educational policies. His salary was reduced and the official flat was taken away from him. The family had to find alternative accommodation, and to pay for it Professor Sklodowski started to take in some of his pupils as boarders. Worse was to come. The eldest daughter, Zosia, died of typhus in 1876, Manya's mother died in 1878 and Professor Sklodowski lost most

The five Sklodowski(a) children. From left to right: Zosia, Hela, Manya, Jozio and Bronya. (Archives Curie and Joliot-Curie)

of the family's savings in a speculative business venture organised by his brother-in-law.

He had always intended to provide the best possible education for all his clever children but he now realised that they would have to fend for themselves and for one another. And they did just that. Joseph, the eldest, trained as a doctor at the University of Warsaw; Bronya, the eldest girl, followed him into that profession, but only after studying at the Sorbonne in Paris because the University of Warsaw was closed to girls; Hela, the least clever but the prettiest daughter, became a teacher; but Manya was to be the star.

She was only 11 years old when her mother died but she was doing brilliantly well at school, and already showing a scientific bent. Even so, when she completed her course, just before her sixteenth birthday, she had no very clear idea as to what she wanted to do so her father arranged for her to have a year's holiday in the country staying with friends and relatives. It was a wonderfully relaxing experience for her but when she returned to Warsaw she was confronted by the harsh, financial reality facing her family so she joined her brother and sisters in earning what money they could by offering private tuition. She soon realised, however, that her meagre pay was not going to swell the family coffers very much so, just before her eighteenth birthday, she advertised her services, through an employment agency, as a governess.

So it was that, on the very cold first day of January in 1886 she travelled, by train and sleigh, 100km north of Warsaw to work for a farming family. Both her employers and the work she had to do were very pleasant, and she had plenty of spare time in which to advance her own education by reading. 'Literature', she wrote, 'interested me as much as sociology and science, but, during those years of work, as I struggled to discover my true preferences, I finally turned towards mathematics and physics.'[4] All went well until Casimir, the student son of the family, came home for his holidays. Manya had been distinctly chubby when at school, but she had now blossomed into an attractive girl. She had a lovely complexion, fine hair, slender ankles, and deep-set, ashen-grey eyes. During her year in the country she had learnt to converse and dance and ride extremely well, and there was a wholesome, fresh, sensitive honesty about her. Above all, there was a tight-lipped mouth and a determined, even stubborn, look. Casimir fell for her, she for him, and they planned to marry. They had much in common, and she thought that his parents liked her. It was then a cruel blow when they let her know, in no uncertain terms, that the son of a wealthy family does not marry a governess.

Manya would have liked to put Casimir and all his family behind her and she expressed vague thoughts of suicide. She knew, however, that her own family needed the money she was earning and that it had already helped Bronya to begin her medical studies in Paris. So she stuck it out until, as the farmer's young children grew up, her services were no longer needed. Even then, she took another similar job, on the Baltic coast, for a further year, all the time sending money home and aiming to save enough to pay for her own further education.

The opportunity came in 1890. By then Bronya had completed her medical examinations in Paris, had married a 34-year-old Polish doctor, Casimir Dluski, and was about to have a baby. Appreciative of how much Manya had helped her, she suggested that she could now reverse the roles. 'You must make something of your life sometime,' she wrote. 'If you can save a few hundred roubles this year you can come to Paris next year and find board and lodging with us.'[5] Consequently Manya enrolled at the Sorbonne in 1891, and chose that auspicious moment to register not as Manya but as Marie Sklodowska, using the female 'ska' ending to her name.

Bronya and her husband had a flat in the rue d'Allemagne (now the Avenue Jean-Jaurès) and Marie was very happy there for some months. The flat was, however, not ideal for Marie. Casimir and Bronya used it as a surgery, and they led a somewhat hectic social life, which Marie found very distracting; worse, the tedious journey to the Sorbonne took an hour of her time and a lot of her money. So, regretfully, she decided to move into the Latin Quarter, closer to her work, and spent the next three years of her life in a variety of not very desirable lodgings. A servant's room in the attic of a six-floor building, with a small skylight, was typical. It was lit by a small oil lamp, water had to be carried from a tap on a nearby landing, cooking was over a minute alcohol heater, and any coal that could be afforded for the small stove had to be carried in a bucket up the six floors. Yet it cost Marie almost one-fifth of her income of around 100 francs per month, and she was left with less than 3 francs a day to pay for her food, clothes, books and university fees.

She could walk to the Sorbonne, and she could eke out her poor living by giving private lessons and by cleaning up in some of the laboratories; many other young students were in the same boat and she was in no mood to let her spartan existence interfere with the opportunity which had opened up for her. Nor did it. She was completely engrossed in her studies and by 1893 she had obtained her first degree in physics, coming top of her class. A year later she took a second degree in mathematics, finishing in second place, and was ready to move on to research.

She began with a project, sponsored by an industrial organisation, on the magnetic properties of steels, but her progress was hampered by the lack of equipment and laboratory space, so she asked for help from a Polish professor of physics who was then visiting Paris. What a stroke of fortune. It led to her first meeting with Pierre Curie, and straightaway, while discussing her work with him, she realised that 'his rather slow, reflective words, his simplicity, and his smile, at once grave and young, inspired confidence'.[6] That confidence took more than a year to grow to the stage where she felt able to accept him as her partner for life, but on 26 July 1895 Marie Sklodowska became Marie Curie in a simple civil marriage ceremony. She could not have known how famous a name it was to become.

They spent their honeymoon on a cycling tour of the Ile-de-France before settling down to married life in an uncomfortable, sparsely furnished three-roomed flat. Marie was allowed to work alongside Pierre but she was not paid so they had to rely on his salary, although this had recently been increased to 500 francs per month so their income did not worry them unduly. They were

Pierre and Marie in their garden at Sceaux during their honeymoon in 1895. (Archives Curie and Joliot-Curie)

blissfully happy, and all the more so when their first daughter Irène was born on 12 September 1897. It had been a difficult pregnancy for Marie but she carried on with as much research as she could manage, and within a few months of Irène's birth she produced her first scientific paper – a monograph on the magnetisation of steels.

What to do next? She was searching for a research project which would enable her, in due course, to produce a thesis which she could submit for a doctor's degree. It is perfectly possible to do research on almost any topic but it is exceedingly difficult to pick a fruitful one. So she turned to Pierre for advice. By chance, Henri Becquerel's discovery of radioactivity had been made in a nearby laboratory, so they knew all about it and they decided, between them, that this was a likely topic to pursue. It was exciting, virgin territory but only time would reveal what an inspired choice it was. Marie set out on her journey of exploration at the end of 1897 and within six years, either alone or in collaboration with Pierre, she had discovered radioactivity in thorium, had found the new element polonium, and had discovered and isolated radium. Becquerel might have discovered radioactivity but the Curies put it on the map. One contemporary scientist described her as 'first in the field, with the rest nowhere'.[7]

Marie's original idea was to see if she could find any signs of radioactivity in chemicals other than the uranium compounds that Becquerel had used. He had detected the invisible radiation by its effect on a photographic plate but the Curies replaced this by a much better electrical method. This depended on the fact, discovered by Becquerel, that air, normally a non-conductor of electricity, became conducting when X-rays, or radiation from radioactive substances, passed through it. Their detector, in which they measured the current, consisted of a pair of parallel, horizontal, circular metal plates mounted one above the other with air in between. The lower plate was connected to a battery and then to the ground, while the upper plate was connected to the ground via an electrometer for measuring current. There was no flow of current because the air between the plates was non-conducting. However,

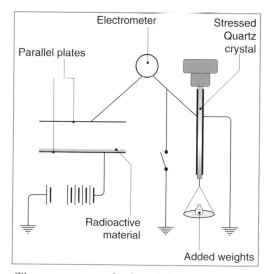

The measurement of radioactivity.

when some crystals of a uranium compound were spread over the top of the lower plate the radiation from them rendered the air between the plates conducting so that what was called an ionising current resulted.

Madame Curie began by testing as many of the metallic and non-metallic elements as she could lay her hands on to see if any of them were radioactive like uranium. She was at first disappointed and it was not until April 1898 that she had any success. Then she found that thorium, a metal first isolated in 1829 by the Swedish chemist J.J. Berzelius, and named after Thor, the Norse God of Thunder, showed signs of radioactivity. This was her first significant discovery but the gloss faded from it to some extent when she found that Gerhardt Carl Schmidt, Professor of Physics at Münster University, had made the same discovery, independently, a few weeks earlier.

Failing in her continued search for any other materials which exhibited radioactivity, she turned to a more detailed study of uranium and thorium compounds with a view to trying to compare the intensity of radiation emitted by various samples. A strong emitter was said to have a high activity; it produced a high ionisation current in the detector. A weak emitter had a low activity and gave a low ionisation current. To measure the activity of a sample, then, it was simply a matter of measuring the ionisation current which it produced in the detector. This was more easily said than done because the current was extremely small – of the order of 10^{-12} amperes – but it was achieved by making use of the piezoelectric effect discovered by Pierre Curie and his brother in 1883. The current to be measured was balanced against the voltage set up in a quartz crystal stressed by hanging weights from it, and the weight required to exactly balance the unknown current gave a measure of its strength. As the currents involved were so minute, it was necessary to design the apparatus, particularly the insulators, with great care so as to avoid electrical leakages. It speaks volumes for the Curies' skills that they were able to use the equipment so successfully over a period of five years while working under far from ideal conditions.

The first thing they established was that the activity of a sample of a uranium compound depended on its uranium content. If it contained 50 per cent of uranium it produced only half the activity of pure 100 per cent uranium metal, and the same held for thorium and its compounds. It was clearly the atoms of uranium or thorium that were causing the radioactivity. They then examined the activities of four naturally occurring uranium minerals – pitchblende, autunite, chalcolite and carnotite. Much to their surprise, they all showed an activity much higher than would have been expected from their known uranium content. One of the samples of pitchblende was, in fact, 3.6 times more active than had been expected.

It was perhaps not very difficult to draw the obvious conclusion. In Madame Curie's words: 'It therefore appears probable . . . that these naturally occurring minerals contain a small quantity of a strongly radioactive substance other than uranium or thorium.'[8] To confirm this conclusion, she made a sample of synthetic chalcolite in the laboratory, by reaction between uranium nitrate, copper phosphate and phosphoric acid. Its activity was 2.3 times less than that of the natural mineral, even though both had the same uranium content. There must therefore be some impurities in the natural minerals that were very highly radioactive, and because it was thought, with some confidence, that *all* the components of the minerals had already been detected by routine chemical analysis, the impurities could only be present in very minute amounts and might well turn out to be hitherto unknown elements. The Curies set about trying to track them down.

The quest was led by Madame Curie because she was more adept in chemical operations than her husband, but he was always close at hand to offer advice and

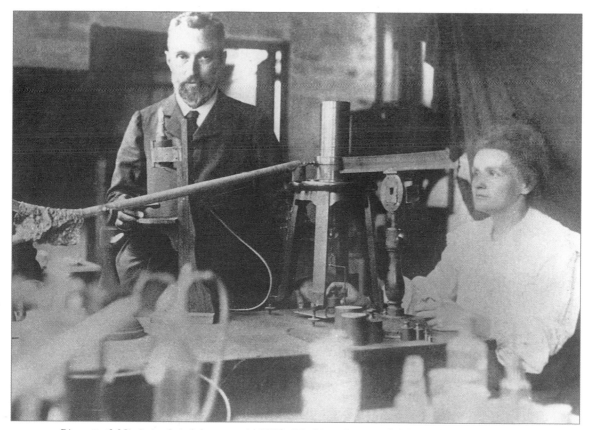

Pierre and Marie in their laboratory in 1898. (Archives Curie and Joliot-Curie)

encouragement, and she also had the help of André Debierne, a close friend of the family, and Gustave Bémant. The omens were not propitious. They were undertaking a 'needle in a haystack' job and the only thing they knew about the 'needle' was that it was highly radioactive. They knew nothing about its chemical properties or its size. Had they realised, as is now known, that their prey was present to the extent of only about 5 parts in a billion, they might well have had second thoughts.

They also had to work in sordid conditions, at first in the glassed-in room alongside Pierre and later in a shed across the alley which had been abandoned by the medical school as an unsuitable place in which to dissect corpses. A contemporary scientist described it as 'a cross between a stable and a potato-store'.[9] It had an asphalt floor and a leaking glass roof and contained only some old pine tables and an antique stove as furniture. It was bitterly cold in winter and unbearably hot in summer. There may, however, have been one saving grace. Unbeknown to anyone at the time, prolonged handling of radioactive substances could be a real health hazard and it may well be that the draughts in the old shed helped to minimise the danger.

Madame Curie was blissfully unaware of this problem as she set to work on material kindly provided, free of charge, by the Austrian government from a pitchblende mine which it owned in Jáchymov. She described it as 'sacks of brown dust, mixed with pine needles' and it consisted of the waste left after most of the uranium had been extracted from the pitchblende. The mining company was accustomed to getting rid of the waste by dumping it in a nearby pine forest. Madame Curie gratefully took delivery of 1,000 kg of it, even though she had to pay for its carriage, and she was pleased to learn that the government had given the mining company permission to sell several more tons if it was needed.

She tackled the problem by using the well-known analytical technique of splitting the various component parts into groups depending on their differing solubilities. The 'brown dust' was known to contain copper, arsenic, antimony, lead and bismuth, together with uranium, thorium, barium and calcium and perhaps an unknown radioactive substance, X. When she dissolved the dust in acid and passed in hydrogen sulphide gas she found, as expected, that the copper, arsenic, antimony, lead and bismuth precipitated out from the solution as insoluble solid sulphides, which could be filtered off. The uranium, thorium, barium and calcium remained in solution. But where was X? Tests on the mixture of solids showed that it had a very much higher radioactivity than the solution, proving that the solids must contain X.

Madame Curie had begun with a mixture of X and nine other elements. In one operation, she had narrowed it down into a mixture of X with only five others.

Similar successive treatments got it down to X plus three, then X plus two, then X plus bismuth. When it transpired that this final mixture had an activity about 400 times higher than that of pure uranium the Curies made a joint announcement, on 18 July 1898, that 'we have recovered a mixture from pitchblende which contains a metal not yet described. If its existence is confirmed, we propose to call it polonium, after the native country of one of us.'[10] Her early years in Poland were never far from Marie's mind.

The Curies did not claim to have obtained pure polonium. They tried to separate it from the bismuth with which it was mixed but came to the conclusion that this was beyond them because the two elements were so very similar. It was like trying to separate identical twins. A much better separation was eventually achieved, in 1902, by Dr Willy Marckwald, a professor at the University in Berlin. He claimed to have obtained a sample of 'polonium' which was some thousand times more active than the Curies' purest sample and his tests on it showed that the new metal was closer to tellurium than to bismuth, so he chose to use his own name, radiotellurium, for it. This did not endear him to Madame Curie, who thought it was 'futile' for anyone to try to replace the name she had chosen. The mild squabble between them ran on until 1906 when Marckwald ended a paper, in which he summarised his case, with the words: 'On these grounds I hold the name radiotellurium to be entirely suitable.' However:

> What's in a name? that which we call a rose,
> By any other name would smell as sweet.

The great services of Marie Curie in the discovery of the radioactive substances justify us in considering her wishes in a question of no wide-ranging importance. For this reason, I propose in the future to replace the name of radiotellurium by polonium'.[11] It was a very gentlemanly withdrawal and perhaps wise, because the lady concerned had a distinctly proprietorial attitude to her discoveries and could be an awkward protagonist when she chose.

Within six months of their correct prediction about the existence of polonium, the Curies had another success to announce. They came to realise that the *total* activity of their starting material could not be accounted for solely by the polonium that it contained. This forced them into searching for a second 'needle' in their 'haystack'. By treating the brown dust with a different series of reagents from those used in the polonium work, they were able to obtain a solid which at first sight appeared to contain none of the elements originally present other than barium. It could not, however, contain only barium, which was not radioactive, because it had an activity 900 times higher than that of pure uranium. In

A page from the Curies' laboratory notebook, June 1898. The left-hand page was written by Pierre and the right-hand one by Marie. (Archives Curie and Joliot-Curie)

December 1898 they reported that 'we believe the new substance contains a new element which we propose to call radium'.[12]

They had already admitted defeat when faced with the problem of separating polonium from bismuth. The challenge now was whether radium could be separated from barium. They were, in many ways, chemical 'twins', but they were not absolutely identical and Marie Curie spent the next four years, and gained immortality, in tearing them apart. They were, she said, 'the best and happiest years of her life'.[13] The method she adopted is known as fractional crystallisation. A mixture of two chemicals, A and B, is dissolved in a hot solvent in which A is less soluble than B. The resulting solution will deposit crystals, when it is cooled, which can be filtered off. Because of the solubility difference, they will be enriched in A. By redissolving these crystals in more hot solvent and then cooling, a second batch of crystals, even richer in A, will form. A third batch will be still richer, and so on. A mixture containing 50 per cent of A and 50 per cent of B might, for example, give a first batch of crystals containing 66.7 per cent of A; the second batch would contain 75 per cent; the third batch, 83.7 per cent; and so on. But that is a favourable example because it starts with a 50–50 mixture and because a considerable difference in solubility between A and B has been assumed.

Radium chloride is significantly less soluble than barium chloride, but Marie was confronted with a mixture containing almost 100 per cent barium chloride with only a trace of radium chloride. It was then an arduous labour which could only be sustained by grim determination and stubbornness, tinged with much hope and confidence. Nor was it a test-tube job. For months on end she toiled away, dissolving the mixture – 20kg at a time – in hot water in cast-iron vats. Constant vigorous stirring with a long iron rod was necessary; then cooling; then filtering off the crystals; then testing their activity to see what enrichment she was getting. And she had to go through the rather dreary process again, and again, and again, hundreds and hundreds of times.

At the end of a day's 'killing work' she was 'broken with fatigue'[14] and it was only a strong inner feeling that she would succeed that kept her going. 'I shall never be able', she wrote, 'to express the joy of the untroubled quietness of the atmosphere of research and the excitement of actual progress with the confident hope of still better results. The feeling of discouragement that I sometimes felt after some unsuccessful toil did not last long and soon gave way to renewed activity.'[15] And when success came it was sweet indeed. One ton of brown dust had yielded only about 100mg of radium chloride, but it was, literally, beautiful to behold. By day, it looked just like common salt but it actually glowed in the dark. 'One of our joys', wrote Madame Curie, 'was to go into our workroom at night; we then perceived on all sides the feebly luminous silhouettes of the bottles or capsules containing our products. It was really a lovely sight and always new to us. The glowing tubes looked like faint fairy lights.'[16]

What is more, the powder not only gave out light but also heat, so that it always had a slightly higher temperature than its surroundings. Where this seemingly endless supply of energy was coming from was a question that was asked but not, at the time, answered. Nor was much concern felt over the dangers now known to be inherent in handling radioactive materials. During the four years' work in her shed Marie had lost over 7kg in weight and both her husband and Henri Becquerel had suffered from skin burns which they thought might be caused by radiation. Indeed, Pierre did some experimental work on its toxic effects on mice and guinea pigs, but the matter did not seem to be taken very seriously.

In 1903 it was the immediate sense of euphoria at what had been achieved, after such a long struggle, that ruled the day. Marie had begun this work on radioactivity in order to get her doctorate. To that end, under the name Mme Sklodowska Curie, she submitted her thesis, entitled 'Researches on Radioactive Substances', to the Faculté des Sciences de Paris in the summer of 1903. Those researches opened up a completely new era in science, but it was the end of a remarkably creative period for her.

Marie's examiners did not have to deliberate for long before granting her a Doctorate of Physical Science, with the mention 'très honorable', and the world-wide acclaim which followed was exemplified by the award of the Nobel Prize for Physics which she shared with her husband and Henri Becquerel in 1903. She was the first Pole to win such a prize. Both she and Pierre treated such awards, however, with some disdain and they were in no way disappointed when their journey to Stockholm to receive the prize had to be postponed because Marie was suffering from anaemia. In many ways, to travel hopefully was, for them, better than arriving. Both were extremely modest and entirely uncompetitive and she wrote that 'our life has been altogether spoiled by honours and fame'[17] and 'with much effort we have avoided the banquets people wanted to organise in our honour'.[18] She thought it quite ridiculous that an American even wanted to name a race-horse after her. When Pierre's friends told him that the Minister was minded to put his name forward for the Legion of Honour he replied: 'Tell him that I do not feel the slightest need of being decorated, but would like a laboratory.'[19] That encapsulated their priorities.

They were, nevertheless, greatly helped financially by the 70,000 francs that came with the Nobel Prize, and their international renown made it much easier for them to raise funds for their research. This was becoming more and more necessary as so far it had been difficult for them to make ends meet and their expenses never seemed to dwindle. They grew even more when, after another difficult pregnancy, their second daughter Eve was born on 10 December 1904. They decided, nevertheless, to forgo the fortune that could well have been theirs had they sought to patent the likely commercial aspects of their discoveries. 'It would', they concluded, 'be contrary to the scientific spirit.'[20]

So they struggled on, with Marie complaining that 'our peaceful and laborious existence is completely disorganised',[21] and Pierre that 'there are days when we hardly have time to breathe'.[22] He had applied for professorial posts at the Sorbonne in 1898 and in 1902, but was rejected both times. Nor was he any more successful when he came to apply for election to the Academy of Sciences. The antiquated procedure involved him in lobbying existing academicians but he was not good at that so he was defeated by a less good, but more loquacious, scientist. Fortunately the family fortunes did begin to improve. Marie and Pierre were welcomed extremely warmly when they went to England to lecture in 1903, and a special chair in radio-physics was created for Pierre at the Sorbonne in 1904 and he was provided with four rooms for his research. Marie became one of his three paid assistants at an annual salary of 2,400 francs. Finally, Pierre was elected to the Academy in 1905.

Alas, it was something of a false dawn. Pierre was off work for almost the whole of 1905 suffering from crippling pains in his legs caused by neurasthenia, and much worse was to follow. Just after lunch on 19 April 1906 he set out to call on his publishers to discuss some proofs but they were closed because of a strike, so he decided to return to his research rooms. It was a rainy, wet day, and he found himself in a narrow street crowded with people and traffic. Perhaps hurriedly, perhaps absent-mindedly, he stepped off the pavement and began to follow a slow-moving cab before crossing the street. As he stepped from behind the cab, he slipped and collided with one of the horses pulling a heavy dray loaded with military uniforms. The horses shied away and the front wheels just missed him, but one of the back wheels hit him on the head. He was killed instantly. He was buried in his family grave at Sceaux.

Marie, now a distraught widow and incurably lonely, went to live with her two daughters and Pierre's 79-year-old father in a small house on the outskirts of Sceaux. Irène was 9 and Ève 2, and Marie began to ease her grief by concentrating on their education and happiness. She rejected an offer of a government pension because, though heartbroken, she still felt that she could and must earn her own living. And she was given the chance to do just that when she was invited to take over her husband's role at the Sorbonne. She was, in fact, the only person qualified to do it but the authorities did not find the decision easy because appointing a woman to such an eminent position was, at the time, a tremendous break with tradition. To ease the transition, she was referred to, at first, as *chargée de cours* but she was known as the Professor from 1908 onwards.

She slowly began to immerse herself, once again, in teaching and research, always seeking to do what she thought Pierre would have done. At 1.30 p.m. on 5 November 1906 she gave her first lecture in the Sorbonne in her new capacity – almost exactly fifteen years to the day since she had enrolled as an impoverished, hopeful student. She began at the precise sentence where Pierre had left off: 'When one considers the progress that has been made in physics in the past ten years . . .'

Her research was never so excitingly fruitful as it had been during those ten years, but now she consolidated and extended her previous work. In particular, she prepared a few decigrammes of very pure radium chloride which she used for three different purposes. First, she measured the relative atomic mass of radium, obtaining a value of 226.4 (which compares well with today's accepted value of 226.05). Secondly, she sealed 21mg of the radium chloride into a glass tube and deposited it in the office of Weights and Measures at Sèvres, near Paris, where it provided an international standard against which the activity of other substances could be measured. Thirdly, in collaboration with her old friend André Debierne, she converted some of the radium chloride into the first ever sample of pure radium metal. It looked just like silver. She also spent a considerable amount of time in editing *The Works of Pierre Curie*, which was published in 1908, and two years later she finished her own magnum opus, a 971-page volume entitled *A Treatise on Radioactivity*.

For all her endeavours she was awarded a second Nobel Prize, this time for Chemistry, in 1911, and it was given to her alone. She took Bronya and Irène with her to Stockholm to collect it but her thoughts were not with them but with the man she had once called 'her true gift of heaven'. In her acceptance speech she emphasised that so much of what she had done had been done with Pierre so that the prize was both a high distinction for her and a homage to his memory.

She was endowed with many other tributes, particularly from overseas, but in France, her adopted country, she was not universally popular. Like Pierre before her, she did not want to be considered for the Legion of Honour, but she did allow her name to be put forward for election to the Academy of Science. Her friends had presumed that this would be a mere formality but they under-estimated the strength of male chauvinism. It might have been tolerable to appoint a woman to a high position in the Sorbonne, when there was no other worthy candidate, but to elect one to the Academy was, for many, going too far. Edouard Branly stood against her and the ensuing controversy was passionate and distinctly distasteful. He was a reasonably successful scientist, if not, by general consent, in the same rank as Marie. But he was also a Catholic, a conservative, a male and French. And he won by two votes.

For a time, too, Marie was subjected to a quite unexpected and completely undeserved campaign of calumny. Its origins are shrouded in some mystery, but it was as though her enormous international acclaim was too much for some French people. Whatever the cause, she was branded as a meddling foreigner and publicly proclaimed to be a Jew; she was plagued with anonymous letters and openly threatened with violence. She also had an unfortunate affair with Paul Langevin, a former pupil of her husband who became a professor at the Sorbonne in 1909. He had been married since 1902 but in July 1910 he left his rather fierce wife, with living-in mother-in-law and four children, and went to share an apartment close to Marie's laboratory. He was decidedly handsome, with a superb, beautifully waxed military moustache, and both their actions and their letters showed that the affair was serious and intimate. But it proved to be nothing but a passing scandal which ruined the reputation of both parties, particularly when their stolen letters were published in the popular press. Langevin challenged one of the editors to a duel, which ended rather farcically with pistols being drawn but no shots fired. Marie's house in Sceaux was besieged by a mob, and the Nobel Prize Committee tried to get her to give up her 1911 award. It was even suggested that Pierre's death might not have been accidental. Paul eventually returned to his family. By an odd quirk of fate, Marie's grand-daughter Hélène married Paul's grandson, Michel, some years later.

It all left Marie suffering from severe depression, and in March 1912 she underwent an operation to cure a kidney disease. She recuperated by hiding away in a private clinic under an assumed name, and spent the summer in England with her old friend and colleague, Hertha Ayrton, under her maiden name. Then she returned to France in October and began work again a month later. It had been a terrible period for her but slowly the clouds began to lift and she was heartened by the decisions, taken both in Poland and in France, to go ahead with the establishment of grand, new laboratories to further her work. She called them 'holy dwellings' and 'temples of the future, of wealth and well-being'. At the opening of the first, in Warsaw in 1913, she received a tumultuous and emotional reception from her native people but she found that they were still under Russian domination. And when she was confronted with the terrible choice as to which organisation she would personally like to direct she chose the Institut du Radium in Paris, despite her recent experiences. Situated in the newly named rue Pierre Curie, it was subtitled Pavillon Curie – and Marie, appropriately, was its first director.

But it was July 1914. Within a month Europe was at war. Sir Edward Grey, the British Foreign Secretary, said: 'The lamps are going out all over Europe. We shall not see them lit again in our lifetime.' Only weeks later the German armies had swept through Belgium and were advancing on Paris. Madame Curie took the precaution of taking her precious supply of 1g of radium to Bordeaux for safe-keeping. Realising that her activities at the Radium Institute would have to be curtailed, she responded to the more immediate challenge by throwing herself wholeheartedly into building up an army X-ray service under the auspices of the Red Cross. She used all her persuasive powers to collect all the available X-ray equipment together and to recruit and train staff to operate it. It was at first set up in hospitals, but later she organised a fleet of twenty mobile units based on a motley collection of private motor cars which she 'borrowed' for the duration. They came to be known as 'little Curies' and she drove one of them – a truck-like

Le Pavillon Curie de l'Institut du Radium in Paris in 1923. (Archives Curie and Joliot-Curie)

Renault – herself. By the end of the war two hundred X-ray units had treated about a million wounded soldiers, so Madame Curie could be well pleased with the contribution she had made to the victory of France and her allies. She was delighted, too, that it led to the freeing of Poland after some 150 years of foreign domination.

After the war Marie entered the twilight of her career. She was in her fifties and her war-time activities had, if anything, increased her fame so that she found herself the honoured guest at more and more ceremonial functions. On her first visit to the United States, in 1921, she was treated just like a queen. Enough money to buy another gram of radium had been collected by the women of America and the precious metal, which had taken 500 men about six months to extract from 600,000kg of ore, was presented to her by President Harding. In 1922 she was elected a member of the Academy of Medicine in Paris. In 1923, the 25th anniversary of the discovery of radium, she was fêted at a great French assembly headed by the President, and her family was granted a pension of 40,000 francs a year. In 1932 she paid her last visit to Poland to open the Curie Radium Institute in Warsaw. And so it went on, with many lesser events to fill the spaces.

Fame did not, however, mean much to her. It was her work and her family that really mattered. 'I could not live', she wrote, 'without the laboratory',[23] and she began to pick up the pieces at the Radium Institute in Paris as soon as she could after the war had ended. She was to some extent more serene and relaxed than in her younger years, taking time off to spend holidays with her children and friends. But she would still work for fourteen hours in her laboratory some days and it is a measure of the Institute's success under her leadership that in the fifteen years after the war almost five hundred scientific papers came from it, thirty-one of which carried Madame Curie's name.

It was a particular joy to her that her daughter Irène made a very significant contribution to that output. Like her mother before her, she had trained as a scientist and had been appointed as an assistant at the Radium Institute in 1918. Working alongside her was the handsome, talkative, high-spirited Frédéric Joliot, who had already established a reputation as one of the most promising young physicists in France. The two were married in 1926, and went on, like Marie and Pierre Curie before them, to win their own Nobel Prize for Chemistry in 1935. But that is another chapter in the story of radioactivity.

Marie Curie did not, alas, live to share their triumph. Signs that she was possibly suffering from the effects of exposure to radiation had first emerged in 1920 when she began to have trouble with her eyes, and blindness was only kept at bay by the use of stronger and stronger spectacles and operations in 1923, 1924 and 1930. She also suffered from painful burns on her hands and in 1933 from a gall-stone, but, as was her wont, she fought against all these disabilities and continued to work very long hours. It was, however, clear to those around her that she was beginning to tire more easily and there were some days when she felt dizzy and weak. Then, in May 1934, she had to take to her bed with a fever. Neither doctors nor X-rays could point to any specific ailment but there were some signs of tuberculosis so she was moved, reluctantly, to a sanatorium at Sancellemoz in the Alps. Her temperature was still very high and further tests revealed that she was in fact suffering from a particularly virulent form of pernicious anaemia. The doctors had never before come across any similar pattern of blood counts and this confirmed their suspicions that the disease was caused by over-exposure to radiation. She died on 4 July 1934 and was buried two days later, at noon, alongside Pierre at Sceaux. There was no formality, no pomp or ceremony, no religious service and no official representations. Only the family were there, and her brother and sister brought some soil from Poland to sprinkle in the grave.

The news of Marie's death spread around the world but all the world could do was marvel, mourn and pay tribute. No one did it with more authority and elegance than Albert Einstein, who wrote:

> It was my good fortune to be linked with Mme Curie through twenty years of sublime and unclouded friendship. I came to admire her human grandeur to an ever growing degree. Her strength, her purity of will, her austerity towards herself, her objectivity, her incorruptible judgement – all these were of a kind seldom found joined in a single individual. She felt herself at every moment to be a servant of society, and her profound modesty never left any room for complacency. . . . Once she had recognised a certain way as the right one, she pursued it without compromise and with extreme tenacity. The greatest scientific deed of her life – proving the existence of radioactive elements and isolating them – owes its accomplishment not merely to bold intuition but to a devotion and persistence in execution under the most extreme hardships imaginable, such as the history of experimental science has not often witnessed.[24]

And there was a final twist in the Curie story in 1995, when the French President François Mitterrand decided that Pierre and Marie should be re-buried under the mighty dome of the Panthéon in Paris. Thus, on 20 April that year, their remains were taken from their shared grave at Sceaux and laid to rest for the second time in a solemn ceremony, and Marie became the first woman to be accorded this signal mark of honour on her own merit. President Mitterrand declared: 'I form the wish, in the name of France, that everywhere in the world the equality of the rights of women and men might progress', and that 'by transferring these ashes of Pierre and Marie Curie into the sanctuary of our collective memory, France not only performs an act of recognition, it also affirms a faith in science, in research, and its respect for those who dedicate themselves to science, just as Pierre and Marie Curie dedicated their energies and their lives to science'.

CHAPTER 4

Lord Rutherford

Ernest Rutherford burst on to the international stage, which he was soon to dominate, in September 1895, the year in which Marie and Pierre Curie were married and Röntgen discovered X-rays. It was a timely, if somewhat fortuitous, entry. He had been doing research into a magnetic method of detecting radio waves at Canterbury College, part of the University of New Zealand at Christchurch, and the thesis he submitted created such a good impression that he was awarded a scholarship provided by funds accruing from the profits of the Great Exhibition of 1851 in London. But he only got it because a preferred competitor withdrew in order to get married. Rutherford was digging potatoes when his mother told him of his success and he flung away his spade and said, laughingly, 'That's the last potato I'll dig.'[1] By chance, at the same time, an important change was made in the regulations regarding entry to Cambridge University. This allowed graduates of other universities to obtain a BA degree without taking the normal examinations, if they were in residence for two years and submitted a thesis 'of distinction as a record of original research'. Ernest Rutherford, with his scholarship behind him, was one of the very first applicants, and so it was that he joined Thomson's small research team at the Cavendish Laboratory.

He was born near Nelson in New Zealand in 1871, the fourth son of James Rutherford, a flax grower of Scottish origin, and his wife Martha, who was the first woman school teacher in New Zealand. There were, eventually, twelve children, though they did not all survive, and the family lived very happily in a humble house amid beautiful countryside. Ernest's early days were spent in a hard, active, open-air life. His early education was in recently established State schools at Brightwater and Havelock, from where he won scholarships first to Nelson College, where he was top of the class in almost every subject, and then to Canterbury College. It was there that he graduated with double first-class honours in mathematics and physics and began his first research project.

He was 24 years old when he arrived in Cambridge. Heavily built and rather clumsy, he had large, fiery, blue eyes, a damp droopy lower lip and a moustache.

A drawing of Lord Rutherford by Illingworth. (ICI)

He was full of energy and confidence, and his loud voice was more akin to Cornish or Cockney than to Scottish or Antipodean. He did not look at all like an intellectual and it was a distinct novelty to have a supposedly clever physicist arriving from the far-away southern hemisphere into the rarefied atmosphere of Cambridge. But his strength of character, his sense of humour, his bonhomie and his gusto saw him through the initial difficulties facing any such newcomer.

At first he continued with his research on radio waves and developed a receiver capable of picking up signals at a distance of about 2 miles, which in its day was something of a record and rivalled the contemporary achievements of the Italian, Guglielmo Marconi. Rutherford was keen to work in this field because he saw the commercial possibilities, which Marconi soon exploited, and he was anxious to make some money so that he could marry his fiancée, Mary Newton, whom he had left behind in New Zealand.

Within a few weeks Thomson had spotted that he was a student of 'quite exceptional ability' and the rumour quickly spread round Cambridge that 'a young rabbit had arrived from New Zealand, who burrows very deep'.[2] It did not take long for his 'burrowing' to be directed away from radio waves and into the general stream of activity at the Cavendish Laboratory, and he turned his attention to the daunting task of trying to unravel the nature of radioactivity. He was in at the start of what he later called the 'heroic age of physics'.[3] His discoveries were to shatter established theory to its very foundations, which were generally believed at the time to be well embedded in solid concrete. Of what did the radiation from uranium, thorium, polonium and radium consist? How did it originate? When Rutherford began his work on what he referred to as 'this promising line', all that was known was that the radiation was penetrating, that it affected photographic plates, and that gases through which it was passed became electrically conducting. It seemed, on the face of it, to have much in common with X-rays. The elucidation of its real nature developed rather like the plot in a detective story with Rutherford, playing the part of the main detective, unearthing and explaining most of the significant clues. When a friend once said to him 'You're always on the crest of the wave', he replied, 'Well, after all, I made the wave didn't I? At least to some extent.'[4]

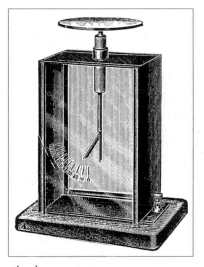

An electroscope.

His first important discovery was that the radiation consisted of at least two different types of rays which he called alpha- and beta-rays, with the latter being much more penetrating than the former. He also hinted that there might well be a third type, which came to light later as gamma-rays. He came to this conclusion after measuring the ionisation currents which samples of uranium compounds could build up in much the same way as Madame Curie had done. But at first he used an electroscope to measure the current. This consisted of two small rectangular pieces of gold or aluminium foil, about the size of a small postage stamp, attached, face to face, at their upper ends, to the bottom of a metal rod. The whole set-up was enclosed in a glass case to protect the foil from draughts. When the metal rod was electrically charged, by touching it with a stick of hard rubber that had been rubbed on a coat sleeve, the two pieces of foil diverged because they carried like charges, and the amount of divergence, which depended on the strength of the charge, could be measured against a calibrated scale placed in front of them. Under normal conditions the pieces of foil held their positions for a long time and only gradually collapsed, because the air surrounding them was a very good insulator and thus they lost their electrical charge only very slowly. But when a radioactive material was brought into the vicinity of the electroscope, the air was rendered conducting so that the pieces of foil collapsed and the rate at which they did so depended on the activity of the radioactive sample. Twice the activity caused twice the rate of collapse, and so on. Measuring the rate of collapse could therefore be used to compare the activity of one radioactive sample with another.

Later, in 1899, Rutherford used a detector consisting of two parallel plates, similar to that used by the Curies, to measure the ionisation current, and he found that the intensity of radiation from a uranium compound was reduced when it was covered by a thin film of aluminium because the metal absorbed some of the radiation. It was reduced further, by the same amount, when a second film was added, and so on. But, much to his surprise, it did not go on like this until *all* the activity had been absorbed by the aluminium. At a certain stage the addition of further aluminium films no longer decreased the intensity of the radiation. It remained steady. Rutherford concluded that the alpha-rays in the radiation were being absorbed by the aluminium but that the beta-rays were still penetrating it. More detailed measurements showed that alpha-rays could only penetrate through about 7cm of air or a thin sheet of aluminium, whereas beta-rays were about a hundred times more penetrating, capable of passing through about 3mm of lead.

These experiments did not, however, supply any information about the make-up of either alpha- or beta-rays, and the first step in that direction came from Rutherford's second discovery. The nature of cathode rays had been resolved when Thomson investigated the effect of a magnetic field on them, and so it was to be with alpha- and beta-rays. Rutherford obtained a narrow beam of the rays by passing the radiation from a uranium compound through central holes in two pieces of metal set some distance apart. When the beam impinged on a photographic plate it made a single mark on the plate. But if it was passed through a magnetic field before reaching the plate then two marks were formed, one to the left and one to the right.

Further investigation revealed that the alpha-rays were deflected rather weakly in one direction, and the beta-rays much more strongly in the opposite direction. Detailed measurement on the extent of the deflection of the beta-rays proved that they consisted of electrons, much like cathode rays. The opposite deflection of the alpha-rays was accounted for by the assumption that they must consist of particles carrying a *positive* electrical charge as opposed to the *negative* charge carried by electrons. The weaker deflection of the alpha-rays also suggested that their particles must be much heavier than electrons. A more detailed measurement of the charge/mass ratio, carried out in 1903, suggested two main possibilities. If the electric charge on the alpha-particle was equal to that on the electron, but positive, then the mass of the particle must be equal to twice that of the hydrogen atom. Alternatively, if the positive charge was twice that of the electron then the mass must be four times that of the hydrogen atom, i.e. the mass of the helium atom. It was the latter option that in due course was proved to be right and linked alpha-rays with helium.

Both alpha- and beta-rays had been shown to consist of particles, because magnetic fields do not deflect light or X-ray-type radiation, so that the term 'ray', originally chosen by Rutherford, turned out to be something of a misnomer though its use has persisted. The particles in the beta-rays had been identified as electrons and those in the alpha-rays were associated with helium atoms. It was, however, important for future experiments that the two 'rays', or types of particle, could be easily separated, either by making use of their different penetrations through metal foil or by the different effect of magnetic fields on them.

* * *

At this stage the scene of the action moved from Cambridge to McGill University in Montreal, Canada. This university had been founded in 1813 by a bequest in the will of James McGill, a Scot who had made a fortune in fur trading. Almost eighty years later another Scottish benefactor, Sir William MacDonald, who had made his money in the tobacco trade, paid for the building of a fine new laboratory and endowed a chair of experimental physics. On Thomson's advice, Rutherford was appointed to the chair when he was only 27 years old, and he set

The MacDonald Physics Building at McGill University in 1906. (From Nature, *19 July 1906)*

sail for Canada in September 1898. His salary was about £500 per year. 'Not bad', he wrote to his mother, and he explained to Mary Newton that 'although we should, of course, have to keep up a certain amount of style, we ought to do it comfortably on £400 and put the rest by'.[5] He was soon able to put his domestic economics to the test because he went to New Zealand to marry Mary in April 1900. She had been a student at Canterbury College and was to be his perfect life-long partner, both as wife and personal secretary. When they returned to Montreal, he set about his work with renewed vigour. He was lucky in that he had good facilities and he was greatly helped by having Frederick Soddy as an associate.

Soddy was born in Eastbourne, England, in 1877, the son of very religious parents, but his mother died when he was young and he was raised in a strong Calvinist tradition by a dominant half-sister, which may account for his rather individual views and somewhat difficult character. He was educated at Eastbourne College and the University of Aberystwyth before going to Merton College, Oxford, in 1896. He took a first-class degree in chemistry after only two years and stayed on at Oxford until he applied for a vacant professorship at Toronto University at the early age of 23. Unusually, he decided to travel to Canada to press his claim. While en route, he read in a newspaper that the position had already been filled so, quite by chance, he decided to call in at Montreal to have a look at the laboratories at McGill. This led to him being offered a lectureship in the Department of Chemistry and to his eventual meeting and partnership with Rutherford. It was particularly fruitful because Rutherford, though an expert in measuring the activity of radioactive substances and in designing the necessary apparatus, knew little about chemical manipulation. Soddy described their work together in glowing terms, writing that 'Rutherford and his radioactive emanations and active deposits got me before many weeks had elapsed and I abandoned all to follow him'.[6]

Their collaboration was short-lived but they contributed greatly to the surge of activity in the years around 1900. In 1899 André Debierne, the intimate friend of M and Mme Curie, had discovered that pitchblende contained not only uranium, radium and polonium but also a fourth radioactive element that he called

The signatures of Rutherford and Soddy.

actinium after the Greek *aktis* meaning ray. A year later Paul Villard discovered the existence of gamma-rays when he was investigating the nature of the radiation emerging from a 0.3mm-thick sheet of aluminium under bombardment by the rays from radium. These gamma-rays were like short-wave X-rays and were able to penetrate a 10cm sheet of aluminium but, unlike alpha- or beta-rays, they could not be deflected by a magnetic field.

Professor F.E. Dorn, a German chemist, also discovered in 1900 that radium emitted a radioactive gas which was at first called radium emanation or niton. It is now called radon and is recognised as being a member of the noble gas group of elements and a component of the atmosphere. Also in 1900, Crookes carried out a very important experiment on a radioactive solution containing a uranium salt and a small amount of a ferric salt which emitted *both* alpha- and beta-rays. When he added a solution of ammonium hydroxide and ammonium carbonate he found that the resulting precipitate was radioactive but emitted *only* beta-rays, whereas the associated solution was also radioactive but emitted *only* alpha-rays. He concluded that he had found a new form of uranium and wrote that 'for the sake of lucidity the new body must have a name. Until it is more tractable I will call it UrX – the unknown substance in uranium'.[7]

So the clues were mounting up but the answers to the puzzles only began to materialise after some further work by Rutherford and Soddy on thorium. In 1899 R.B. Owens, Professor of Electrical Engineering at McGill University, noticed that the activity of a sample of a thorium compound, which he was measuring, seemed to be very much affected by draughts. Moreover, objects in the vicinity were found to be to some extent radioactive – a phenomenon that came to be called induced or excited radioactivity. These observations led to the hypothesis that some kind of radioactive gas was being emitted by the thorium compound; it was at first called thorium emanation but is now known as thoron.

When a sample of the emanation was collected, by passing a stream of air over the thorium compound contained in a glass tube, it was discovered that the activity of the emanation rapidly faded away. After 54 seconds, only half the original activity was left; after 108 seconds, only one quarter; after 162 seconds, only one eighth; after 216 seconds, only one sixteenth; and so on. After 6 minutes the sample had lost just over 99.8 per cent of its original activity. This was the first occasion that a falling-off in radioactivity over time had been recorded but it soon became clear that this was the norm rather than an exception. The phenomenon came to be known as radioactive decay and the rate of the decay for any particular substance was measured by its typical half-life – that is, by the time it took for its radioactivity to be reduced to half its original value. That quantity is

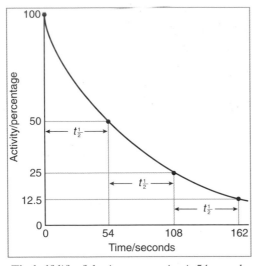

The half-life of thorium emanation is 54 seconds.

unaffected by any change in temperature or pressure, and is independent of the original amount of material. Whether you use 100 grams of emanation or 1 gram, both lose half their activity in 54 seconds.

Half-life values for radioactive substances are now known to vary between a few seconds and millions of years. Those substances with a small value are said to be short-lived; those with a high value are long-lived. That the idea of radioactive decay did not come to light earlier, when uranium, thorium, polonium, actinium and radium were discovered, was due to the fact that they all have high half-lives so that their radioactive decay is extremely slow and very difficult to spot. The half-life for uranium, for example, is about 4,510,000,000 years.

The big breakthrough came in 1901 when Rutherford and Soddy discovered that there were two sorts of thorium atom, which they called thorium and thorium-X, just as Crookes had found two sorts of uranium atom. They found that adding aqueous ammonia to a solution of what was thought to be simply thorium nitrate formed insoluble thorium hydroxide, which could be filtered off leaving a solution behind. To everyone's surprise, the solid was found to be much less radioactive than the solution and Rutherford and Soddy suggested that this was perhaps because the *solid* contained thorium atoms whereas the *solution* contained thorium-X atoms.

The Christmas holidays intervened at this stage and the laboratories were shut, but on their return to work Rutherford and Soddy found that all the radioactivity in the solution had 'disappeared' whereas that in the solid had returned to its normal value. Further investigation showed that the thorium-X in the solution had a short half-life of only about four days so it had 'run out' over the Christmas holidays. But, simultaneously, the solid had regained its radioactivity at the same rate as the solution had lost its. What is more, it was found that the thorium-X emitted only alpha-rays while that the thorium emitted both alpha- and beta-rays; that the thorium emanation came from the thorium-X and not from the thorium atoms; and that the radioactivity induced on other surfaces by the thorium emanation always had a half-life of about eleven hours.

A page of Rutherford's laboratory notebook of March 1902 concerning the radioactivity of thorium hydroxide.

To account for these observations, Rutherford and Soddy suggested, in a paper entitled 'The Cause and Nature of Radioactivity', published in 1902 in the *Philosophical Magazine*, that a series of spontaneous atomic changes must be taking place which were, they wrote, 'of a different order of magnitude from any that have before been dealt with in chemistry'.[8] They did not fully understand the details of all the changes but they summarised the three about which they did know as follows:

Thorium $\longrightarrow$ Thorium-X $\longrightarrow$ Thorium emanation $\longrightarrow$ Induced radioactivity
Uranium $\longrightarrow$ Uranium-X
Radium $\longrightarrow$ Radon

It was a revolutionary suggestion because it implied that one atom could split up and form another one. Atoms could no longer be regarded as the immutable particles on which so much chemical theory had been based for almost a century. The indestructible atom had become distinctly ephemeral. Sir William Ramsay put it in rhyme:

> So the atoms in turn, we now clearly discern,
> Fly to bits with the utmost facility:
> They wend on their way, and, in splitting, display
> An absolute lack of stability.

Such startlingly new ideas were received in many quarters with scepticism and opposition. It was even suggested at McGill that they had brought discredit on the university. Both Becquerel and Madame Curie were critical, and Lord Kelvin wrote that 'the disintegration of the radium atom is wantonly nonsensical'.[9] But Rutherford stood his ground and, in the words of Sir Henry Tizard, 'marshalled all his evidence, direct and circumstantial, with the skill of a great lawyer, and drove his points home one by one until he got a unanimous verdict'.[10]

The idea of a spontaneous, unstoppable process of change from one atom to another, with the loss of alpha-, beta- or gamma-rays, came to be known as radioactive disintegration or decay, and the original atom was referred to as the parent and its decay product as the daughter. An extensive search for possible new products began, but the McGill partnership was broken when Soddy left in 1903 to go to University College in London to work with Sir William Ramsay, who was already famous as the discoverer of the noble gases – helium, argon, krypton and xenon – and as the winner of the 1904 Nobel Prize for Chemistry. In no time at all they demonstrated that helium gas, which they detected spectroscopically, was formed from radium, which provided further evidence to support the view that alpha-rays were associated with helium atoms.

At the same time Otto Hahn, a promising young chemist from Germany who had come to work with Ramsay in order to improve his English before going back home to work for the firm of Kalle & Company, discovered radiothorium as a disintegration product between thorium and thorium-X. Recommended by Ramsay as 'a nice fellow, modest, completely trustworthy, and very gifted',[11] he went in 1905 to work with Rutherford who was still at McGill. He took with him his sample of radiothorium and quickly added thorium A, thorium B and thorium C to his list of discoveries of new radioactive species. Hahn returned to Germany in 1906 to join the Chemical Institute at the University of Berlin under the direction of Emil Fischer. Because radioactivity was not recognised as a conventional subject he could not be given an official post and no room could be found for him to work in, until he was eventually fitted into the carpentry shop in the base-ment of the building. It was

Otto Hahn. (UKAEA)

from there that he grew into one of the world leaders in radioactive research.

Soddy only stayed in London for two years before becoming a lecturer in chemistry at Glasgow University in 1904, while Rutherford left McGill in 1907 to become the Langworthy Professor of Physics at Manchester University. By then the idea of radioactive disintegration taking place through what Soddy called a 'cascade' was well established and it came to be realised that all the known naturally occurring radioactive species could be summarised in three radioactive series known as the thorium, uranium and actinium series.

The thorium series is the simplest and, using the old historical names, it is represented as follows. (The series using modern names is given on page 63.)

Thorium → Mesothorium 1 → Mesothorium 2 → Radiothorium →
Thorium-X → Thorium emanation → Thorium A → Thorium B →

Thorium C → Thorium C' → Thorium D
Thorium C → Thorium C" → Thorium D

Each of the atoms listed has its own particular half-life value, which shows that each is different from the others. Thorium, for example, has the longest, at 2.2×10^{10} years, and thorium C' has the shortest, at about 10^{-11} seconds. Details of the uranium and actinium series are given in the Appendix on page 221.

The ideas of the half-life of a radioactive substance and of the existence of various disintegration series were the main outcome of the Rutherford–Soddy collaboration. They had only worked together at McGill for about eighteen months but it had been a singularly fruitful partnership and both men looked back on it with much satisfaction. Rutherford wrote that 'he kept turning up to the lab five nights out of seven till 11 or 12 o'clock, and generally made things buzz along'[12] and commented 'I have to keep going as there are always people on my track',[13] while Soddy recorded that 'scientific life became hectic to a degree rare in the lifetime of an individual, rare perhaps in the lifetime of an institution'.[14] But neither of them was burnt out and they both had much more to offer when they returned to Great Britain.

CHAPTER 5
Inside the Atom

Rutherford left McGill University in a blaze of glory. Shortly before, he had written proudly to his mother that: 'I had the largest audience they had ever raised at McGill. They were stored everywhere, including some who were looking through a ventilator in the top of the roof.'[1] He had, indeed, established an international reputation as a researcher, teacher and lecturer, and his modesty and bonhomie had made him universally popular. He paid generous tribute, as was his wont, to Canada and McGill when he returned to Toronto for a British Association meeting in 1909, and said 'I owe much to this country for the unusual facilities and opportunity for research so liberally provided by one of her great universities'.[2] Yet he was happy to move to Manchester University as the Langworthy Professor of Physics because this brought him closer to the scene of contemporary scientific activity. As at McGill, he found everything very much to his liking. Sir Arthur Schuster, the professor since 1888, had designed a new laboratory which had only been completed in 1900. There was an exceptionally capable laboratory assistant in William Kay, and there was also Hans Geiger, a young researcher who had come over from Erlangen in Germany in 1906 and who was to take over Soddy's role as Rutherford's right-hand man.

Rutherford and his wife, with their only daughter, 6-year-old Eileen, settled into a new house and their natural hospitality, even though no alcohol was allowed, ensured a warm welcome for any guests. He found, too, that he had much in common with the Lancastrians who surrounded him, and the whole area was bustling and thriving with all sorts of activity. If he needed any further encouragement to get on with his work, it came in the award of the Nobel Prize for Chemistry in 1908, 'for his investigation into the disintegration of the elements and the chemistry of radioactive substances'. On accepting the prize he commented that he had studied many rapid transformations but had seen nothing so quick as his change from a physicist to a chemist.

He had spent only nine years at McGill, and his collaboration with Soddy had lasted less than two years, but in that time over fifty papers had been published

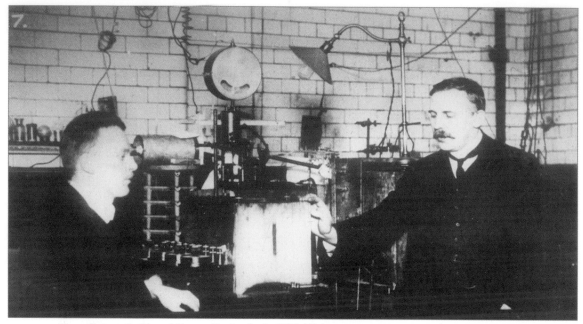

Hans Geiger (left) and Ernest Rutherford. (UKAEA)

recording a host of new and surprising facts. This meant that many established scientific ideas had had to be reassessed and none more so than the existing idea of an atom, which had been introduced in 1808 by John Dalton. He was the son of an impecunious weaver and had begun his working life running a preparatory school in Kendal, along with his brother. In his atomic theory, published in his book *A New System of Chemical Philosophy*, he suggested that all matter was made up of atoms which were indivisible and could neither be created nor destroyed. He regarded each of the thirty-three elements he knew about as having its own particular type of atom, with its own particular mass. It was not possible, at the time, to measure the actual mass of any one atom but it did gradually become possible to measure how much heavier any atom was than the atom of hydrogen, which was the lightest, and that became known as the relative atomic mass of the atom. The value for hydrogen was 1; for carbon it was 12; for iron, 56; and for silver, 108. Dalton used a number of different geometrical shapes as symbols to represent the atoms of the elements but they were replaced by the present letter symbols introduced by the Swedish professor, J.J. Berzelius, in 1818.

Dalton's indestructible atoms were the basis on which chemistry had developed for a hundred years. Rutherford himself wrote that he had been brought up to 'look at them as nice hard fellows, red or grey in colour, according to taste',[3] and

Newton had them as 'so very hard, as never to wear or break in pieces: no ordinary power being able to divide what God himself had made One, in the first creation',[4] while a schoolboy once wrote of them as 'very small, hard marbles invented by Dr Dalton'. The discovery that radioactive atoms were continually splitting and that nothing could stop them made any such idea of an atom quite untenable. But what was to replace it?

The existence of electrons in both cathode rays and beta-rays suggested that they might be a component part of all atoms and that idea was supported by two other facts. First, it had been known since around 1883 that electrons are given off from a hot metallic wire, as in a thermionic valve, and secondly Heinrich Hertz had discovered in 1887 that electrons are also emitted when light of appropriate wave-length falls on to some metals. Such facts led J.J. Thomson to put forward the idea of what is sometimes called the 'currant-bun' or 'plum-pudding' model of an atom in which he envisaged a number of electrons embedded in a surrounding sphere of positive charge, though at the time he preferred to call the electrons 'corpuscles' because he was not clear as to their exact nature. The total negative charge on the corpuscles had to be balanced by the surrounding positive charge so that the atom as a whole could be electrically neutral, and as Thomson regarded this positive charge as having no mass the mass of any atom had to be made up of the total mass of its corpuscles. This meant that atoms had to contain thousands of corpuscles, and they were thought to exist in spinning rings. In Thomson's own words:

As these corpuscles are all negatively charged, they will repel each other, and so if an atom is a collection of corpuscles, there must in addition to the corpuscles be something to hold them together; if the corpuscles

Dalton's symbols for the elements.

form the bricks of the structure, we require mortar to keep them together. I shall suppose that positive electricity acts as the mortar.[5]

And in a letter to Rutherford in 1904 he wrote that 'I think a spinning top is a good illustration of the radium atom'.[6] Such ideas seem fanciful today but Thomson developed them into a sophisticated model of an atom which attracted a good deal of support and held the stage for seven years until 1911. It was then replaced by a model in which most of the mass of the atom is in a small, positively charged central nucleus around which the electrons circulate. Such a new idea was first put forward, without any solid experimental backing, by the French scientist Jean Perrin in 1901; by Hantaro Nagaoka, a Japanese physicist, in 1904; by Sir Oliver Lodge, Professor of Physics at Liverpool University and later the Principal of the University of Birmingham, in 1906; and by John W. Nicholson, a mathematical physicist at the Cavendish Laboratory, in 1911.

These early, tentative suggestions were then developed in three main stages, following work by Rutherford, Niels Bohr and James Chadwick, into today's widely accepted atomic model of an atom. First, between 1909 and 1911, Rutherford carried out what came to be called his scattering or bombardment experiments in collaboration with Geiger and Ernest Marsden. They discovered that a parallel beam of beta-rays directed towards a thin sheet of metal passed through the metal but that the beam was diverged. This was explained as being due to the repulsion of the electrons in the beta rays by those in the atoms of the metal. The measured divergence indicated that the number of electrons in the metal atom was approximately half its relative atomic mass. Aluminium, for example, with a relative atomic mass of 27, had about 13 electrons in its atom. This proved that the major part of the mass of an atom must be in its positive part because the electrons weighed so little.

In a second experiment a parallel beam of alpha-rays was directed towards a piece of gold foil, 6×10^{-5}cm thick, and their position was picked up by the flashes of light each particle made when it struck a screen coated with zinc sulphide. It was found that most of the rays passed through the foil and were deflected in varying amounts but, much to everyone's surprise, it transpired that a few of them (about 1 in 8,000) were deflected back through angles greater than

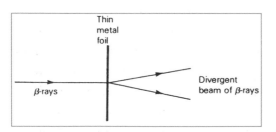

The divergence of a beam of beta-rays on passing through a thin metal foil.

90 degrees. This back-deflection was not simply a reflection from the front surface of the foil because the number of back-deflections increased as thicker pieces of foil were used. When Rutherford was first told about the results of this experiment he said: 'It was quite the most incredible event that has ever happened to me in my life. It was almost as incredible as if you fired a 15-inch shell at a piece of tissue paper and it came back and hit you.'[7] He

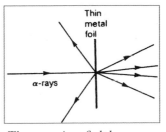

The scattering of alpha-rays by a sheet of thin metal foil.

realised that the heavy alpha-particle could only be deflected through large angles by a near-collision with something of its own charge and greater mass. He was able to calculate that the measured deflections could only be accounted for on the assumption that an atom had a positively charged nucleus, of diameter about 10^{-12}cm, carrying a positive charge equal in number to about half the relative atomic mass of the atom concerned. That meant that the positive charge on the nucleus of the atom was equal in magnitude to the total negative charge carried by its electrons.

Rutherford's original atomic model, then, had a central positively charged nucleus that contributed most of the mass and it was surrounded by an array of electrons sufficient in number to neutralise the charge on the nucleus, so that the atom as a whole was electrically neutral. This model of an atom was not widely accepted but it could be used very effectively to explain the nature of Mendeleev's classification of the elements. In 1869, when he was only 35, Dmitri Ivanovich Mendeleev, Professor of Chemistry at St Petersburg University, had classified all the sixty-six elements known to him, listing them in their order of relative atomic mass in what came to be known as the periodic table. It was a massively bold enterprise which showed that the chemical elements were not 'mere fragmentary, incidental facts of nature, but that they form successive units in the sublime harmony of the universe'.[8] Hydrogen, with a relative atomic mass of 1, came first, followed by helium (4), lithium (7), beryllium (9), boron (11) and so on, up to uranium (238), which in 1869 was the atom with the highest relative atomic mass. He noticed that many of the elements fell into vertical groups with similar chemical properties, exhibiting what he called periodicity, but he did not know why this should be. At that time he had to leave some gaps in his table to meet that chemical requirement, but he predicted, quite rightly, that the gaps would be filled as new elements were discovered. So it was that radium, polonium and actinium, all the noble gases and a number of other elements were in due course fitted into the overall scheme. There are now 115.

Rutherford's notes on atomic structure. (Cavendish Laboratory)

The numerical order in which the elements were placed came to be known as the atomic number of the element. Thus hydrogen was 1, helium 2, lithium 3, and so on, up to uranium at 92, and when necessary the symbol for the element was written with the atomic number (A_r) as a subscript and the relative atomic mass (Z) as a superscript. The hydrogen atom, for example, is written as $_1^1H$; helium as $_2^4He$, lithium as $_3^7Li$ and uranium as $_{92}^{238}U$.

The simplest atom, hydrogen, contains one electron outside the nucleus which gives the atom a charge of -1 unit. The nucleus has a balancing charge of +1 unit to make the atom electrically neutral and a mass of 1 unit to give it a relative

Group 1 A	Group 1 B	Group 2 A	Group 2 B	Group 3 A	Group 3 B	Group 4 A	Group 4 B	Group 5 A	Group 5 B	Group 6 A	Group 6 B	Group 7 A	Group 7 B	Group 8 A	Group 8 B
H															
Li		Be		B		C		N		O		F			
Na		Mg		Al		Si		P		S		Cl			
K		Ca		Sc		Ti		V		Cr		Mn		Fe Co Ni	
	Cu		Zn		Ga		Ge		As		Se		Br		
Rb		Sr		Y		Zr		Nb		Mo				Ru Rh Pd	
	Ag		Cd		In		Sn		Sb		Te		I		
Cs		Ba		La (Ce Er)										Os Ir Pt	
						Hf		Ta		W					
	Au		Hg		Tl		Pb		Bi						
						Th				U					

Periodic table of the sixty-six elements known in 1890. The radioactive elements are underlined.

atomic mass of 1; it is referred to as a proton. The small mass of the electron – 1,840 times lower than that of the nucleus – is, for most purposes, neglected.

	Relative mass	Electrical charge
Proton (p)	1	+1
Electron (e)	1/1840 (0)	–1

When it came to the helium atom, however, there was a problem. The atom had two electrons outside the nucleus so that it had to have two protons in the nucleus to balance the negative charge. But this did not provide a relative atomic mass of 4. The solution suggested was that the nucleus contained four protons and two electrons and this was the model adopted for all other atoms. The number of extra-nuclear electrons was equal to the atomic number and the number of protons in the nucleus was equal to the relative atomic mass. The nucleus also contained enough electrons to maintain electrical neutrality. For example:

Hydrogen, $_1^1\text{H}$ Helium, $_2^4\text{He}$ Lithium, $_3^7\text{Li}$ Uranium, $_{92}^{238}\text{U}$

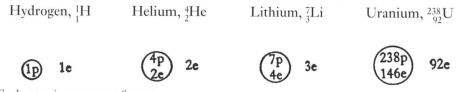

Early atomic structures of atoms.

At this stage the limitation of Rutherford's atomic model lay in the fact that little or nothing was known about the extra-nuclear electrons around the nucleus. Rutherford regarded them as making up a homogeneous atmosphere of negative electricity, not unlike the positive electricity of Thomson's atom, but that was far too vague to be very helpful. Knowing that the Group 1 elements lithium, sodium, potassium, rubidium and caesium had, respectively 3, 11, 19, 37 and 55 electrons outside the nucleus did not, for instance, suggest any obvious reason why they should be chemically alike. But the matter was elegantly resolved by an inspired suggestion from Niels Bohr, a Danish scientist who had spent a year in 1911–12 working first with Thomson in Cambridge and then with Rutherford in Manchester. When Bohr pointed out that existing spectroscopic data could be interpreted on the basis that the electrons in an atom were arranged in different orbits around the nucleus, like the planets around the sun, everything became clearer. The similarity of the elements in Group 1 of the Periodic Table, it transpired, was due to the fact that they all had one electron in their outermost orbit while those in Group 2 had two; those in Group 3 had three; and so on. The detailed arrangement of the electrons in their orbits is shown, for example, as follows:

Group 1		Group 2		Group 3	
Li	2.1	Be	2.2	B	2.3
Na	2.8.1	Mg	2.8.2	Al	2.8.3
K	2.8.8.1	Ca	2.8.8.2	Ga	2.8.8.3
Rb	2.8.18.8.1	Sr	2.8.18.8.2	In	2.8.18.8.3
Cs	2.8.18.18.8.1	Ba	2.8.18.18.8.2	Tl	2.8.18.18.8.3

It is the outermost electrons in any atom that largely determine its chemical nature because it is those electrons that interact when two or more atoms combine together to form compounds. That is why, for example, the formula of sodium chloride is $NaCl$, magnesium chloride is $MgCl_2$ and aluminium chloride is $AlCl_3$.

Bohr was the son of a professor of physiology at the University of Copenhagen and he spent most of his life as director of the Institute of Theoretical Physics in the same city. He was commonly referred to as the 'Great Dane' and is regarded by many as second only to Albert Einstein in the contribution he made to modern physics. One of his associates described him as the 'wisest and most lovable of men'[9] and he was both a great scientist and a great humanist – and, when young, a very good footballer. He won the Nobel Prize for Physics in 1922, and his son Aage won it in 1975. The father's gold medal is unique because in 1943, when he felt threatened by the Germans occupying Denmark (his mother was a Jew), he escaped to Sweden in a fishing boat. Fearful of the fate of his medal he dissolved it in concentrated nitric acid and put the solution in a safe place. It was recovered at the end of the war and the gold was extracted from it and re-cast into a new medal.

The combination of Rutherford's and Bohr's ideas produced a very useful atomic model, but there was still one outstanding problem because the packing together of unequal numbers of protons and electrons in a small atomic nucleus was recognised as being unsatisfactory so far as electrical forces were concerned. At the time it was not

Niels Bohr. (UKAEA)

known how to overcome this problem and the matter was not resolved until 1932, when James Chadwick discovered that a new atomic particle was produced by bombarding beryllium with alpha-particles obtained from a silver disc coated with polonium; he called it a neutron and announced its birth in a letter to *Nature* dated 17 February. His final experiments had taken ten days, during which he slept for only three hours each night; when it was over, he said: 'Now I want to be chloroformed and put to bed for a fortnight.'[10]

He was born in 1891 at Bollington in England and educated at Manchester Grammar School. After graduating in physics at Manchester University in 1911, he stayed there as one of Rutherford's assistants before moving to Berlin in 1913 to work with Geiger, who had returned to that city to become the director of the newly established radioactivity laboratory at the Physikalische-Technischen Reichsanstalt. Because he delayed his departure from Berlin, at the onset of war in 1914, Chadwick was unlucky enough to be interned as an enemy alien for the duration of the war and he had to live, with five others, in a box intended for two horses on Ruhleben race-track. On his return to England, with only £11 in his pocket and a severely disrupted digestive system, he joined Rutherford in the Cavendish Laboratory in Cambridge.

Sir James Chadwick in 1958. (Cavendish Laboratory)

In 1935 he won the Nobel Prize for Physics and soon after moved to Liverpool University as the Lyon Jones Professor of Physics. His department there became a leading centre of atomic physics and he was heavily involved in the early stages of deciding whether the building of an atom bomb might be a practical possibility. Later, from 1943, he led the British team working in America on developing just such a bomb. Back in Liverpool after the war, he was knighted in 1945, and he continued his research while also acting as an adviser on nuclear matters to the government. From 1948 to 1958 he was Master of Gonville and Caius College in Cambridge, and he died in 1974.

Chadwick's neutron was electrically neutral and it had a mass of 1 unit. Rutherford had in fact suggested the possible existence of such a particle in 1920 but had not pursued the matter. It is interesting to reflect on what might have been if the neutron had been found in 1920, particularly if it had been found in Germany, because of the essential role it played in the development of the atomic bomb. Its more immediate role, however, was as a component of atomic nuclei. Instead of them containing protons and electrons it was realised that they contained protons and neutrons. The number of protons was equal to the number of extra-nuclear electrons, and sufficient neutrons were added to make up the necessary relative atomic mass. For example:

Hydrogen, $_1^1$H   Helium, $_2^4$He   Lithium, $_3^7$Li   Uranium, $_{92}^{238}$U

$\left(\overline{1p}\right)$ 1e $\binom{2p}{2n}$ 2e $\binom{3p}{4n}$ 3e $\binom{92p}{146n}$ 92e

Atomic structures of atoms.

And this model for the structure of an atom soon came to be widely accepted.

CHAPTER 6
Ten Sorts of Tin

The atomic model built up by Rutherford, Bohr and Chadwick could account extremely well for the changes taking place in radioactive transformations, but only after Rutherford finally determined the precise nature of the alpha-particle, which he originally did in experiments carried out in collaboration with Geiger. Use was made, as in the bombardment experiments, of the fact that alpha particles caused a visible flash of light whenever they impinged on a screen coated with zinc sulphide. In a device that came to be called a spinthariscope, which was invented by Crookes in 1903, a small specimen of radium was supported in front of such a screen, which was viewed through an eye-piece fitted with a lens. The number of particles hitting the screen was counted and the total electrical charge built up on a similar but uncoated metal screen was also measured. This enabled the electrical charge on a single alpha-particle to be calculated. It turned out to be twice the charge on an electron, and this, in conjunction with the known charge/mass ratio for the alpha-particle, demonstrated that the particle must be the nucleus of a helium atom. That is, a particle consisting of 2 protons and 2 neutrons, with a mass of 4 and an electrical charge of +2.

This conclusion was confirmed by using an electrical method to count the alpha-particles. The apparatus consisted essentially of a thin, central anode wire stretched along the axis of a surrounding metal cylinder which served as the cathode. A high potential difference of over 1,000 volts was maintained between the anode and the cathode. Every time an alpha-particle passed into the cylinder there was a small

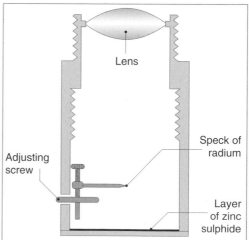

A spinthariscope.

Lens

Speck of radium

Adjusting screw

Layer of zinc sulphide

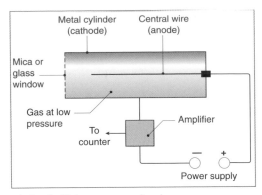

A simple Geiger counter circuit.

pulse of current between the anode and the cathode and this could be amplified so that it could be recorded as a click on a microphone or on an automatic counter. This piece of apparatus was later developed by Geiger and one of his students, W. Müller, into the Geiger–Müller counter, which is almost a household name nowadays. It is capable of measuring the intensity of alpha-, beta- and gamma-rays and it has been an indispensable instrument in all modern work on radiation.

The final verification of the association of alpha-particles with helium came much later, in an experiment carried out by Rutherford and Thomas Royds in 1909. A small amount of radium emanation was compressed into a thin-walled capillary tube, which was then sealed and placed in an outer, evacuated, glass container. After a few days the spectrum of helium was clearly visible when an electric discharge was passed through the contents of the outer container.

When a radioactive atom loses an alpha-particle, $_{2}^{4}$He, its atomic number decreases by 2 and its relative atomic mass by 4. The newly formed atom therefore lies in a group two places to the left in the periodic table. For example:

$$_{92}^{238}\text{U} \longrightarrow {}_{90}^{234}\text{Th} + {}_{2}^{4}\text{He}$$

$$_{88}^{224}\text{Ra} \longrightarrow {}_{86}^{220}\text{Rn} + {}_{2}^{4}\text{He}$$

When there is a loss of beta-rays, i.e. of electrons, $_{-1}^{0}$e, the atomic number increases by 1 but there is no change in the relative atomic mass. There is a move of one group to the right in the periodic table. For example:

$$_{88}^{228}\text{Ra} \longrightarrow {}_{89}^{228}\text{Ac} + {}_{-1}^{0}\text{e}$$

$$_{84}^{216}\text{Po} \longrightarrow {}_{85}^{216}\text{At} + {}_{-1}^{0}\text{e}$$

All the changes taking place in any of the disintegration series can, therefore, be recorded and this is done below for the thorium series, using modern symbols instead of the historical names given on page 49.

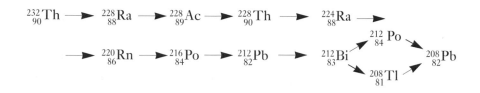

The consequential changes in place in the periodic table are shown in the diagram below, and the details for the uranium and actinium series are given in Appendix I on page 221.

In 1910, when he was in Glasgow, it occurred to Soddy that one of the consequences of understanding the nature of the changes taking place in a disintegration series was the realisation that atoms with the same atomic number but different relative atomic masses were sometimes formed. They occupied the same position in the periodic table and therefore had similar chemical properties but they had different masses and Soddy called them isotopes (from the Greek ισος τοπος meaning *the same place*). Examples from the thorium series are provided by $^{228}_{90}$Th and $^{232}_{90}$Th; $^{224}_{88}$Ra and $^{228}_{88}$Ra; $^{212}_{84}$Po and $^{216}_{84}$Po; and $^{208}_{82}$Pb and

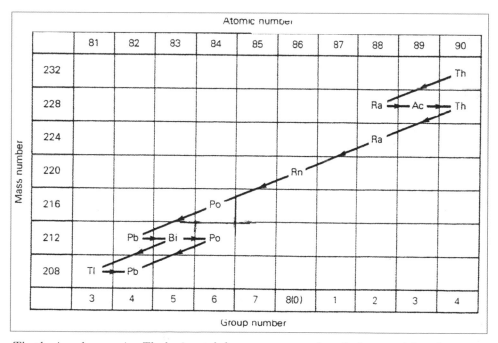

The thorium decay series. The horizontal changes represent a loss of a beta-particle and an increase in atomic number of 1. The diagonal changes represent a loss of an alpha-particle and a decrease in atomic number of 2 and in mass number of 4.

$^{212}_{82}$Pb. It is like having identical twins who differ only in their weight or, as Soddy himself put it, like 'having atoms with identical outsides but different insides'.[1]

Soddy's work was interrupted by the First World War between 1914 and 1918 but, when that was over, he became Dr Lee's professor of chemistry at Oxford in 1919. This was a new chair and many thought that it should have been filled from within, so Soddy was not welcomed with open arms and his appointment turned out to be something of a disaster for everyone. The Old Chemistry Department, of which he was in charge, was ill-equipped and lived up to its name, and he was obliged to do much more lecturing than he expected. But, more importantly, he lost much of his interest in radioactivity and he produced no papers during his time at Oxford. His attitude also became very arrogant and abrasive, particularly after he was awarded the Nobel Prize for Chemistry in 1921, 'for his contributions to the chemistry of radioactive substances and his investigation into the origin and nature of isotopes'. Consequently, he had few friends and he antagonised so many people that even when he did make good suggestions for change no one took any notice. He also became very touchy. He felt strongly, for instance, that radioactivity had been hi-jacked by physicists; he thought that what became nuclear physics should have been nuclear chemistry; and he wrote that he 'was sick to death of the efforts of the Cambridge clique to try to falsify the whole history of the subject so as to concentrate the limelight on the Cavendish Laboratory'.[2] He was also very dissatisfied with what he thought was the anti-science attitude in the ancient universities, and with the undemocratic way in which the Royal Society was organised.

Because of his early upbringing, he had always held strong views on social and moral issues. He had been profoundly disturbed by the First World War, and had became more and more concerned that science was 'proving as much a curse as a blessing to mankind',[3] so he turned his attention to social and economic matters and what he took to be the ills of the world. He put forward, in particular, the idea of a new monetary system based not on money but on energy. He wrote that 'the energy available for each individual man is his income'[4] and regarded money as a 'purely conventional symbol of wealth'.[5] Part of his solution to the problems was to nationalise the banks, but in general his ideas attracted very little support. This made him feel all the more isolated and, following the death of his wife in 1936, after twenty-eight years of marriage, he resigned from his Oxford professorship and undertook a long tour of India and the Far East with the intention of developing a new process for extracting thorium from monazite sand. But nothing came of it and he returned to England where he continued to propound his pet, and by now rather cranky, theories through his extensive writings. He eventually retired to Brighton where he lived a lonely, despondent and embittered life until he died on 22 September 1956 at the age of 79. Few people have enjoyed such an interesting and varied career. Professor Paneth, the Director of the Max Planck Institute in Germany, who worked closely with Soddy, wrote of his complex personality and of his suspicions of nearly everyone in authority, but asked his readers to 'honour the memory of a brilliant intellect, and experimenter second to none among the founders of radiochemistry, and an uncompromising champion of his ideals'.[6]

Very shortly after Soddy's announcement of the existence of *radioactive* isotopes, J.J. Thomson discovered that neon, which is not

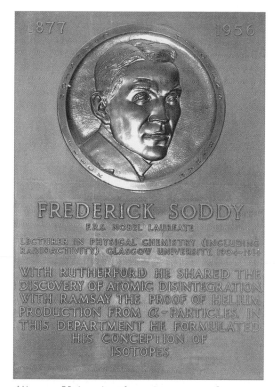

Glasgow University plaque in memory of Frederick Soddy. (Glasgow University)

radioactive, also had two isotopic forms. This discovery arose out of some much earlier work in 1886 by Eugen Goldstein, a German physicist who worked at the Berlin Observatory, on what he called canal rays (*Kanalstrahlen*). He found that the cathode rays formed in a discharge tube with a perforated cathode were associated with another set of rays that emanated from the holes in the cathode in the opposite direction to the cathode rays. In 1897 Wilhelm Wien, the Professor of Physics at Aachen, measured the charge/mass ratio of the rays by deflecting them in a magnetic field, and this showed that they consisted of positively charged particles more than a thousand times heavier than electrons. It was thought that they consisted of positively charged particles formed by the loss of electrons from the atoms or molecules of the gas in the discharge tube.

J.J. Thomson reinvestigated these rays, which he called positive rays, in 1913, using the same technique of applying magnetic and electrical fields that he had developed for measuring the charge/mass ratio of the electrons in cathode rays. In this way all the particles in the positive rays with the same charge/mass ratio were deflected in the same way and could be picked out from those with different

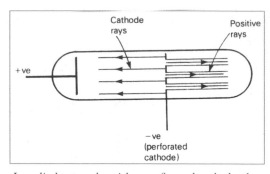

In a discharge tube with a perforated cathode, the cathode rays are associated with positive rays flowing in the opposite direction.

charge/mass ratios. Using a discharge tube containing neon gas, with a relative atomic mass of 20.183, Thomson discovered that the positive rays actually contained two particles, one with a mass of 20 and the other of 22, with the former predominating to give an *average* mass of 20.183. They were the first two *non-radioactive* isotopes to be discovered, but another isotope, of mass 21, later came to light.

Thomson then set one of his assistants, F.W. Aston, the task of trying to see if he could separate these two components of neon. It was realised that the two isotopes would have identical *chemical* properties but it was hoped that slight differences in their *physical* properties might make separation possible. Aston's first attempt was to make use of possible differences in boiling point but even after 3,000 fractionations he had no success. He then turned to possible density differences which would give different rates of diffusion through a clay pipe, and this enabled him to get a partial separation of the two isotopes which provided him with two samples of neon, one with a relative atomic mass of 20.16 and the other with a value of 20.28.

Aston was born in Harborne, England, in 1893 and was educated at Malvern College and at Mason College, which later became Birmingham University. His early research work was carried out not only in that university but also in an attic of his private house, when he worked for a while in a brewery. He joined the team at the Cavendish Laboratory in 1910 but worked at the Royal Aircraft Establishment at Farnborough during the First World War, investigating the treatment of aeroplane fabrics with lacquers (dopes). He was lucky enough to work with G.P. Thomson, J.J.'s son, and to escape injury when an experimental plane crashed in 1914. The change of scene and activity from that associated with a university laboratory greatly increased Aston's engineering experience and enabled him to develop Thomson's positive ray apparatus into a new instrument, which he called a mass spectrograph, when he returned to the Cavendish Laboratory in 1918. The third model he built, which could measure masses to 1 part in 10^5, has been developed into a commercially available instrument, which can measure to 1 part in 10^9, and this has played an important role in radiochemistry, nuclear physics and organic analysis.

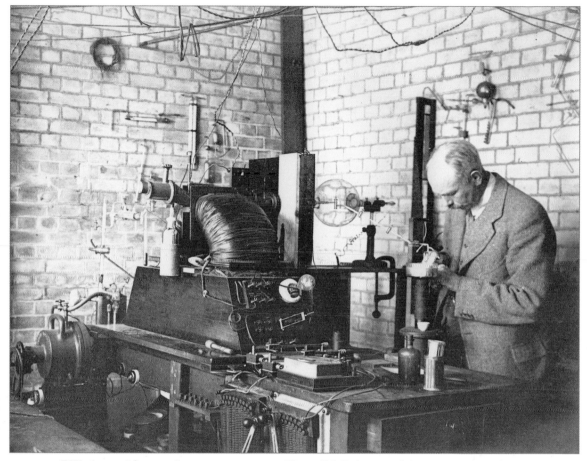

F.W. Aston with an early mass spectrometer. (Cavendish Laboratory)

His first success with his new equipment was the discovery of two isotopes of chlorine – with an expected atomic mass of 35.5 – with masses of 35 and 37, and within a few years he had examined around fifty elements. Almost all the elements have now been found to have stable, non-radioactive, naturally occurring isotopes and many have a wide variety, with tin having ten. Dalton's idea that all atoms of the same element were alike had been proved to be just as wrong as his idea that they were indestructible.

Hydrogen has two main isotopes; it is made up of 99.985 per cent of hydrogen or protium (^1_1H) and 0.015 per cent of heavy hydrogen or deuterium (^2_1H or D). Tritium (^3_1H or T) can also be made but it is doubtful whether it occurs naturally in ordinary hydrogen. Oxygen also has three isotopes, $^{16}_8O$, $^{17}_8O$ and $^{18}_8O$, which means that there are nine possible sorts of water molecule. The commonest variety is formulated as $^1H_2{}^{16}O$, and what is known as heavy water, or deuterium oxide, is $^2H_2{}^{16}O$ or $D_2{}^{16}O$. The three isotopes of uranium – uranium-238, uranium-235 and uranium-234 are also very important:

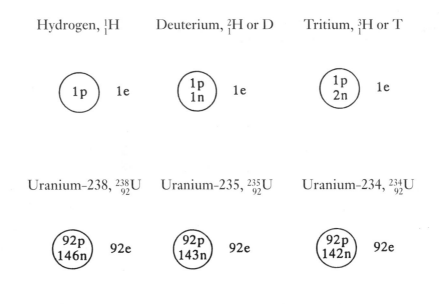

Hydrogen, ^1_1H Deuterium, ^2_1H or D   Tritium, ^3_1H or T

Uranium-238, $^{238}_{92}U$ Uranium-235, $^{235}_{92}U$ Uranium-234, $^{234}_{92}U$

Atomic structures of isotopes.

From 1918 Aston lived for the rest of his life as an elegant but reserved bachelor fellow in Trinity College, Cambridge. He won the Nobel Prize for Chemistry in 1922, but he had many other interests. He was skilful enough to make a home-made vacuum pump; he was fond of travel and sport; he was a good enough musician to be the music critic of the *Cambridge Review* for many years; he was keen on astronomy; he was a very good photographer; and he had sufficient financial know-how to build up the money left to him by his father so that he was very rich when he died in 1945. His obituary notice in the *Proceedings of the Royal Society* summarised his life as a 'chain of uninterrupted success'.

CHAPTER 7
Artificial Radioactivity

Rutherford was knighted in 1914 and he wrote to a friend that 'it is, of course, very satisfactory to have one's work recognised by the powers that be, but the form of recognition is also a little embarrassing for a relatively youthful and impecunious Professor like myself. However, I will trust it will not interfere with my future activities.'[1] The outbreak of war in that same year did in fact cause some interruption to his planned activities. Not only was he involved in a research programme concerned with trying to improve the methods for detecting submarines, but he was also a member of the Board of Inventions and Research, and he spent quite a lot of time in the United States as a member of the British Mission there.

He did, nevertheless, find time to begin an investigation into the effect of bombarding a number of light elements with alpha-particles. He knew from his earlier experiments that alpha-particles were scattered by the nuclei of heavier elements but he hoped that they might have a more marked effect on the nuclei of lighter elements which carried lower positive charges. 'I am also trying', he wrote, 'to break up the atom by this method.'[2] He therefore experimented with passing the alpha-particles from radium C through a number of different gases on to a zinc sulphide screen on which he hoped to pick up some possible scintillations. When the screen was close to the radium C it showed many scintillations caused by the alpha-particles passing straight through the gas, but when it was taken further away these scintillations disappeared because the particles had insufficient energy to pass through more gas. Surprisingly, however, he still observed scintillations on the zinc sulphide screen when he used air as the gas, and he concluded that they were caused by protons (the nuclei of hydrogen atoms). Because there were no similar scintillations when the air was replaced by pure oxygen, he concluded that the protons must have come from collisions between alpha-particles and nitrogen atoms in the air. He interpreted the change – wrongly, as it later transpired – as involving the formation of carbon-13 and alpha-particles along with the protons:

$$^{14}_{7}N + ^{4}_{2}He \longrightarrow ^{1}_{1}H + ^{13}_{6}C + ^{4}_{2}He$$

Once again he showed a masterly touch in his choice of research project, and when he announced its result in 1919 it was the first ever example of the artificial disintegration of an atomic nucleus. It was also the last project that he undertook at Manchester. In October 1919 he succeeded Sir J.J. Thomson as Cavendish Professor at Cambridge University and it was there, in 1923, that Patrick Blackett demonstrated that the new process discovered by Rutherford did actually involve the formation of oxygen-17 along with protons:

$$^{14}_{7}N + ^{4}_{2}He \longrightarrow ^{1}_{1}H + ^{17}_{8}O$$

Blackett, born in Croydon, Surrey, joined the Royal Navy as a cadet in 1912, at the age of 15, and was present at the battles of Jutland and the Falkland Islands. His scientific bent came to light when he designed a new gun-sight, and at the end of the war he went to study science at Cambridge, eventually joining the team at the Cavendish Laboratory where he helped to develop a piece of equipment called a cloud chamber. This had been invented in 1912 by a colleague, C.T.R. Wilson, who was born in 1869 on a Scottish farm. Following his father's death when Wilson was only 4 years old, the family moved to Manchester and Wilson studied biology at Owens College (now Manchester University). He taught at Bradford Grammar School for four years before becoming a lecturer, and eventually the Jacksonian Professor of Natural Philosophy, at Cambridge. He was awarded the Nobel Prize for Physics in 1927

C.T.R. Wilson. (Cavendish Laboratory)

and Blackett wrote of him that 'of
the great scientists of this age he was
perhaps the most gentle and serene,
and the most indifferent to prestige
and honour. His absorption in his
work arose from his immense love of
the natural world and from his
delight in its beauties.'[3]

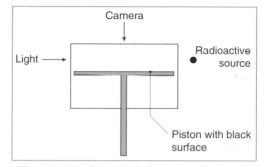

The principle of the cloud chamber.

The idea for the cloud chamber,
which Rutherford is reported to
have described as 'the most original apparatus in the whole history of physics',[4]
had grown out of Wilson's interest in atmospheric electricity and cloud
formation, which had developed during visits to Ben Nevis in Scotland in 1894
and 1895, and led him to investigate methods of forming artificial clouds by the
sudden expansion of moist air. His cloud chamber consisted of a glass cylinder,
about 130cm in diameter, full of damp air or some other gas, and fitted with a
piston with a black upper surface. A downward movement of the piston caused

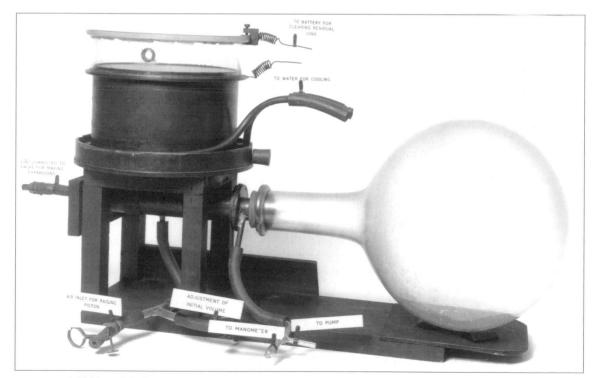

A 1911 model of Wilson's original cloud chamber. (Cavendish Laboratory)

Typical cloud chamber photographs. (Top left) Tracks of alpha-particles from thorium-C showing different ranges. (Top right) Tracks of electrons in a magnetic field. (Bottom left) A collision between an alpha-particle and a helium atom. Because they both have the same mass, their paths after collision are at right-angles to each other. (Bottom right) An alpha-particle hits a nitrogen atom to form an oxygen atom and a proton. The path of the proton is shown by the lighter, longer track and that of the oxygen atom by the heavier, shorter one. (Photos by P.M.S. Blackett)

the damp gas to expand and cool, which resulted in it becoming supersaturated with water vapour. Charged particles passed through the gas at this stage formed nuclei on which the water could condense to form vapour trails like those sometimes observed from the tail of an aeroplane. These trails could be photographed so that a permanent track of the movement of the particles could be recorded. In practice, the piston was moved by connecting it, through a valve, to a large evacuated glass globe; when the valve was opened, the piston was sucked downwards. The cloud chamber was used to measure the penetration of different particles, to show the effect of a magnetic field on their path, and the effect when they collided with other atoms. Blackett used it, for example, in 1923 to photograph Rutherford's 1919 artificial atomic transmutation of nitrogen into oxygen by collision with an alpha-particle, but he had to take more than twenty thousand pictures before he discovered what he was looking for because only very few alpha-particles brought about the change.

Light elements, other than nitrogen, also lost protons when bombarded by alpha-particles but that did not happen with heavier elements because the particles did not have enough energy to break through the higher positive charges on their nuclei. Consequently John Cockcroft and Ernest Walton had the idea of building what came to be known as a particle accelerator to provide high-energy particles with which to bombard atomic nuclei. They were encouraged to do this by two Russians – George Gamow and Peter Kapitza – who were working alongside them. Cockcroft was particularly well equipped to do this. After an early education in his birthplace of Todmorden in Yorkshire, he had read mathematics at Manchester University, and had then gone on to serve as a signaller in the army. He subsequently trained as an electrical engineer at Manchester College of Technology and worked as an apprentice for the engineering firm Metropolitan-Vickers before joining Rutherford in 1924. He became the Jacksonian Professor at Cambridge in 1939 and played an outstanding role both as a scientist and administrator in the development of the atomic bomb during the Second World War and of peaceful uses of nuclear power after the war, and in 1959 was elected as the first Master of the newly formed Churchill College in Cambridge. Ernest Walton was born in Dungarvon, County Waterford, in 1903 and educated at the Methodist College in Belfast and at Trinity College, Dublin, before joining the staff at the Cavendish in 1927. He returned to Trinity College, Dublin, in 1934 and was the Professor of Natural and Experimental Philosophy there from 1947 to 1974 when he retired.

The first particle accelerator designed by Cockcroft and Walton and built at a cost of £500 – a record high, in its day, for a single piece of equipment at the Cavendish Laboratory – provided a beam of high-energy protons. They were produced initially in the positive rays of a discharge tube containing hydrogen and they were then energised by passing in succession through high-intensity electrical fields in three cylindrical electrodes. When the energised protons were passed through a hole in a piece of mica they emerged as a well-focused beam and when Cockcroft and Walton directed the beam on to lithium or boron they found that alpha-particles were formed:

Sir John Cockcroft (UKAEA) and his signature on a Nycomed–Amersham mural. (Photograph by Ed Lorch)

E.T.S. Walton. (UKAEA)

$$^1_1H + {^7_3}Li \longrightarrow {^2_4}He$$

$$^1_1H + {^1_{15}}B \longrightarrow {^3_4}He$$

The formation of the alpha-particles was confirmed by photographing their tracks in a cloud chamber, and Cockcroft and Walton announced the result of their experiment on 16 April 1932. At the same time, in the United States, Robert Van de Graaff at Princeton and Ernest Lawrence at the University of California were both working on new ways of generating high voltages, and in due course Cockcroft and Wilson's accelerator gave way to cyclotrons, synchrotons and cosmotrons, all designed to provide particles with higher and higher energy so that nuclei could be bombarded more and more effectively. Cockcroft wrote that 'we are living in the Golden Age of Physics, so rapidly did discoveries come along'.[5]

One of them occurred in 1933, when the first artificially radioactive isotopes of non-radioactive elements were made by Madame Curie's daughter Irène and her husband Frédéric Joliot. Irène was born in Paris in 1897 and educated first in a

An accelerator built by Cockcroft and Walton at the Cavendish Laboratory in 1932 being operated by Walton. (Cavendish Laboratory)

cooperative school organised by her mother for the children of her friends and then at a private school, the Collège Sévigné. During the First World War she helped her mother to run mobile X-ray units. Thereafter, she worked with her mother in the Radium Institute and graduated from there after writing a thesis on the nature of alpha-radiation from polonium. Frédéric was also a Parisian, born in 1900, the youngest of six children. After attending the Lycée Lakanal, he decided to train as an engineer and studied at the École Lavoisier for two years before moving to the School of Physics and Chemistry in Paris where M and Mme Curie had discovered radium. He graduated from there in 1923 and after working for a year as an engineer in a steel factory and doing his military service he was appointed as an assistant to Madame Curie at the Radium Institute in 1925. A year later he married Irène, and to maintain the Curie name the couple adopted their married name of Joliot-Curie. This led to their nickname, the Jolly-Curios, which reflected in particular Frédéric's lively personality. They were interested not only in scientific research but in contemporary social and political matters, and they played a major role in the activities of the Popular Front which arose after the anti-Republic riots of 6 February 1934.

Their major joint discovery was that phosphorus, with a relative atomic mass of 31, had a radioactive isotope with a mass of 30, which was formed when aluminium was bombarded with alpha-particles. The nuclear reaction involved is represented by the equation:

$$^{27}_{13}\text{Al} + ^{4}_{2}\text{He} \longrightarrow ^{30}_{15}\text{P} + ^{1}_{0}\text{n}$$

The isotope was also unusual in that it decayed to a stable isotope of silicon by losing a positron, which was a particle with the same mass as an electron and a positive charge of the same magnitude. This new particle had been observed at the California Institute of Technology by Carl D. Anderson in 1932 while he was studying the tracks made in a cloud chamber by cosmic rays, and its existence had been confirmed soon after by Patrick Blackett.

The Joliot-Curies were awarded the Nobel Prize for Chemistry jointly in 1935 but their collaboration ended soon after when Irène followed her mother as Professor and Director of the Curie Radium Laboratory at the Sorbonne and Frédéric became the Professor at the Collège de France. He was particularly active in the French Resistance movement during the war and was twice arrested by the Nazis. After the war he developed the National Centre for Scientific Research and became High Commissioner of the French Atomic Energy Commission, in which capacity he was responsible for building the first French

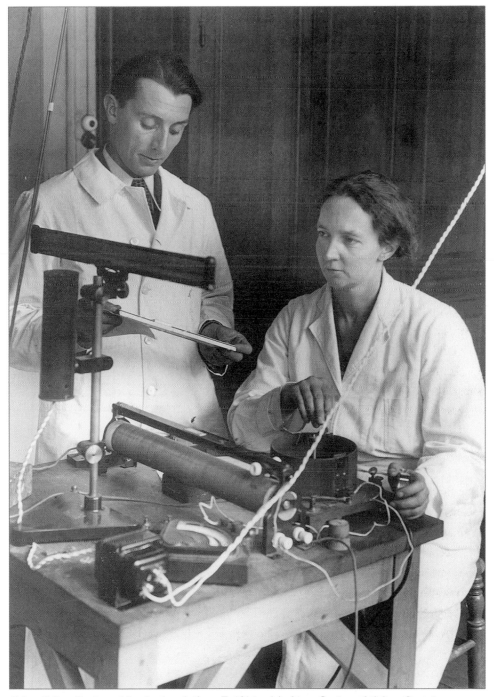

Irène Joliot-Curie and her husband, Jean Frédéric. (Archives Curie and Joliot-Curie)

nuclear reactor in the Fort de Chantillon in 1948. He was, however, dismissed from that job in 1950 because of his membership of the Communist party. He returned to academic life at the Collége de France and became President of the Communist-sponsored World Peace Council, being awarded the Stalin Peace Prize in 1951. Irène died in 1956 of leukemia, probably caused by long exposure to radiation, and he succeeded to her chair in the Sorbonne, but died after two years as a result of an accident.

The year after the Juliot-Curies won their Nobel Prize, Enrico Fermi was appointed, at the age of 25, to a newly created post as Professor of Theoretical Physics at the University of Rome. Setting up the new professorship was, in the main, the idea of Orso Mario Corbino, a senator of the Kingdom of Italy as well as the Director of the Physics Institute in the University of Rome. He was concerned that science was at such a low ebb in the country, which had not won any Nobel prize since that awarded to Marconi in 1909, and he hoped that Fermi's appointment would 'enable Italy to regain with honour its lost eminence'.[6]

Fermi was the son of a high-ranking civil servant, and had been educated at the select Reale Scuola Normale Superior in Pisa and at the University of Pisa, where he gained his doctorate for a thesis on X-rays before working at Göttingen, Leiden and the University of Florence. His interest in physics had begun when, at the tender age of 14, he bought a second-hand book on the subject in the market of Campo dei Fiori. His initial interest was encouraged by a friend of his father's who lent him other books. By the time he was 17 he was familiar with such abstruse topics as the generalised theory of relativity, and it was the mathematical and theoretical aspects of physics which he most liked.

Enrico Fermi. (Argonne National Laboratory)

He was, nevertheless, a very good experimentalist and in his new post he continued at first the work that was already going on in spectroscopy and atomic physics.

Because his was a new post, however, he was free to choose his own research project. Influenced by the results recently announced by Rutherford and by the Joliot-Curies, he opted to investigate the effect of irradiating elements with neutrons in the hope that he would be able to make radioactive isotopes. It was an inspired choice and one of the best examples of how the best researchers seem able to choose the right topic for their research at the right moment. It had been known for some time that neither alpha-particles nor protons, as used by Rutherford and the Joliot-Curies, were ideal bombarding particles because they carried positive charges and so were repelled by the positive nuclei at which they were aimed. So Fermi thought that 'neutrons would be much better'[7] and he and his team – the 'Pope' and the 'boys' as they were called – set to work with a glass tube containing radon, a source of alpha-particles, and powdered beryllium to provide the neutrons, using home-made Geiger counters to detect any radioactivity.

They were at first disappointed because there was no sign of any radioactivity when they bombarded water (containing hydrogen and oxygen atoms), lithium, beryllium, boron and carbon with neutrons – but everything changed with their next target, calcium fluoride. After irradiation with neutrons for only a few minutes there was some short-lived reaction in a nearby Geiger counter. Thereafter they tested over sixty other elements and found positive results in forty cases, with a new radioactive isotope being found every few days. Fermi's team later looked back to this as the most glorious and satisfying period of their lives. They had made the manufacture of a wide variety of radioactive isotopes relatively simple and by 1948 more than a thousand were known.

They also made another extremely significant discovery when they found, in October 1934, that the effect of neutrons as bombarding particles was greatly affected by their speed. Most people thought that speeding up the neutrons would increase their effectiveness, but Fermi decided to try slowing them down. To that end he originally planned to pass the neutrons through a piece of lead but, feeling mysteriously dissatisfied with that idea, he replaced it, at the last moment, with a piece of paraffin. He wrote that 'with no advance warning, no conscious, prior, reasoning, I immediately took some odd piece of paraffin . . . and placed it where the piece of lead was to have been'.[8]

The paraffin slowed down the neutrons – 'moderated' them was the final technical term that came to be used – and, surprisingly, increased their ability to produce radioactive isotopes in many cases. Fermi interpreted this as meaning that the bombarding neutrons sometimes simply bounced off one nucleus on to another; sometimes they split the nucleus and converted it into another, which might be radioactive; and sometimes the nucleus 'captured' a neutron and was converted into a heavier one. What actually happened seemed to depend both on the speed of the neutrons and the size of the nucleus being bombarded. Because there were so many possibilities it was difficult to interpret all the experimental results fully and those obtained when uranium was irradiated with neutrons were especially perplexing.

Fermi thought that some of the uranium nuclei might be capturing neutrons and that new trans-uranium elements with nuclei heavier than uranium might be being formed, and he even suggested that they could be called ausonium and hesperium. This possibility was announced as a certainty in June 1934, and widely claimed as a great triumph for the Fascist culture of Mussolini's Italy. But Fermi was mistaken and it was not until 1939 that others – notably Otto Hahn, Lise Meitner and Fritz Strassman – clarified the situation. By then Fermi had won the Nobel Prize for Physics in 1938 for his 'use of neutron irradiation to produce new elements and the discovery of nuclear reactions induced by slow neutrons'. And because his wife, Laura, was Jewish, Fermi took advantage of his visit to Stockholm to receive the prize and the family emigrated to the United States, where he played a predominant role in the development of the atom bomb (which had in fact been made possible by his earlier neutron research). Professor Corbino's hopes had been more than fulfilled.

By then there had been real progress in making trans-uranium elements and this was the final achievement in the discovery of new radioactive species. The first two, neptunium and plutonium, were made in 1940 by E. McMillan and P.H. Abelson, at the University of California at Berkeley, by bombarding uranium with neutrons. This was the method by which Fermi thought he had made a trans-uranium element in 1934, but the difference was that the neutrons used by McMillan and Abelson came from the cyclotron recently constructed by Ernest Lawrence. The $^{238}_{92}U$ atom initially captures one neutron:

$$^{238}_{92}U + ^{1}_{0}n \longrightarrow ^{239}_{92}U$$

and the resulting heavier isotope of uranium decays in two stages to form a plutonium isotope:

$$^{239}_{92}U \longrightarrow ^{239}_{93}Np + ^{0}_{-1}e$$
$$^{239}_{93}Np \longrightarrow ^{239}_{94}Pu + ^{0}_{-1}e$$

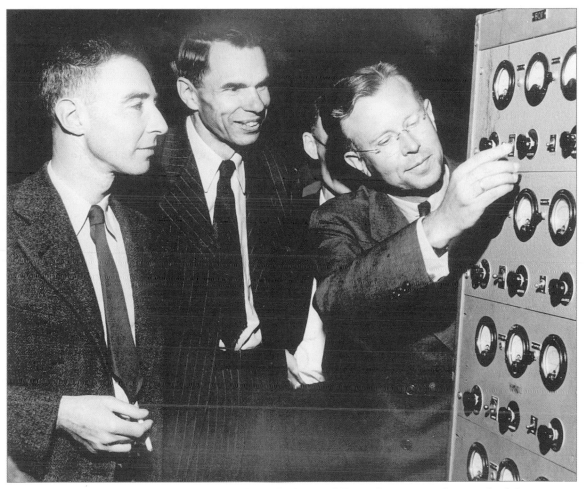

(Left to right) Robert Oppenheimer, Glenn Seaborg and Ernest Lawrence at the controls of the 184-inch cyclotron magnet in the Lawrence Berkeley Laboratory. (Ernest Orlando Lawrence Berkeley National Laboratory)

At about the same time, a team led by Glenn T. Seaborg prepared another isotope of plutonium by bombarding uranium oxide with high energy deuterons produced in a cyclotron:

$$^{238}_{92}U + ^{2}_{1}H \longrightarrow ^{238}_{93}Np + 2^{1}_{0}n$$
$$^{238}_{93}Np \longrightarrow ^{238}_{94}Pu + ^{0}_{-1}e$$

The ^{239}Pu and ^{238}Pu isotopes both disintegrate with the loss of an alpha-particle into different isotopes of uranium, the former with a half-life of 24,390 years and the latter with one of 92 years:

Between 1944 and 1958 all the elements with atomic numbers between 95 and 103 were made by similar methods. They are called, in turn, Americium (Am), Curium (Cm), Berkelium (Bk), Californium (Cf), Einsteinium (Es), Fermium (Fm), Lawrencium (Lr), Mendeleevium (Md) and Nobelium (No). Seaborg was the leading light in this work, though he had a number of close associates. Born in Ishpeming, Michigan, in 1912 of Swedish immigrant parents, he went to school in Los Angeles and received his doctor's degree in 1937 at the University of California, with which he was associated all his life. During the Second World War he carried on his research as a section head at the Metallurgical Laboratory at Chicago University, but he returned to California as the Professor of Chemistry in 1945. He was awarded the Nobel Prize for Chemistry jointly with Edwin McMillan in 1951 and was Chairman of the US Atomic Energy Commission from 1961 to 1971.

More recently, other new, highly radioactive elements – sometimes known as super-heavy elements, with relative atomic masses higher than the 260 value for lawrencium – have been made by high-energy collisions between two smaller atoms or ions. The new elements are, however, ephemeral, with half-lives of just a fraction of a second; only a few atoms of them have ever been made and only under very artificial conditions, and the very existence of some of them is in doubt.

This new advance began in 1964, when a new element, with an atomic number of 104, was made both at the Joint Institute for Nuclear Research at Dubna in the USSR and at the Lawrence Radiation Laboratory in the University of California at Berkeley. The Russians made it by collision between plutonium-242 and neon-22 and called it kurchatovium after Igor Kurchatov, who was appointed lecturer in nuclear physics at Leningrad University in 1938 and moved to the newly formed Soviet Atomic Energy Institute in 1942. The Americans used a collision between californium-249 and carbon-12 and called it rutherfordium, after Lord Rutherford. Other similar discoveries followed both in Russia and America and also in the Gesellschaft Für Schwerionforschung (GSI, or the Society for Heavy Ion Research) in Darmstadt, Germany, and the Paul Scherrer Institute in Switzerland. The discovery of all but three of the elements up to the atomic number 118 has been claimed, but there has been considerable confusion and argument about the names to be used for them. The International Union of Pure and Applied Chemistry (IUPAC) originally suggested temporary names based on

H																	He
Li	Be											B	C	N	O	F	Ne
Na	Mg											Al	Si	P	S	Cl	Ar
K	Ca	Sc	Ti	V	Cr	Mn	Fe	Co	Ni	Cu	Zn	Ga	Ge	As	Sc	Br	Kr
Rb	Sr	Y	Zr	Nb	Mo	Tc'	Ru	Rh	Pd	Ag	Cd	In	Sn	Sb	Te	I	Xe
Cs	Ba	* Lu	Hf	Ta	W	Re	Os	Ir	Pt	Au	Hg	Tl	Pb	Bi	Po	At	Rn
Fr	Ra	+ Lr	Rf	Db	Sg	Bh	Hs	Mt	Uun	Uuu	Uub		Uuq		Uuh		Uuo

*	La	Ce	Pr	Nd	Pm	Sm	Eu	Gd	Tb	Dy	Ho	Er	Tm	Yb
+	Ac	Th	Pa	U	Np	Pu	Am	Cm	Bk	Cf	Es	Fm	Md	No

Modern periodic table showing 115 elements.

the atomic number of the element. On this basis, kurchatovium or rutherfordium was named unnilquadium (Unq), and elements with successively higher atomic numbers, up to 109, were called unnilpentium (Unp), unnilhexium (Unh), unnilseptium (Uns), unniloctium (Uno) and unnilennium (Une). After considerable controversy between Europe and America it was, however, eventually agreed that these elements should be named as rutherfordium (Rf) for element number 104, dubnium (Db) for 105, seaborgium (Sg) for 106, bohrium (Bh) for 107, hessium (Hs) – after the Latin for the German state of Hess – for 108 and meitnerium (Mt) for 109. Newly claimed elements with atomic numbers between 110 and 118 are, temporarily, called ununnilium (Uun) for 110, unununium (Unu) for 111, ununbium (Uub) for 112, ununquadium (Uuq) for 114, ununhexium (Uuh) for 116 and ununoctium (Uuo) for 118.

* * *

It is a measure of the importance of all this remarkable work on radioactivity and the structure of the atom that between 1908 and 1951 it resulted in nine Nobel prize winners in chemistry and ten in physics; even more remarkable was the fact that eleven of them had worked under Rutherford. He had been showered with honours for his own contribution and these were capped successively by the award of the Order of Merit in 1925, by being appointed President of the Royal Society, a position he held between 1925 and 1930, and by elevation to the peerage in 1931 when he became Baron Rutherford of Nelson, commemorating his birthplace. He sent a cable to his 89-year-old mother, with whom he had always kept in close touch, which read: 'Now Lord Rutherford, more your honour than mine.'[9]

Lord Rutherford's coat of arms. (Photograph by Colin Flood)

His armorial bearings were supported on the dexter side by a figure representing Hermes Trismegistus, the Egyptian god of wisdom who may have written books on alchemy, and on the sinister side by a Maori brandishing a club. The escutcheon was quartered by two curved graphs showing the matching decay and growth of a radioactive parent and daughter element. This typified the majestic nature of Rutherford's character and achievements but it said nothing of the sadness that he and his wife had to endure. In 1930 their daughter, who was married to Professor R.H. Fowler, the Cambridge physicist, died just a week after giving birth to her fourth child. Rutherford never really got over this loss, but found some consolation in his two granddaughters and two grandsons.

He died, after a sudden and short illness, on 19 October 1937, aged 66, and was buried in Westminster Abbey. *The Times* reported that he had been 'a living force in academic life and both intellectually and socially all things will be slower and weaker for want of his ubiquitous and enthusiastic energy'. And James Chadwick wrote that 'the world mourns the death of a great scientist but we have lost our friend, our counsellor, our staff and our leader'.[10]

CHAPTER 8
Early Uses

The first X-ray photograph was taken by Wilhelm Röntgen, after dinner on the evening of 22 December 1895, when he asked his wife Bertha to come down to his laboratory and place her hand on a photographic plate beneath a beam of X-rays. He called it a shadow photograph and when it was developed it showed the bone structure of her hand, showing some signs of arthritis, together with two rings on one finger. A few weeks later, in January 1896, an X-ray of a patient with a needle stuck in the foot was taken at the London Hospital in Britain, and the use of this new technique, now known as radiography or diagnostic radiology, spread rapidly around the world. Today, the 'picture' can be shown up on a fluorescent screen or on photographic film; it is estimated that every year about half the people in the industrial world have an X-ray. In the United Kingdom some 25 million medical X-rays and 10 million dental ones are taken every year.

Taking X-rays in the early days was both hit-or-miss and dangerous. The equipment was very rudimentary and unreliable, and the operator, who had to experiment with different techniques as he or she went along, was liable to be seriously harmed. There was, nevertheless, rapid progress. The first radiograph was taken in England

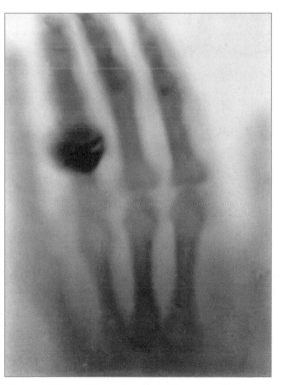

X-ray of Frau Röntgen's hand. (Deutsches Röntgen-Museum)

by the engineer A.A. Campbell Swinton, on 8 January 1896; just a few weeks later, on 15 February 1896, the first was published in the USA in the *New York Medical Record*; also in the same year William Morton produced a textbook in the USA, *The X-ray*, containing forty-seven photographs. Also in 1896 electrical departments were opened in several London hospitals and it was announced that X-rays would be used in all hospitals in Belgium. In 1987 the Röntgen Society was formed in Britain, and in 1898, during the Sudanese campaign, Surgeon-Major J.C. Battersby took sixty X-ray pictures using the first two army–issue sets under the most difficult of circumstances. The wax insulation in the induction coil threatened to melt in the heat of the desert and the batteries operating the coil had to be recharged by a pedal-cyclist. A year later there were nine army sets and 22,000 X-rays were taken during the South African War.

At first the penetration of the X-rays was very limited and it was necessary to use a long exposure to get a picture. It took 30 minutes, for example, to take the first ever chest X-ray of a 10-year-old girl at St Thomas's Hospital in London in 1896, and it took William Morton the same time to take a whole-body X-ray in 1897. But that problem was solved by using higher voltages in the X-ray tubes, even though it eventually involved cooling the tubes, and by the invention in 1913 of a new type of tube (known as a thermionic tube) by W.D. Coolidge, an American physical chemist who worked for the General Electric Company at Schenectady, New York. The invention of various pre-treatments also greatly extended the scope of radiography. The barium meal, for example, was invented by an American doctor, Walter Bradford Canon, in 1897. The patient swallows a suspension of barium salts, which is opaque to X-rays, so that the digestive system can be investigated. In the early 1920s Sickard and Forestier injected a mixture of iodine and poppy seed into the bronchial tubes to render chosen parts more opaque; this procedure is now called bronchography. Likewise, the gall bladder was rendered opaque to X-rays by injection in 1924; vessels in the brain in 1927; and in the translumbar region in 1929.

Another very important step forward came in the 1930s with the invention of tomography – a word derived from the Greek *tomos* (a slice) and *graphein* (to draw). A conventional X-ray picture is a two-dimensional picture of a three-dimensional structure, and thus it has no depth. Tomography aims to produce a three-dimensional picture by building up a series of pictures of thin slices of a part of the body. This is done by arranging for the X-rays to be focused on to points in one plane and to arrange the detectors so that they can only pick up rays from those points. When that has been done the process is repeated for points in a different plane. Both the source of the X-rays and the detectors have to move in unison. The first and simplest way of doing this was invented in the 1930s by Professor Bernard Zeidses des Plantes and came to be known as plain tomography.

X-rays also came to play another important role when doctors examining the deleterious effects of X-rays on the skin of people using them realised that, because they could kill off human cells, they might be used for therapeutic as well as diagnostic purposes. In November 1896, for example, the Austrian doctor Leopold Freund removed an unwanted hairy growth from a birthmark on the back of a 5-year-old girl by treatment with X-rays for 2 hours per day over a period of 16 days. The idea was taken up, particularly by W.S. Hedley, who was in charge of the electrotherapeutics department at the London Hospital and by Dr John Macintyre, the Medical Electrician at the Royal Infirmary in Glasgow. Much had to be learnt. What doses and exposures were necessary to deal with all the different situations that arose? How could damage to healthy tissues be kept to a minimum? How could X-rays with sufficient energy be obtained? Over the years, however, it has grown into a major method of cancer treatment and a main component of oncology, the study of tumours.

Until the discovery of radium there was little demand for radioactive substances and their only uses were in making coloured glass and gas mantles. The glass-making had been invented by Josef Riedel in Bohemia in the 1830s and used uranium compounds for making yellow and green glasses which glowed in some lights. In 1885 Baron von Welsbach found that a mantle made from silk or cotton impregnated with a mixture of 99 per cent thorium oxide and 1 per cent cerium oxide greatly improved the illumination when placed over a gas light.

The Curies and others realised that radium was likely to be very useful and they did not patent their extraction process because they did not want to impede its manufacture. Nevertheless, its applications could only be developed very slowly because it was in such short supply, and at a price of $180,000,000 per gram it was more expensive than the finest gemstone. Factory-scale production began in 1902 in a plant of the Central Chemical Products Company in Paris, which had been opened with a grant of 20,000 francs from the French Academy of Sciences and was supervised by André Debierne. Later, in 1904, Armet de Lisle, a French manufacturer of quinine, built a factory at Nogent-sur-Marne to the east of Paris where radium was made and, soon after, the Austrian government opened a plant at Jáchymov. Madame Curie, though generally presented as a pure scientist interested only in research, kept in close touch with all this industrial activity and always hoped that a national centre for making radium would be set up in France.

That never happened and by the start of the First World War only about 12 grams of radium had been made world-wide, almost all of it coming from Europe. Most of it had been made from such a low-grade pitchblende ore that it could take as much as 400 tons to provide 1 gram of radium, but a search for richer ores soon brought much better results and radium production advanced in three clear stages. First, carnotite found in western Colorado was used to establish an American industry which made almost 200 grams of radium, some of it at a price as low as $38,000 per gram, between 1913 and 1923. But that collapsed when rich pitchblende ores, giving 1 gram of radium for 10 tons of ore, were found in the Belgian Congo. They were mined by the Union Minière du Haut Katanga mainly from the Chinkolobwe mine, and processed at Oolen in Belgium, that country becoming the main supplier of radium between 1922 and 1933. Then, in 1931, similar pitchblende ores were found along the shores of the Great Bear Lake in Canada, and new companies set up there could compete with the Belgians. In 1938 the two countries, with a combined output of several hundred grams per year, divided up the world market and stabilised the price at about $40,000 per gram. Canadian production went on until 1954 and the Belgian until 1960, but by then the demand for radium had declined as it was replaced by artificially radioactive isotopes.

Throughout that time radium therapy came to be widely used as an alternative to surgery or X-ray treatment of cancers. This came about because early workers with radium found that they suffered from burns on their skin in the same way as X-ray workers. And this was confirmed, in April 1901, when Becquerel borrowed a tube containing radium from the Curies and carried it in his waistcoat pocket for 6 hours while attending a conference. Nine days later he noticed a red area on his skin, adjacent to the radium, and he went to see Dr Besnier, a dermatologist, who identified it as an X-ray-like burn. And so it came to be realised that the radiation from radium could perhaps be used to treat cancer and other diseases instead of X-rays. Consequently a number of pioneers, such as William Rollins, a Boston dentist; Robert Abbe, a New York surgeon; Drs Rehns and Salmon at the Pasteur Institute in Paris; and Dr Danlos, Dr Wickham and others at the Hôpital St Louis in Paris, experimented with its use.

The progress made by the workers at the Hôpital St Louis was so encouraging that Armet de Lisle decided to pay for the establishment of a new research centre, the Laboratoire Biologique du Radium, which was opened in the rue d'Artois in Paris on 1 July 1906. It was staffed by a group of workers from the Hôpital St Louis, led by Dr Wickham, and de Lisle provided it with radium. The laboratory worked out dosage rates for different treatments, designed and tested new technical equipment, began to take note of necessary safety precautions, and published a constant flow of articles and papers. They also developed new techniques, including that of the 'cross fire' method which involved directing two or more different beams of radiation on to a cancer so as to limit the amount of radiation passing through any one part of the body. Between 1905 and 1909 nine hundred patients were treated and in 1906 Wickham and one of his assistants, Paul Degrais, published *Radium Therapy*, which was the first textbook on the subject. It was illustrated in colour, described many case histories and was published in an English translation in 1910.

Other research institutes like the Laboratoire Biologique were set up in France, the USA, Great Britain and Germany both before and after the First World War so that by the 1920s the medical use of radium in what had come to be called radiotherapy (or, for a while, Curietherapy) was well established. It had the great advantage over X-rays of being more portable and pliable so that it could be used in two different ways, which are now known as external beam radiotherapy or teletherapy (from the Greek *tele*, 'far') and brachytherapy (from the Greek *brachy*, 'near'). In teletherapy, radium or radon contained in what was called a radium bomb (because it looked like a small hand-grenade made of lead) was used to direct a beam on to a body from a distance. In brachytherapy radium was used in treating skin cancers by the patient holding a radium applicator up against the growth, or by fixing a specially designed container, holding the radium, adjacent to the growth. Later it was inserted, in suitably shaped containers, into body cavities such as the uterus, or it was embedded close by a growth that needed to

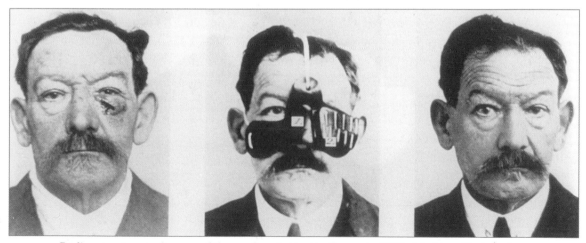

Radium treatment of cancer of the eye for a patient in France in 1920. (Archives Curie and Joliot-Curie)

ON NE VIEILLIT PLUS
MIEUX ON. RAJEUNIT

LA
CRÈME ACTIVA
radioactive

*provoque une activité particulière de
la vie des tissus; la peau mise en état
de jeunesse constante devient plus fine
et plus blanche et les rides disparaissent*

ENVOI D'ESSAI · Un pot (durée 1 mois) plus que suffisant
pour constater des resultats deja surprenants, est
envoye franco, sans marques exterieures, avec notice
contre mandat de 2'95 adressé à
Compagnie francaise de Vulgarisation
41, RUE D'AMSTERDAM, PARIS 8ᵉ
EN VENTE DANS BONNES PARFUMERIES & GRANDS MAGASINS

*La Crème Activa. Advertised in 1919, it was
claimed to promote youthful skin and remove
wrinkles.*

be controlled. The various methods of treatment were very successful for many years until artificial radionuclides, which were much more effective, became increasingly available in the second half of the twentieth century and almost completely replaced radium.

There was a less satisfactory medical use for radium in the early years of the twentieth century because its magical properties led many to suppose that it must be a cure-all for every ill. It was therefore promoted as a component of many quack remedies which claimed to cure anything from sexual impotence to insanity. It was possible to buy equipment which contained an 'insoluble preparation impregnated with radium' for making so-called radioactive water in the home. There was a radium compress, which it was claimed could be applied to almost any part of the body to cure almost any diseases. There were hair tonics, face creams, suppositories, ointments and mouthwashes, and even a glass rod coated at one end, which was designed to be hung over one's bed to 'disperse all thoughts and worries about work and troubles and bring contentment, satisfaction and body comfort that soon results in peaceful, restful sleep'.[1] And in the baths at the spa at Jáchymov it was possible to soak in radium-containing water and to breathe radon-containing air at the same time.

All these medical and quasi-medical uses had to compete for their fair share of the available radium against the demands made for it by the manufacturers of a new type of luminous paint. This quickly replaced the older paint which suffered from the disadvantage of having to be pre-exposed to light to stimulate the luminescence of the calcium sulphide which it contained. In the new radium paints the radiation from a minute amount of radium was sufficient to maintain the luminosity of zinc sulphide, which was the other component of the paint. In

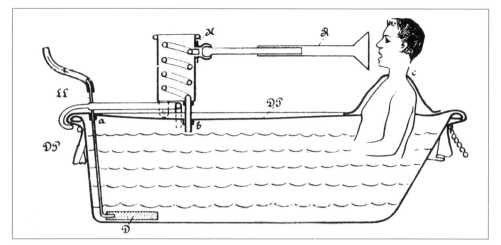

An early bath treatment at Jáchymov. The patient wallows in water containing radium and inhales radon.

1903 the Tiffany gem expert George F. Kunz painted the figures and hands on a watch with the new paint and the idea of being able to tell the time in the dark became very popular. It was estimated that, by 1920, 4 million luminous clocks and watches were produced in the United States. It seems odd that such an expensive material could be used so widely in such a relatively cheap product but it required only about 9 grams of radium. The luminous paints were also widely used in other areas such as motor-car instruments, door plates, key-hole covers and theatre seat numbers. Military applications in aircraft instruments, ships' compasses and gun-sights, particularly during the First World War, required so much radium that some doctors and hospitals were persuaded to sell their supplies to the paint manufacturers.

It slowly came to light, however, that people working with luminous paints became ill, and a few even died; on investigation, it transpired that they were in the habit of licking their paint brushes with their tongues to bring the brush to a sharp point. The amount of radium that entered their bodies was very small but it gradually built up in the jaw bones where it replaced calcium and caused cancer. The use of radium in paints was therefore banned, and modern luminous paints contain promethium-147. Pedoscopes, in which X-rays were used to test the fit of a shoe, were also banned because of possible health dangers to the users from exposure to the X-rays.

A very different use of radioactive materials involved their use as what are nowadays called tracers. The idea was that an object or a substance could be

A 1930s pedoscope for testing the fit of a shoe. Similar machines were first used in 1920, but their use was banned in the 1950s. (Clarks)

'labelled' with a very small amount of a radioactive substance, either attached to it or incorporated in it, so that it could be readily detected by picking up the radiation. It is like asking a man in a crowd to carry a flag. The new technique was pioneered by George Hevesy, who was born in Budapest in Hungary in 1885, and who won the Nobel Prize for Chemistry in 1943. He was a very experienced scientist who had discovered a new element, hafnium, in 1922, and whose working life saw him attached to nine major research centres in seven different European countries before he ended his career as Professor of Chemistry at Stockholm in Sweden, a country to which he had fled from the German occupation of Denmark in 1943. He was closely associated in his work with the Austrian Fritz Paneth, who was in turn Director of Chemistry at the University of Königsberg, guest reader and lecturer at Imperial College in London, Professor of Chemistry at Durham University, and finally the Director of the Max Planck Institute for Chemistry in Mainz, Germany. Hevesy and Paneth wrote an important book, *A Manual of Radioactivity*, which was published in Germany in 1923 and translated into Russian in 1924, Hungarian in 1925 and English in 1926.

It was while he was working in Manchester with Rutherford between 1911 and 1913 that Hevesy became interested in radioactivity, and when he returned to Vienna he used a tracer technique for the first time to measure the solubility in water of lead chromate. This is a very insoluble solid and it was not possible to detect the minute amounts of chromate that did dissolve by normal chemical analysis. But by using lead chromate containing some radioactive lead-210, which was produced as a disintegration product of radium, it was possible to detect the small amount of radioactivity in a solution of the substance.

Hevesy also used lead-210 to study the absorption of lead nitrate in beans; phosphate fertilisers containing radioactive phosphorus-32 to examine the uptake of phosphorus in plants, and other phosphates to do the same thing for animals; radioactive calcium impregnated in mice to show that about 1 in 300 of the calcium atoms present in a mouse at birth are passed on to the next generation; and the radioactive labelling of red blood corpuscles to measure blood volumes. A contemporary use for investigating possible cardiac problems in a patient involved the injection of a solution containing radium C into a vein in his or her arm and the measurement of the time it took to move into the other arm.

George Hevesy.

Radioactive substances also played an important role in the measurement of geological time. James Hutton, a Scottish gentleman-farmer and physician, who had made his fortune by exploiting a process for extracting ammonium chloride from soot, and who is generally regarded as the father of modern geology, wrote a paper entitled 'Theory of the Earth' in 1788, in which he suggested that the earth was eternally old. There was, he wrote, 'no vestige of a beginning' and 'no prospect of an end'[2] but such an idea was very controversial as it was contrary to the biblical account of the creation of the universe by God at some fixed point in time. Hutton's view won much support but some scientists, notably the German Hermann von Helmholtz and the Scot William Thomson, later Lord Kelvin, both of whom were involved in the development of new ideas about heat energy and the new science of thermodynamics, set out in the middle of the nineteenth century to try to re-estimate the probable age of the earth. They based their calculations on the idea that the earth had grown out of hot material originating from the sun and they attempted to work out the time that would be necessary, with certain rates of cooling, for the earth to reach existing temperatures. In 1854 Helmholtz suggested a figure of 25 million years; Kelvin began with one of 100 million years in 1862, but revised it to 24 million in 1897.

Their figures were, however, thrown into disarray with the discovery of radioactivity because they had not known of the presence of heat-producing radioactive substances in the earth and had taken no account of the considerable input of heat involved in their cooling calculations.

This was an unexpected set-back, but there was some compensation because the discovery of radioactive substances provided three completely new methods of studying geological time. The first depends on the fact that the alpha-particles from disintegrating uranium end up as helium gas, and in 1 year 1 gram of uranium will produce 11×10^{-8} millilitres of the gas. If it is presumed that it all remains trapped within a uranium-containing mineral then measuring the volume of helium per gram of uranium in the mineral enables its age to be calculated. It can, however, only be a lower limit for the age, as some of the helium formed within a mineral is likely to escape. Early measurements were made by both R.J. Strutt, later the 4th Lord Rayleigh, who was Professor of Physics at the Imperial College of Science in London from 1908 to 1919, and by Rutherford. The former measured the helium content of a sample of radium bromide in 1905 and calculated that its age must be two billion years, and the latter estimated the minimum age of a number of ores at 400 million years.

The second way of measuring the age of some minerals depends on the fact that alpha-particles produce coloration in minerals such as quartz, mica, rock salt, fluorite and garnet, the intensity of the colour depending on the number of particles traversing the mineral and the time involved. It is possible, then, for each mineral, to draw up a scale of coloration associated with the mineral being subjected to different amounts of radiation for different times. A strong dose for a short time will produce the same colour as a weak dose for a long time. If a sample of a mineral contains any small inclusion of a radioactive element that emits alpha-particles, they will cause coloration in the mineral within a sphere of radius equal to the range of the alpha-particles. When cut into thin sections, these colorations show up as circles with radii of the order of 0.02 mm; they are called pleochroic haloes. By discovering what radioactive material is present in the mineral sample, measuring how much of it there is, and measuring the intensity of the colours in the pleochroic haloes in the mineral it is possible to estimate its age. Such studies were carried out by Rutherford and on larger scale by John Joly, the Professor of Geology and Mineralogy at the University of Dublin.

The third method depends on the fact that when uranium disintegrates, it loses eight alpha-particles and ends up as radium G, an isotope of lead, with 1 gram of uranium producing 1.21×10^{-10} grams of radium G in 1 year. If a uranium-containing mineral is found to contain that amount of radium G for every gram of uranium, it must be approximately 1 year old. Similarly, if it contains 1.21×10^{-2} grams of radium G it must be approximately 100 million years old. The figure is only approximate because it does not take into account the slight decrease in the amount of uranium caused by the disintegration but this can be allowed for if necessary. It is also necessary to make a correction if the original mineral contains some natural lead; if it also contains some thorium, the radioactive lead formed from that element must similarly be accounted for. Such measurements dated a sample of pitchblende from Tanganyika as 700 million years old and one of zircon from Mozambique as 1,500 million years. And in 1931 Arthur Holmes, a pupil of Strutt, collated the results of nearly thirty years of investigation all over the world to estimate the probable age of the earth. He wrote: 'No more definite statement can therefore be made at present than that the age of the earth exceeds 1,460 million years, is probably not less than 1,600 million years, and is probably much less than 3,000 million years.'[3]

In more modern methods of radiometric dating of minerals the measurement of uranium-lead ratios in the mineral is replaced by those of potassium-40 to argon-40, uranium-238 to uranium-234, rubidium-87 to strontium-87, or samarium-147 to neodymium-143. And taking all these measurements, along with those from other non-radioactive methods, into account, the generally accepted value for the age of the earth today is 4,600 million years.

CHAPTER 9
The Fission of Uranium

It was always a great joy to Pierre and Marie Curie to see their first sample of radium chloride glowing in the dark, and in 1903 Pierre found that a sample of radium was always at a temperature several degrees higher than its surroundings. The radium atom seemed to be a miniature power station providing an endless supply of light and heat, and Pierre estimated that a sample of radium would be able to melt its own weight of ice in the course of a year. This was found to be typical of most radioactive elements, but as the energy was released so slowly it was not easy to see how it could be put to any great practical use. There was, nevertheless, a possibility that in due course ways and means might be found of utilising it.

Soddy drew attention to this in 1904, when he wrote that 'if it could be tapped and controlled what an agent it would be in shaping the world's destiny! The man who put his hand on the lever by which a parsimonious nature regulates so jealously the output of this store of energy would possess a weapon by which he could destroy the earth if he chose.'[1] And in a lecture on 'The Internal Energy of the Elements' in 1906, he said 'that by the expenditure of about 1 tonne yearly of uranium, costing less than £1,000, more energy would be derived than is supplied by all the electric supply stations of London put together. One little step, so easily anticipated in imagination, divides us from this great inheritance.'[2] Rutherford, too, had written in 1903 that 'could a proper detonator be found, it was just conceivable that a wave of atomic disintegration might be started through matter, which would indeed make this old world vanish in smoke'.[3] He even said, in jest, that 'some fool in a laboratory might blow up the universe unawares'.[4]

H.G. Wells dramatised such ideas in his book *The World Set Free*, published just before the start of the First World War. He envisaged an international conflict, set in 1956, in which the major cities of the world were destroyed by atom bombs. That was science fiction on a grand scale in 1914 but it became something of a reality in 1945, eleven years before Wells had prophesied, when atom bombs were dropped on the Japanese cities of Hiroshima and Nagasaki. But

the reality dawned only slowly and neither Soddy nor Rutherford were prepared
to put much money on it in the early years. The former 'trusted Nature to guard
her secret'[5] and as late as 1933 the latter said that 'anyone who looks for a source
of power in the transformation of atoms is talking moonshine'.[6]

They were not, at the time, aware of Fermi's experiments on bombarding
uranium with neutrons and it was the correct interpretation of the results of those
experiments that opened the door to the use of nuclear energy. That explanation
came from two Germans, Otto Hahn and Fritz Strassman, and two Austrians,
Lise Meitner and her nephew Otto Frisch. After working with Rutherford at
McGill for a year, Hahn had returned to Germany, where he became the Director
of the Kaiser-Wilhelm Institute for Chemistry in 1912. He was involved in the
early stages of the German attempts to build an atom bomb, but he once told a
friend that he had contemplated suicide when he first realised that the fission of
uranium might lead to a bomb. As he was also anti-Nazi he quietly opted out to
continue his own research.

Hahn was handsome, sporty and debonair; he did not take himself too
seriously; he liked beer and cigars; and, though happily married to Edith, he was
fond of the ladies. No wonder, then, that he struck up a formidable professional
relationship and a platonic friendship with Lise Meitner, the slight but attractive
girl who came from Vienna to work with him in 1907. Born in 1878, she was the
daughter of an attorney, who forced her to qualify as a French teacher, so that she
could reliably earn a living, before allowing her to study physics. Her strength of
character was shown by the fact that within two years she became only the second
female to gain a doctorate in science in Vienna. She regarded physics as a 'battle
for final truth'[7] which she was determined to win. Later, too, she was one of the
few nuclear scientists who refused to have anything to do with atom bombs
because she thought there ought not to be any. She had originally intended to stay
with Hahn for two years but such was their rapport that she was still with him in
1938 when Germany annexed Austria and she automatically became a German
citizen. Fearing that her Jewish origins would put her job at risk she escaped, first
to Holland and then to Copenhagen, where she was looked after by Niels Bohr
who found her a job in Sweden at the Physical Institute at the Academy of
Sciences paid for by the Nobel Foundation. She accepted Swedish citizenship in
1949 and stayed there until 1960 before retiring to Cambridge, England, where
she died on 27 October 1968. Albert Einstein, temporarily forgetting her origins,
described her as 'the German Madame Curie'.

Meitner's nephew Otto Frisch had a similarly successful career. He was born in
Vienna in 1904 and educated at the university in that city before going to work in

Lise Meitner. (UKAEA)

Germany, first in Berlin and then in Hamburg. Like his aunt, he was forced to flee from Nazi persecution in 1933, and he moved to Birkbeck College in London and later to work with Niels Bohr in the Institute of Physics in Copenhagen in Denmark. When that country was threatened by the German armies in 1939, he moved again, this time to Birmingham University.

Fritz Strassman, a young chemist, had joined Hahn as an assistant in 1935, and in 1938 the four of them, excited but puzzled by Fermi's results, put their existing research projects to one side and set out to try to discover what actually happened when uranium was bombarded by neutrons. Like Fermi, they found that there were a number of radioactive products (perhaps as many as ten), some of which they were able to identify, but at first they also agreed with him that some of them were probably new trans-uranium elements. The unexpected break-through came in December 1938 when Hahn and Strassman concluded that one of the products was, in fact, barium. There were two reasons why it had at first eluded them in the complex mixture of products they were dealing with. First, they had found it difficult to distinguish it from its fellow Group 2 element, radium, and secondly, they had never anticipated that an atom almost half the mass of a uranium atom could possibly be formed because in all previous cases of splitting a nucleus by bombardment it had simply been a matter of chipping small fragments off it. It was comparable to a marksman, accustomed to his bullets making small holes in his target, suddenly finding that they had torn it in two.

The dramatic conclusion was published in the 6 January 1939 edition of *Naturwissenschaften*. Hahn described it as 'horrifying' and wrote to Meitner, who was spending Christmas with friends at Kungälv near Gothenburg, saying that 'it contradicted all previous experiences in nuclear physics'.[8] She found it difficult to believe, as did her nephew Frisch, when he came to join her for Christmas. They were, however, reluctant to think that Hahn, with all his experience, could have got it wrong, and, while discussing the matter during a walk in the nearby forest, they came to realise that the uranium nucleus must in fact have split into a number of other nuclei, one of which was barium. After Christmas Meitner returned to Stockholm and Frisch to Copenhagen, and over the phone they drafted a paper with the title 'A New Type of Nuclear Reaction', which was published in *Nature* on 11 February 1939.

They visualised the splitting of the uranium atoms in terms of the liquid drop model of a nucleus, which had originally been proposed by Niels Bohr, and suggested that when the drop was hit by a neutron it began to oscillate before it elongated, with the formation of a waist, and finally broke apart. Likening the process to that of cell division in biology they christened it uranium or nuclear fission. Frisch was so excited that he wrote to his mother saying: 'I feel as if I had caught an elephant by its tail, without meaning, while walking through a jungle. And now I don't know what to do with it.'[9] More importantly, he realised that the fission of a uranium atom released a considerable amount of energy; it was rather like firing a gun, cutting a compressed spring or setting off a mouse-trap. And he was able both to calculate and to measure the amount of energy involved and was happy to find that Frédéric Joliot's calculations and experiments agreed with his.

As news of this remarkable phenomenon spread around the world, physicists rushed to get on the bandwagon and the department at Princeton was likened to 'a stirred up anthill'.[10] There was even more excitement when it was mooted by a number of workers that during the fission of a uranium nucleus by a single neutron more neutrons were produced; these were called secondary neutrons. If this could be confirmed, and if one bombarding neutron produced more than one secondary neutron, then it was immediately apparent that it would be possible to build up a chain reaction. If the fission of one uranium atom produced, say, three secondary neutrons then each of them might be able to split three more atoms producing nine more secondary neutrons, and so on. In this way a single neutron might lead to the fission of millions of uranium atoms and the release of energy as each fission took place would build up in geometric progression – 1 to 3 to 9 to 27 to 81 to 243 to 729 to 2187 to 6561 to 19683 and so on.

The increase in the number of secondary neutrons – 3 in the example quoted – came to be called the multiplication factor. For a chain reaction to be feasible, it was essential that this factor be greater than 1, and Fermi and Szilard in the United States and Frédéric Joliot and his colleagues in France carried out experiments which confirmed that it was. The French results were published first

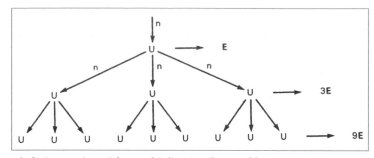

A chain reaction with a multiplication factor of 3.

in letters to *Nature* on 15 March and April and practical use of nuclear energy became a real possibility. If the chain was allowed to build up rapidly, it might release enough energy to make an atom bomb. If the build-up of the chain could be controlled, a completely new source of power for peaceful purposes would be attainable. Such conclusions were an eye-opener to most people, including many scientists who had poured a lot of cold water on the whole idea.

Leo Szilard. (Argonne National Laboratory)

But Leo Szilard, one of the central Europeans who played important roles in the development of nuclear energy, was not surprised. Born in Hungary in 1898, he had studied electrical engineering before serving in the Austro-Hungarian army during the First World War. Thereafter he moved to Germany and read physics at the University of Berlin, where he stayed until 1933 when he felt forced to leave owing to the anti-Semitism of Hitler's regime. It is interesting to reflect on what the result of the Second World War might have been if Germany had not forced so many scientists out. Szilard, like many of the others, moved to London and then, in 1938, to the United States. As early as 1934, influenced by the writings of H.G. Wells, he began to file a number of patents relating to the 'liberation of nuclear energy for power production and other purposes' and it would appear that he had foreseen the possibility of a chain reaction involving neutrons and uranium some time before it became a reality. He was an enthusiastic, imaginative, eccentric idealist with strong political views and somewhat utopian ideas for changing the world. Worried about the possible impact of his ideas, he assigned his patents to the British Admiralty so that they could be kept secret. When he found, in 1938 and 1939, that the idea of using nuclear energy was being widely discussed he thought that 'the world was headed for grief'; supported by a fellow Hungarian scientist, Edward Teller, he strove to keep the information under lock and key. Together they approached Albert Einstein and asked him to write to President Roosevelt to warn him of the impending dangers. He did this on 2 August 1939 and his letter is reproduced in Appendix II on page 222.

But it was all too late. Hitler's armies had marched into Czechoslovakia on 16 March 1939 and into Poland, which Britain had pledged to defend, on 1 September. Two days later, at noon, Neville Chamberlain, the British Prime Minister, announced in the House of Parliament that 'this country is now at war with Germany. We are ready.' This caused the immediate protagonists – Britain, France and Germany – to mobilise their military forces to wage war, and their scientists to make the discoveries that would lead to the manufacture of an atom bomb against which it was thought there would be no defence. It was not difficult to see that the countries that could do that first would probably win the war. But there were formidable problems to overcome.

The first was to get hold of enough uranium. It was not, at the time, regarded as a very useful material and was only used in research projects and for making glass with an attractive greeny-yellow colour. Consequently, there was a rather unseemly rush to corner the uranium supplies that were available both from the Belgian company, Union Minière, with mines in the Belgian Congo (now the Democratic Republic of Congo), and from the Canadian firm, Eldorado Gold Mines Ltd, with mines at Great Bear Lake almost on the Arctic Circle. So far as Great Britain and America were concerned there was a good deal of hassle and suspicion and ill-feeling until a Declaration of Trust was eventually signed on 13 June 1944 to 'insure the acquisition at the earliest practicable moment of an adequate supply of uranium and thorium ores'.[11]

Any hope that it would be easy to achieve a chain reaction were dashed when Bohr suggested, rightly, that the two main isotopes of uranium reacted differently to neutrons with different speeds. Slow neutrons are very effective in fissioning uranium-235 atoms but they are simply captured by uranium-238 atoms without causing fission. Faster neutrons will also fission uranium-235 atoms, though less readily than slower ones, but they are preferentially captured by uranium-238 atoms, again without causing any fission. It does, in fact, require very fast neutrons to fission uranium-238 atoms. If, then, a block of natural uranium containing over 99 per cent of uranium-238 atoms and only 0.72 per cent (1 part in 140) of uranium-235 atoms is bombarded by a beam of neutrons, fission is caused in the uranium-235 atoms, mainly by the slower neutrons, but the faster ones are mainly captured by the uranium-238 atoms and none of the secondary neutrons is fast enough to fission those atoms.

The immediate efforts to overcome the problem centred around trying to slow down – moderate – the secondary neutrons so that more of them would be able to bring about fission of the relatively scarce uranium-235 atoms. To that end the research teams all turned their attention to building assemblies in which the uranium was in some way embedded within a material which would function as a moderator. The idea was that a secondary neutron from one fission would be slowed down by travelling through the moderator before it hit another uranium atom. Fermi, for example, suspended about fifty cans of uranium oxide in a tank of water; the French team embedded lumps of paraffin wax into some uranium oxide; and G.P. Thomson, the son of J.J. and the Professor of Physics at Imperial College, London, tried immersing spheres of uranium oxide in water. Some progress was made and it was discovered that it was best to have the uranium arranged in a regular array of separated rods within a moderator, as is done in today's nuclear reactors.

It also became clear that neither water nor paraffin wax were ideal moderators because they both absorbed too many neutrons, but the choice of a replacement, which lay between graphite and heavy water, was not an easy one. Graphite was quite abundant and cheap, but had to be used in a particularly pure form which was not easy to obtain, while heavy water was ideal but rare; the only reliable source was a chemical plant at Vemork, near Rjukan, to the west of Oslo in Norway, which was owned by the Norwegian Hydro-Electric Company. Fermi and Szilard in the United States opted for graphite, and used it to great effect. The German team, led by Werner Heisenberg and Carl von Weizsäcker, chose to use heavy water but their efforts to buy the Norwegian stocks came to naught when Norway realised what they wanted it for. Thereafter the Germans never had enough of the precious liquid to meet their needs, even though they invaded Norway, and their nuclear research project rather petered out and was replaced by rocket development. There is some evidence, too, that Heisenberg and von Weizsäcker, neither of whom were great supporters of Hitler, did not actually want to make a bomb and were more interested in peaceful uses of nuclear energy. But if they had originally chosen graphite as their moderator, instead of heavy water, history might well have been very different.

The French, too, chose heavy water, like the Germans, but were treated much more favourably by the Norwegians who gave them all the local supplies – 185kg on condition that they would be repaid in kind or at cost after the war. The valuable cargo was driven away from Vemork in twenty-six cans and reached Paris, via Edinburgh, on 16 March. It had been a close-run thing because another plane, which the Germans believed was carrying the precious cargo, had been forced down over Hamburg. Alas, the French research was coming to an end because the German armies occupied Paris on 14 June and an armistice was signed on 22 June. Joliot decided to stay in France but he took the precaution of burning all his papers and of sending his two assistants, the Austrian Hans von Halban and the Russian Lew Kowarski, to England on 18 June. The Earl of Suffolk, who was a Scientific Liaison Officer with the French government, also organised the transfer of the French supplies of heavy water, valued at £22,000, to England. The twenty-six cans were transported on a Royal Navy destroyer from St Nazaire to Falmouth, from where they were taken to Wellington Barracks in London by a platoon of Coldstream Guards. As the duty officer was uncertain what to do with such an unexpected cargo he sought advice and the heavy water was moved to Wormwood Scrubs prison (then occupied by the War Office) before being taken to Windsor Castle where it was looked after by the librarian.

The two Frenchmen were able to pass valuable information to the English about their work, but an alternative approach to that of relying on the use of moderators had been suggested in an important report submitted from Birmingham University in March 1940. Very important secret work was being carried out there by James Randall and H.A.H. Boot on perfecting a cavity magnetron which was vital for the successful development of the British radar defence system. But under the direction of the Professor of Physics Mark Oliphant, who had come from Adelaide to Trinity College, Cambridge, and had worked at the Cavendish Laboratory on the nuclear disintegration of lithium, the university was also to become the starting point of the atom bomb. Oliphant, a Rutherford-like fellow with a great zest for life, a loud voice, a hearty laugh and a remarkable skill as an experimenter, had been appointed in 1937 and as well as being involved with the magnetron research had also begun to build a cyclotron and was working on how best to convert uranium oxide into the pure metal.

Mark Oliphant. (Ernest Orlando Lawrence Berkeley National Laboratory)

He persuaded the university to establish a new chair for a Professor of Mathematical Physics, and arranged for it to be occupied by the German-born Rudolf Peierls, who, after research in Rome, had gone to Cambridge on a Rockefeller Fellowship in 1933 and decided to stay in England. And in the summer of 1939 they were joined by Otto Frisch, who left Copenhagen when Denmark was threatened by the German armies, to avoid having to work for them or, perhaps, being sent to a concentration camp.

The coming together of this trio was fortuitous but timely, and it paid off well. They were, in fact, the first group to make a positive, practical suggestion as to how an atomic bomb might be made, and naturally enough they all played important roles in building it during the war. Thereafter Oliphant returned to Australia where he directed nuclear research at the University of Canberra between 1950 and 1963 and was Governor of South Australia from 1971 to 1976. He died, aged 98, in 2000. Peierls went back to Birmingham before becoming in turn the Professor of Physics at Oxford University and at the University of Washington in Seattle. Frisch became the Deputy Chief Scientific Officer at the British Atomic Energy Research Establishment at Harwell near Oxford. In 1947 he was appointed Professor of Natural Philosophy at Cambridge University. He retired in 1971 and died in 1979 following an accident.

In the early days at Birmingham, Frisch, who was a bachelor, was taken into their home by Peierls and his Russian wife Genia, and the two men became very friendly. Both of them were, in law, enemy aliens until they took British citizenship in 1940 and 1943 respectively, but this had no effect on their scientific work. They decided to follow up a suggestion, first made in 1939 by Niels Bohr, that it was the uranium-235 atoms that were of major importance in what was loosely referred to as the fission of uranium. So Frisch set about trying to see

Otto Frisch and Sir Rudolf Peierls. (UKAEA)

whether he might be able to separate the uranium-235 from the uranium-238 atoms in natural uranium. He hoped to use a relatively simple process of thermal diffusion, invented by the German Klaus Clusius, which involved a long, vertical glass tube with an electrically heated wire running down its axis. When a gaseous compound of uranium, such as hot uranium hexafluoride, was introduced into the tube, the gas molecules containing the lighter isotope would diffuse to the hot central region and be carried upwards by convection currents. The molecules with the heavier isotope would move to the colder, outer region and be carried downwards. In this way the lighter molecules would collect at the top of the tube and the heavier ones at the bottom.

For his experiments Frisch designed a slightly modified tube, which was made for him by the university glass-blowers. But he made very slow progress because he had only a small room in which to work and the glass-blowers could not help him much because they were so heavily involved in their radar work. He did enough, however, to realise that only a very partial separation of uranium-235 and uranium-238 atoms could be achieved using only one tube but he concluded that 'with something like a hundred thousand similar separation tubes it might be possible to produce a pound of reasonably pure uranium-235 in a modest time, measured in weeks'.[12] And he wrote that 'the cost of such a plant would be insignificant compared with the cost of the war'.[13]

With this possibility in mind he and Peierls then asked themselves the question as to what might happen if a block of relatively pure uranium-235 did become available and was bombarded by neutrons. One possible answer was distinctly alarming because, as there are always neutrons floating around in the atmosphere, a chain reaction might be set up and the block might blow up spontaneously. Fortunately Peierls was able to calculate that the block could only blow up if it was above a certain critical mass or size. He argued that in a small block so many of the secondary neutrons would escape from its surface that a chain reaction could never build up. In a larger block, above the critical size, fewer neutrons would escape so that a chain reaction would be possible and Peierls calculated that the critical size would be close to that of a golf ball.

Frisch and Peierls submitted their ideas to Professor Oliphant in two short reports which, for reasons of security, were typed by Peierls himself, with only one carbon copy. The first, three pages long, was headed 'On the construction of a super-bomb based on a nuclear chain reaction in uranium'. It concluded that a 5 kg bomb would be equivalent to several thousand tons of dynamite and that it could be constructed from two pieces of uranium-235, each below the critical size, which could be rapidly brought together, perhaps by the use of springs, to make a piece above the critical size in order to set the bomb off. The report said that protection from the bomb would be 'hardly possible' and that a by-product would be radiation that would be 'fatal to living beings even a long time after the explosion'.[14] In a second, shorter and less technical report headed 'Memorandum on

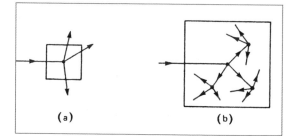

Critical size. (a) The secondary neutrons escape without causing fission. (b) The secondary neutrons cause fission and set up a chain reaction.

the properties of a radioactive super-bomb' they again raised the hazard of the radiation, writing that 'owing to the spreading of radioactive substances with the wind, the bomb could probably not be used without killing large numbers of civilians, and this may make it unsuitable as a weapon for use by this country'.[15]

Oliphant, convinced by their arguments, wrote that 'the whole thing must be taken rather seriously'[16] and sent the reports to Sir Henry Tizard, the civilian chairman of the Committee on the Scientific Survey of Air Defence, who was an experienced scientific administrator. Born in 1885, he had been educated at Westminster School and Magdalen College, Oxford; he served with the Royal Air Force during the First World War and was the assistant comptroller of Aeronautical Research from 1918 to 1919. Later he was made secretary to the Department of Scientific and Industrial Research and Chairman of the Aeronautical Research Committee. He was elected President of Magdalen College in 1942, becoming the first scientist to hold such an office in any Oxford college.

His preliminary view on the work of Frisch and Peierls was that he 'was prepared to take a bet that there would be certainly no military application in this war'.[17] Nevertheless, he set up a committee, chaired by G.P. Thomson, consisting of James Chadwick and his assistant P.B. Moon together with John Cockcroft; they were joined later by Patrick Blackett. The committee, which met for the first time on 10 April 1940, came to be called the MAUD committee to try to hide its real purpose. The name originated in a telegram which Niels Bohr sent to Frisch when Denmark was overrun by the Germans early in 1940. It ended with the words 'Tell Cockcroft and Maud Ray Kent'. This was a reference to Maud Ray, formerly governess to Bohr's children, who lived in Kent. But Frisch was unaware of her existence and interpreted the words as a secret, anagrammatic message to be read as 'taken radyum' to indicate that the Germans had captured the Copenhagen stocks of that element. Because Maud had so puzzled him he suggested it as a name to provide security for the committee – but the truth will out and it was soon taken to mean Military Applications of Uranium Disintegration.

After some fifteen months the committee, which had begun by being somewhat sceptical, produced its final report on 15 July 1941. In summary, it said that building an atom bomb was practicable and that it would 'lead to decisive results in the war'. It predicted that a bomb containing about 12 kg of uranium-235 would have the same effect as abut 2,000 tonnes of TNT and that it would cost around £5 million to build a plant capable of making sufficient uranium-235 to build three bombs per month. The material for the first could be ready by the end of 1943. The committee envisaged that a bomb could be made by using conventional explosives to fire two 5 kg masses of uranium–235, each below the critical size, into each other from the opposite ends of a sealed gun-barrel. They would meet at about 4,000 miles per hour, and form a mass of uranium–235 larger than the critical size which would be exploded by stray neutrons.

The committee echoed Frisch and Peierls in making clear their concern regarding the hazards to be expected from the radiation which exploding the bomb would produce, writing that it 'seems certain that the area devastated by the explosion would be dangerous to life for a considerable time. The physiological effects of these radiations are delayed and cumulative so that great care would have to be taken in working anywhere near.'[18] Despite that warning and the advice of his chief scientific adviser, Lord Cherwell (formerly Professor Lindemann), that the odds against success were only two to one or even money, Winston Churchill, the British Prime Minister, accepted the committee's recommendation 'that work should continue with the highest priority'. He wrote that 'although personally I am quite content with the existing explosives, I feel we must not stand in the way of improvement'.[19] To that end formal contracts were signed by the government with the university departments at Cambridge, Birmingham, Liverpool and Oxford to allow them to speed up their research programmes, and Imperial Chemical Industries were brought into the fold. Thomson's committee, loaded with academics, was replaced by a new division within the Department of Scientific and Industrial Research called the Directorate of Tube Alloys to shield its real activities. It was directed by W.A. (later Sir Wallace) Akers, the Research Director at Imperial Chemical Industries, and it held its first meeting at the beginning of November 1941. This organisational change did not please all the scientists, some of whom were left out in the cold, and Oliphant was particularly angry that the work which he had originated should be put in the hands of 'commercial representatives completely ignorant of the essential nuclear physics upon which the whole thing is based'.[20] It reflects well on Akers that he was quickly able to draw everyone together.

The Maud committee also recommended that 'the present collaboration with America should be continued and extended'.[21] It would have been timely for a joint Anglo-American project to be set up with both partners as equals but this did not happen, mainly because the British were hesitant. America was not at war so the British were concerned about possible security risks; at the time the British were well ahead of the Americans in their research programme and did not want to lose control; and awkward questions as to what might happen at the end of the war, particularly when commercial organisations were involved, remained unanswered.

With hindsight, it is clear that a great opportunity was lost and it was not until 30 July 1942 that the British Chancellor of the Exchequer, Sir John Anderson, realising the difficulties of building even small pilot plants in a country under constant air bombardment and with limited industrial and man-power resources, recommended to Churchill that Britain should move her design work and the people involved to the United States. The British die was cast but it is a measure of the difficulties involved in resolving the details that it was not until 19 August 1943 that a formal agreement 'Governing the Collaboration between the Authorities of the USA and the UK in the matter of Tube Alloys' was signed by Mr Churchill and President Roosevelt at Quebec.

CHAPTER 10
Hiroshima and Nagasaki

The letter written by Einstein to President Roosevelt, on 2 August 1939, warning of the potential danger of atom bombs, was not delivered to him until 11 October because his advisers thought that he was far too busy to be bothered with it. It was but one of many examples of the lack of any great sense of urgency in the United States following the outbreak of war in Europe on 3 September 1939, but when Roosevelt did see the letter he took immediate action in setting up an Advisory Committee on Uranium under the chairmanship of Lyman J. Briggs, the Director of the National Bureau of Standards. The committee, which included military and naval representatives as well as Szilard and Fermi and other scientists, was divided as to the likelihood of being able to develop a chain reaction in uranium. The army representative said that there was already a large prize on offer to the inventor of a death ray which could kill a goat but that there had been no claimants. Many of the scientists did not see uranium as a solution to any wartime problems, and the committee as a whole was clearly thinking more of a controlled nuclear chain reaction perhaps powering a submarine than blowing anything up. It did, however, recommend, on 1 November, that 'adequate support be given for a thorough investigation'.[1]

Despite the general air of pessimism, there was a good deal of important research work being carried out, independently and to some extent casually, in a number of universities on nuclear matters. In February 1940, for example, at the University of Minnesota, Alfred Nier used a mass spectrometer, similar to that designed by Frederick Aston, to separate uranium-235 from uranium-238. This enabled John R. Dunning, a colleague of Fermi at Columbia University, to show that it was the uranium-235 atoms and not the uranium-238 atoms that were fissioned by slow neutrons. Four months later E.M. McMillan and P.H. Abelson announced that they had made plutonium by bombarding uranium with neutrons, and the first suggestions that this new element might be easily fissionable and might well be a substitute for uranium-235 in making atom bombs began to surface.

The main American project, however, organised by Fermi and Szilard, was the building of what came to be called an atomic pile. The idea was to build up a lattice structure from blocks of graphite in which lumps of natural uranium oxide and/or uranium were embedded. Any neutrons entering the pile would fission some of the uranium-235 atoms and produce some secondary neutrons which would be slowed down (moderated) by passing through the graphite before, it was hoped, fissioning other uranium-235 atoms. In a small pile, sufficient neutrons might escape from the surface so that a chain reaction would not be set up, but as the pile got bigger and bigger it would eventually reach a critical size so that a chain reaction would result. Because the uranium-235 atoms are very thinly spread in natural uranium, the critical size of the pile would be much larger than that of the golf ball predicted for *pure* uranium-235 by Peierls.

The Briggs committee agreed to grant $6,000 to Szilard and Fermi at their first meeting and work began on the seventh floor of the Pupin Laboratories at Columbia University where the physicists soon came to resemble coal-miners as they bored holes in 4 tons of graphite bricks. The results of their early work were encouraging but overall the American nuclear programme, if it in fact deserved that name, was uncoordinated and badly organised, with the Briggs Committee being singularly ineffective. In May 1940 A.V. Hill, a scientific adviser at the British Embassy in Washington, reported that the general opinion in America was that 'to turn to uranium as a war investigation . . . was probably a wild goose chase'.[2] And Szilard was complaining that if each necessary step required ten months of deliberation then obviously it would not be possible to carry out the work efficiently. By the summer of 1941 there was even some talk of abandoning all work on nuclear fission.

Some reorganisation was clearly needed and on 12 June 1940 the Briggs Committee was absorbed into a new National Defense Research Council – the NDRC. Vannevar Bush, who had moved from being Vice-president of the Massachusetts Institute of Technology to become President of the Carnegie Institute, a private research organisation, was the chairman and James B. Conant, a distinguished organic chemist who was elected President of Harvard at the age of 40, was his deputy. A further review of the situation, instigated by the National Academy of Sciences, was undertaken in May 1941 by A.H. Compton, who, after working with Rutherford at the Cavendish Laboratory in Cambridge, became a professor at the University of Chicago and shared the Nobel Prize for Physics in 1927 with C.T.R. Wilson. This led to Bush moving to a new organisation, the Office of Scientific Research and Development, while Conant ran the NDRC.

There was really no time to judge whether or not these changes were beneficial because events took over and led to more positive decisions and actions. On

22 June the German armies advanced eastwards in an attack on Russia and a day later the British MAUD committee produced its first draft report. Details of this filtered through to the Americans but seemed to have no effect until Oliphant flew across the Atlantic in August to reinforce the message. He was 'amazed and distressed'[3] to find that Briggs had not shared the information available to him and had locked many of the reports in his safe. But Oliphant was able to influence events in private meetings with Lawrence and Conant, who passed on his views to Compton and Bush.

So the ground was prepared for action when the MAUD report was finally delivered to the United States government on 3 October 1941, and within six days President Roosevelt had appointed a Top Policy Committee to explore thoroughly whether or not an atomic bomb could be built. Its members were the Vice-President, Henry Wallace; the Secretary of War, Henry L. Stimson, and the Army Chief of Staff, George C. Marshall, together with Bush and Conant. In November the National Academy of Sciences submitted a report that broadly agreed with the conclusions of the MAUD committee. It emphasised that the destructive effect of the radiation resulting from the atom bomb 'may be as important as the explosion itself'[4] but if there were any lingering doubts as to the best course of action they were swept aside by the news of the Japanese attack on the American fleet at Pearl Harbor on 7 December. Within three days the United States was at war and all the resources on both sides of the Atlantic were committed to building an atom bomb.

The most immediate advance came from work on the pile. Once preliminary studies had shown that the idea was feasible, Fermi began construction of the latest model in a double squash court under the West Stand of Stagg Field Stadium in the University of Chicago in May 1942. It was referred to as CP-1 (Chicago Pile number 1). A bottom layer of blocks of pure graphite was covered with two layers of blocks containing lumps of uranium and/or uranium oxide. Then came another layer of pure graphite followed by two uranium-containing layers – and so on. The pile was supported on a wooden structure, and cadmium sheets, which could be moved up or down within the pile, were incorporated to act as control rods. Cadmium is a very good absorber of neutrons so that there could be no chance of any chain reaction when the rods were fully inserted in the pile. Withdrawing the rods enabled the neutrons to 'go into action' but a chain reaction capable of producing energy could not take place until the pile was larger than the critical size and the rods, which could be used to control it, were sufficiently withdrawn.

The pile was built in the shape of a large balloon lying on its side and it reached the critical size when it contained fifty-seven layers and was 7.7m long and 6.1m

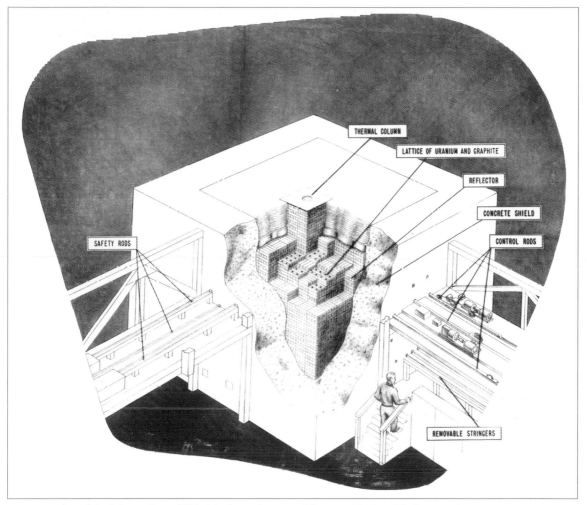

THERMAL COLUMN

LATTICE OF URANIUM AND GRAPHITE

REFLECTOR

CONCRETE SHIELD

CONTROL RODS

SAFETY RODS

REMOVABLE STRINGERS

A model of the replica of CP-1 built at Argonne. (Argonne National Laboratory)

across. It contained 385 tons of graphite, 6 tons of uranium and 34 tons of uranium oxide, but with the control rods fully inserted it was inactive. At 2 o'clock on 2 December, Fermi, standing on the balcony originally intended for spectators of a squash match but now housing a panel of control instruments, began to withdraw the control rods. An assistant stood by with a bucketful of concentrated cadmium nitrate to throw over the pile if anything should go wrong but it was not required and, as Fermi withdrew the rods, bit by bit, surrounded by an awesome silence from the spectators, it eventually went critical and produced energy. It was only enough to light a small torch bulb – but it was enough to convince one of those present that 'he had seen a miracle'. The controlled release of nuclear power had been successfully achieved for the very first time and Fermi proclaimed that controlling the power was 'as easy as driving a car'. The pile had also opened up a way of making plutonium because some of the uranium-238 atoms in the pile had captured some of the available neutrons and been transformed into that element. Those privileged to be present drank a little Chianti out of paper cups but there was an eerie feeling and only muted elation. Szilard, indeed, said that the occasion would 'go down as a black day in the history of mankind'.[5]

It is a measure of the confidence of its designers that they were prepared to build CP-1 in the centre of a crowded city such as Chicago and to commemorate the event a plaque was erected on the site which read:

ON DECEMBER 2, 1942
MAN ACHIEVED HERE
THE FIRST SELF-SUSTAINING CHAIN REACTION
AND THEREBY INITIATED THE
CONTROLLED RELEASE OF NUCLEAR ENERGY

Twenty-five years later, when the site had been demolished and redeveloped, a bronze sculpture by the British artist Henry Moore was erected. Called 'Nuclear Energy', it is 3.7m high, stands on a granite base 2.9m in diameter, and weighs 3 tonnes. In 1989 Hiroshima City bought a replica of the sculpture for their Museum of Contemporary Art.

Following the outstanding success of the first atomic pile, the American research effort gathered momentum but it was still spread between a number of different universities and largely directed by individual professors, until Bush and Conant realised that, as the project was rapidly moving away from the research stage into large-scale industrial activity, new people and new methods were required. So the giant chemical firm E.I. du Pont de Nemours and the army, with the Boston construction firm of Stone & Webster alongside, were brought into play. As with the earlier introduction of ICI and Akers in England, this displeased some of the scientists, but it was an essential step forward.

On 17 September 1942 a 46-year-old colonel in the Corps of Engineers, Leslie R. Groves, was chosen to lead what became known as the Manhattan Project. He had trained as an engineer at the Massachusetts Institute of Technology before joining the army and had been responsible for building the Pentagon in Washington. He was a ruthlessly hard worker, who thought that most scientists were indecisive and argumentative; he was a tactless loner and something of an

Anglophobe, and was regarded by his second-in-command as the 'biggest sonofabitch he had ever met'.[6] Yet he knew that his job was to build an atom bomb, and that is what he did.

Within three days of his appointment he had bought 1,250 tons of rich pitchblende (which had been stored at Port Richmond on Staten Island since being shipped there, in 1940, from the Belgian Congo by the Union Minière company in 1940 to take it out of the reach of the Germans); he had finalised the long-delayed acquisition of a 52,000-acre site on the Clinch River in Tennessee, which came to be known as Oak Ridge; and he had been promoted to brigadier. That was how it went on. In November he acquired

This sculpture, 'Nuclear Energy' by Henry Moore, was erected in 1967 on the site of the old football stand at the University of Chicago where the first atomic pile was built in 1942. The bronze sculpture is 3.7m high and weighs 3,050kg. It stands on a base of black polished granite which is 2.9m in diameter. (University of Chicago)

a site at Los Alamos in New Mexico, and in January 1943 still another at Hanford on the Columbia River in the State of Washington.

The plan was to extract uranium-235 from natural uranium at Oak Ridge; to make plutonium at Hanford; and to use Los Alamos as a central laboratory where the actual atom bombs would be designed and produced. Security was a major consideration and isolating each site from the others was a major part of the overall security plan. Los Alamos in particular, 48km away from Santa Fe in a region of extinct volcanoes and strips of flat ground on the tops of high cliffs

General Groves. (UKAEA)

separated by deep canyons, was very isolated and not easily accessible – so much so that Szilard said: 'Nobody could think straight in a place like that, and everyone who goes there will go crazy.'[7]

Fortunately, Julius Robert Oppenheimer, who was appointed by Groves to direct the programme at Los Alamos, prevented that from happening. He was the 38-year-old son of a German Jew who had emigrated to the United States in 1898 and had prospered as an importer of textiles. Robert, in his early years, was very clever but delicate and he suffered from loneliness and lack of confidence to the extent that he was, at times, suicidal. But he worked his way through what he called 'his almost infinitely long adolescence' until, while holding joint professorial posts at the California Institute of Technology and the University of California, he established an international reputation in the field of quantum theory.

It was a bold but inspired move by Groves to appoint Oppenheimer as the two did not, at first sight, appear to have much in common. Groves was very much overweight, super-confident, hyperactive and decisive, whereas Oppenheimer was tall and skinny, with a shambling gait, a lugubrious expression, a nervous approach, an overall air of lethargy and no experience of large-scale organisation. There was also a question mark about Oppenheimer's political views because he had supported left-wing causes and his brother, his first fiancée and many of his close friends were, or had been, members of the Communist party. The straightforward action-man Groves and the complex deep-thinking Oppenheimer did, nevertheless, turn out to be a dream team, and despite his lack of experience the latter rapidly transformed himself from a 'theorist into a most effective leader and administrator'[8] and built up at Los Alamos a group of highly talented international scientists described by Groves as 'the greatest collection of eggheads ever'.[9] They operated in what a visitor described as a 'unique intellectual atmosphere'.[10]

They had many problems to solve and it was necessary to solve them quickly because no one knew with any confidence how far ahead the Germans were with their own nuclear research programme. Roosevelt decreed that 'time was of the essence' and nothing was allowed to impede possible progress. Where there was more than one possible way of solving a problem no preliminary time was to be spent on trying to find the best option. They were all fully investigated right from the start and no pilot plants were used. This involved some costly and, in Conant's phrase, 'Napoleonic decisions'.[11]

The policy was demonstrated very clearly in the separation of uranium-235 from uranium-238 at Oak Ridge. Frisch, in Birmingham, had originally suggested that the two isotopes should be separated by the process of gaseous thermal diffusion but the MAUD committee had recommended an alternative process of gaseous diffusion. This involves the passage of gases through a porous membrane, such as a porous pot. A lighter gas will pass through more rapidly than a heavier one. Professor Simon, another refugee from Germany who had actually served in the German army in the First World War and had been one of the first poison gas casualties, had done some work at Oxford University on developing this process. In the electromagnetic method of separation, developed mainly by Ernest Lawrence at the University of California, isotopes were separated, as in Aston's original mass spectrometer, by using the effect of electric and magnetic fields on a beam of charged uranium atoms. The lighter atoms are deflected more than the heavier ones, just as a cross-wind has a greater effect on light cars than on lorries. In the centrifugal method, pioneered by Jesse W. Beams, a friend of Ernest Lawrence, at the University of Virginia, isotopes are separated by using a high-speed centrifuge to throw the heavier isotopes further out than the lighter ones. Finally, a fifth method, that of liquid thermal diffusion, was investigated by Abelson, the discoverer of neptunium and plutonium, at the Naval Research Laboratory at Anacostia. In this method liquefied uranium hexafluoride was passed under pressure into an annular tube which was heated on the outside by steam and cooled on the inside by cold water. As in gaseous thermal diffusion, the lighter isotope moves to the hotter, outer wall and rises to the top of the tube, while the heavier isotope moves to the colder, inner wall and falls to the bottom.

The apparent profligacy of investigating so many different processes simultaneously paid good dividends in the end because it was only by using the partially enriched uranium from one process as the feed-stock for another that adequate supplies of uranium-235 were obtained. In the end rather more than 40kg of 80 per cent pure uranium-235 was delivered to Los Alamos by 24 July 1945. It was less than three years since General Groves had bought the Oak Ridge site and a newly built town with a peak population of 75,000 had been involved.

The scientists at Los Alamos had been working out how best to make a practical bomb from uranium-235 by refining the original idea of Frisch and Peierls of shooting two pieces of uranium-235, each below the critical size, into each other so as to form a piece above the critical size. Measuring the precise critical size was therefore of the utmost importance and the necessary work was undertaken by the Critical Assembly Group working in a separate building in Omega Canyon, remote from the main site. In one set of experiments, designed by Frisch, slugs of uranium hydride containing uranium-235 were dropped through a ring of the same material. As they passed through, the assembly became super-critical for a fraction of a second, simulating a small bomb, and it was possible to measure the output of energy. Frisch referred to the exercise as 'twisting the dragon's tail'.

Similar experiments caused the first two fatal disasters at Los Alamos. An alternative to Frisch's method involved building up an assembly of small cubes of uranium-235 until the critical size was approached. Because this was clearly a hazardous operation, it was agreed that no one would carry it out on their own. Moreover, to avoid the risk of accidents caused by dropping a single cube, all of them would be added to the assembly from the bottom and not from the top. Failure to keep to these rules caused the death of Harry Daghlian, on 21 August 1945. Working alone one night, he dropped a cube down into his assembly. He swept it aside as quickly as he could and although he felt no immediate ill-effects he soon became sick and ambulance took him to hospital. Later his hands became gangrenous, his hair fell out, he complained of severe internal pains, and he became delirious before he died twenty-four days later. His sufferings were watched, helplessly, by Laura, Enrico Fermi's wife, who worked part time in the hospital as a nurse.

A fellow worker, the Canadian physicist Louis Slotin, was killed in a similar incident after the war had ended. He was experimenting with sliding two hemispheres of uranium-235 towards each other along a rod and measuring the output of neutrons as they got closer and closer. He used two screwdrivers to manipulate the hemispheres and he had carried out the experiment many times before, but on 21 May 1946 one of the screwdrivers slipped and the assembly became critical. Slotin, who had fought in the Spanish Civil War as a member of the Abraham Lincoln Brigade and had been a pilot in the Royal Air Force in the early years of the Second World War, instantly tore the two hemispheres apart with his hands to try to save the lives of his five colleagues present in the room. He also had the presence of mind to tell them to go back to where they had been standing at the moment of disaster and drew a diagram of their positions on the blackboard so that doctors could assess the radiation dose to which each had been exposed. They all survived, but Slotin died after nine days of terrible agony.

Frisch finished his experiments on 12 April, the day that President Roosevelt died at the age of 63, and reported the results to Oppenheimer. Thereafter, making a bomb from uranium-235 was relatively straightforward, though the original idea of shooting two pieces of uranium into each other to 'detonate' the bomb was replaced by shooting one piece into another stationary one. The designers were so confident that, particularly in view of the relative shortage of uranium-235, they decided that it was not necessary to carry out any preliminary tests. The bomb, which weighed 4,100kg and was about 3m long and 0.75m in diameter, was code-named Little Boy. It could have been made ready for use at almost any time but it was decided to wait for a second type of bomb to be ready for use as a back-up.

That bomb was code-named Fat Man because it was bigger and podgier than Little Boy; it was egg-shaped, weighed 4,536kg and was 3.5m long with a maximum diameter of 1.5m. It was a completely different animal from Little Boy, being made of plutonium rather than uranium-235 and having a different basic design. The plutonium for the bomb was made at Hanford in a two-stage process. First, it had to be made within a pile (or a reactor as it was sometimes called) by the bombardment of uranium-238 by neutrons, but as only a small part of the uranium-238 was converted into plutonium there had to be a secondary process to extract the pure plutonium. Three piles were built, at 10km intervals, alongside the Columbia River. They were based on Fermi's original CP-1 built in Chicago but were much bigger, used purer graphite and uranium and operated at 200 megawatts instead of 1 megawatt. Operating the piles required extensive shielding which involved steel plates, concrete walling and special high-density wood barriers, together with massive cooling which took 350,000 litres of water out of the nearby river every minute. After about seven weeks the slugs of uranium, clad in aluminium tubes embedded in cylinders of pure graphite, contained about 250 parts per million of plutonium.

The tubes containing the mixture of uranium and plutonium were stored in water for about eight weeks to allow the short-lived radioactivity to decline and the mixture was then dissolved in nitric acid. The plutonium was extracted from the mixture in a series of chemical operations carried out in stainless steel tanks contained in one of three huge concrete structures, 234m long, 20m wide and 24m high, which were known as 'Queen Marys' after the big British ship of that name. The walls of each structure were 2.1m thick and the roof was 1.8m thick

Fat Man (top) and Little Boy. (Los Alamos National Laboratory)

and the radiation was so intense that every operation had to be carried out by remote control through the concrete walls using periscopes, television cameras and automated handling equipment. It was a fantastic achievement involving 55,000 people, yet only two years after work began in the summer of 1943, enough plutonium to make two bombs had been delivered to Los Alamos and more was in the pipeline.

The scientists at Los Alamos, led by Emilio Segrè, had, however, come up against a problem that led them to conclude that the 'gun-method' of firing two small pieces of material into each other, which worked well with uranium-235, would not work for plutonium. It would not be possible, they decided, to fire two pieces of plutonium together rapidly enough to avoid pre-detonation. This was due to the fact that the plutonium-240 atoms, present along with the predominant plutonium-239 atoms, fission far too readily. The problem had been to some extent foreseen and Seth H. Neddermeyer had worked out a possible solution, which came to be known as the implosion method, in April 1943. The idea was that two touching hemispheres of plutonium forming a sphere which was below the critical size would be surrounded by explosive charges which, when detonated, would compress the sphere into about half its original size. This smaller sphere would be super-critical because the atoms in it would be much closer together so that the neutrons responsible for bringing about a chain reaction would have to travel much shorter distances before colliding with other atoms.

This was a completely new field of research which necessitated a very inventive approach. The surrounding explosive had to be made into specially designed shapes so that they would focus the detonation wave in much the same way as lenses focus light waves. Over a period of two years over 20,000 castings and 50,000 machining operations had to be carried out to achieve the required result. There was, too, a further complication because there was some doubt as to whether, under the conditions, there would be enough stray neutrons to trigger off a chain reaction so it was thought necessary to incorporate an initiator in the centre of the plutonium sphere. This consisted of a mixture of polonium-210, as a supplier of alpha-particles, and beryllium. It was estimated that it would produce 95 million neutrons per second but as it was unknown territory, and as the supply of plutonium was plentiful enough to allow it, it was decided that it would not be wise to use Fat Man without a preliminary test.

The test, which was code-named Trinity, took place on 16 July 1945 on the edge of the Alamogordo bombing range in the south of New Mexico. The test bomb was suspended at the top of a 30m high metal tower and there were strongly shielded observation posts between 9 and 10km to the north, west and south of it, together with a viewing platform for VIPs 32km away. The bomb exploded in the dark 15 seconds before 5.30 a.m.; it went off with a burst of searing light which lit up the whole area and this was followed by a blast of hot air, which knocked some of the observers over, and a thunderous roar. Thereafter an enormous ball of red, orange and yellow flames leapt up into the sky and grew into a mushroom-shaped cloud of dust which rose to a height of almost 11km before being dissipated in all directions by the winds.

General Thomas F. Farrell, Groves's deputy, wrote of the 'strong, sustained,

Monument at the Trinity Test site. (Los Alamos National Laboratory)

awesome roar which warned of doomsday and made us feel that we puny things were blasphemous to dare to tamper with the forces heretofore reserved to the Almighty'.[12] And Oppenheimer, the chief architect, wrote: 'We knew the world would not be the same. A few people laughed, a few people cried. Most people were silent. I remembered the line from the Hindu scripture, the *Bhagavad-Gita*: Vishnu is trying to persuade the Prince that he should do his duty and to impress him he takes on his multi-armed form and says, "Now I am become Death, the destroyer of worlds."[13] I suppose we all thought that, one way or another.' Groves congratulated Oppenheimer with the words 'I am proud of you all'[14] and told Farrell that the war would be over after two bombs had been dropped on Japan.

Within three weeks, that had happened. The war in Europe had ended on VE-Day, 8 May 1945, but the war in the Far East was far from over. The Japanese armies were being rolled back after their initial far-flung advances towards Australia but it involved some very heavy fighting. In recapturing the island of Okinawa over 12,500 Americans and 100,000 Japanese were killed in twelve weeks of fierce conflict and it was estimated that there might be 200,000 American casualties if they attempted a direct assault on the Japanese home islands. To avoid that, President Harry Truman, who had succeeded President Roosevelt on 12 April, had decided on 1 June that the atom bombs were to be dropped on Japan when they were ready. Winston Churchill agreed with this decision, and, after Truman and Churchill met the Russian leader Joseph Stalin at Potsdam a declaration was issued. It read: 'We call upon the Government of Japan to proclaim now the unconditional surrender of all Japanese armed forces, and to provide proper and adequate assurances of their good faith in such action. The alternative for Japan is prompt and utter destruction.'

The date was 23 July. The Japanese did not respond, so Little Boy was dropped on the city of Hiroshima at 10.15 a.m. on 6 August. As there was still no surrender, Fat Man was dropped on the city of Nagasaki at 11.05 a.m. on 9 August. The Japanese military leaders still wanted to fight on, but on 14 August Emperor Hirohito intervened and a surrender was arranged. The Japanese did not know that there were no more bombs available for immediate use.

Conventional bombs were generally fused to explode when they hit the ground. Consequently they made a big crater but much of their blast effect was directed upwards into the air. In contrast, the much more powerful atom bombs were exploded above ground at a height of about 580m so that much of the blast wave was directed downwards on to the ground below. At Hiroshima, 60 per cent of the city was destroyed and an area of 9 sq. km of buildings, many of which had been built to withstand the effects of earthquakes, was flattened in the initial blast. But the damage caused by the blast was outdone by that caused by the heat and the radiation. There was a tremendous flash as the bomb went off and people as far as 4km away were badly burnt, while granite 600m away was partially melted. Much of the city was aflame for days. Those who were not blown or burnt to death thought that they had survived but within a short time they began to feel unwell. Few realised that they were suffering from the effects of the radiation emitted by the bomb, about which little was known at the time.

There were about 350,000 people in Hiroshima when the bomb went off. Shortly after, the Japanese authorities estimated that 71,000 had been killed and 68,000 injured, but over the years the mortality figures grew until it became clear

Hiroshima after the bomb. (Los Alamos National Laboratory)

that more than 50 per cent of those present on the fateful day were dead. Similar figures applied at Nagasaki even though Fat Man was more powerful than Little Boy. The bomb was, however, dropped slightly off target and the surrounding terrain was much hillier than at Hiroshima.

Large numbers of casualties in air raids was, on its own, nothing new. Bombing of Japanese cities had been going on for some time with increasing ferocity. On the night of 9 March 1945 1,600 planes dropped some 2,000 tons of incendiary bombs on Tokyo and more than 100,000 people were killed, a million were injured and a million lost their homes. Follow–up raids on Nagoya, Osaka and Kobe over the next ten days killed at least 50,000 more. In Europe on the night of 13 March and throughout the following day, 800 British Lancaster bombers and 400 American B–17s killed almost 130,000 people in Dresden. These awesome results were only achieved, however, by saturation bombing using large numbers of planes, many of-which failed to return. What was different about the atomic bomb raids was that only two planes and only two bombs were needed, and there was the added horror of the fall-out of radiation which could cause such long-term lingering death and could mean that the children of those irradiated might be born with severe malformations.

The nuclear age had arrived with a very big bang. Neither warfare nor even life itself would ever be the same again.

CHAPTER 11

Aftermath

The great majority of scientists who had been involved in making the atom bombs were overjoyed when they heard that both Little Boy and Fat Man had exploded according to plan, and there were great celebrations. But the mood quickly changed when the full enormity of what had happened began to dawn and there was much soul-searching as the vast scientific problems that they had conquered were replaced by moral issues. Stimson wrote: 'The world is changed and it is time for sober thought . . . The focus of the problem does not lie in the atom. It resides in the heart of man.'[1] And those accustomed to dealing with neutrons, isotopes, critical size and implosion came face to face with death, destruction, fall-out and radiation sickness.

There was a full range of individual reaction. Truman rated dropping the bombs as 'the greatest thing in history'[2] but Szilard, who had fought long and hard to try to control the development and use of the bomb, said that 'using it against Japan is one of the greatest blunders of history'.[3] General Groves had no doubt that developing the atom bomb had been necessary but when asked whether atomic energy is a force for good or evil he replied 'As mankind wills it'.[4] Frisch felt some 'unease, indeed nausea' and recorded that 'it seemed rather ghoulish to celebrate the sudden death of a hundred thousand people even if they were enemies'.[5] Peierls wrote that 'nobody could look at the reports and the pictures about Hiroshima and Nagasaki with anything but horror, and nobody would feel any pride at having had a hand in bringing this about. But this was war, and in war, death, suffering and destruction are unavoidable.'[6] Such a view was, in general terms, matched by Curtis LeMay, the commanding general of the Strategic Air Command, long after the event, when he wrote: 'Killing Japanese didn't bother me very much at the time. It was getting the war over that bothered me . . . Every soldier thinks something of the moral aspects of what he is doing. But all war is immoral, and if you let that bother you, you're not a good soldier.'[7]

No one agonised more than Oppenheimer because no one had been through the mill more than he had. He had lost about 9kg in weight during his time at Los

Alamos and he used phrases such as 'the physicists have known sin' and 'we have blood on our hands'.[8] And when Otto Hahn, captured in Germany by the advancing allied troops and temporarily interned along with Heisenberg, Weizsäcker and six other German physicists in a large house near Cambridge, heard the news he said: 'I was almost unnerved by the thought of the great new misery it meant, but glad that it was not the Germans but the Anglo-Americans who had made and used this new instrument of war.'[9]

Whatever the individual views might have been, what had happened soon passed into history though there has been a continuing debate ever since as to whether the bombs should have been dropped or not. But, as it was, 'What happens next?' became the question of the day. There was at first a serious exodus of scientists from Los Alamos, and Norris Bradbury succeeded Oppenheimer as the Director in October 1945. Other nuclear centres also lost staff because they thought their job was done and they wanted to return to their old university-based, peaceful research projects. They certainly wanted to get away from military control and the associated excessive secrecy. Many of them, too, hoped for some sort of new world order in which there would be completely free dissemination of all information and international rather than national thinking and planning.

One immediate step forward was the founding, at the end of August 1945, of the Association of Atomic Scientists at Los Alamos which was the first of many pressure groups to be formed within the nuclear energy field. It had about a hundred members and was led by Willie Higinbotham, a 34-year-old electronics engineer, who was the son of a Protestant clergyman. He had feelings of guilt about what he had done at Los Alamos and told his mother that he was 'not a bit proud of the job we have done . . . and that he now knew the meaning of mixed emotions'.[10] The aim of his association, which by the middle of November had grown into a national Federation of Atomic Scientists, was to enlighten the general public as to what was going on and to lobby the politicians. Their pressure was in the end successful when they managed to get the May–Johnson Bill, which would, if passed by Congress, have kept control of nuclear matters in the hands of the military, replaced by the McMahon Act. This took time and the Act was not passed until July 1946 and it was the end of that year before Truman set up the US Atomic Energy Commission (AEC). It consisted of five commissioners with equal powers and equal voting rights, with David E. Lilienthal, who had been the first chairman of the Tennessee Valley Authority, as chairman. There was an associated General Advisory Committee of nine members with Oppenheimer in the chair, together with a Military Liaison Committee of which Groves was a member.

The AEC took over the administration of the Manhattan Project on 31 December 1946 and set about trying to revitalise its activities. The main military aims were to improve the designs of Little Boy and Fat Man and to investigate the possibility of making still more powerful bombs, which became known as fusion, thermonuclear, super- or hydrogen bombs. They depended not on the *fission* of large atoms such as uranium or plutonium but on the *fusion*, at very high temperatures, of very small atoms such as the isotopes of hydrogen. Edward Teller was the bomb's main

Edward Teller. (Lawrence Livermore National Laboratory.)

advocate and it was his single-minded tenacity that eventually led to it being built. He was another in the long line of Jewish refugees who contributed so much to physics. He was born in Budapest on 15 January 1908, the son of a prosperous lawyer, and he found his way to the United States in 1935, after training and working in Budapest, Karlsruhe, Munich, Leipzig, Göttingen, Copenhagen and London. He was the Professor of Physics at the George Washington University until 1941, when shortly after becoming an American citizen he moved to Columbia University to work with Fermi and Szilard.

It was at Columbia, in the spring of 1942, while he was having lunch with Fermi, that Teller first discussed his idea for a new bomb. It was known that the enormous amount of energy liberated by the sun came from fusion reactions at very high temperatures, and Teller's idea was that a fission bomb might be used to heat a mixture of small atoms to such a high temperature that they would fuse together and liberate still more energy. The fission bomb would, in effect, be the detonator for the fusion bomb. The small atoms of hydrogen, deuterium or tritium – ^1_1H, ^2_1H or ^3_1H – were thought to be the most likely to undergo fusion reactions and they could be packed around a central fission bomb to make a fusion bomb as large and as powerful as required.

Fermi was not greatly excited by the idea but, after some initial doubts as to its feasibility, it became something of an obsession for Teller. He had been one of the first to join the Los Alamos team in April 1943 but he did not get on well with Oppenheimer and, because everyone was so busy designing fission bombs, he found little support for his new idea. He was, however, put in charge of a small group which was set up to study the idea more thoroughly and by the end of the war he was confident that it would be possible to build a bomb with the power of 10 million tonnes of TNT by surrounding a fission bomb with about 1 cu. m of liquid deuterium with some tritium to act as a booster. At the end of the war Teller, somewhat disappointed and with the feeling that he had been sidelined and not fully appreciated, left Los Alamos to join Fermi at the University of Chicago, but he kept in touch and was invited in April 1946 to chair a secret meeting to review the progress being made on the super-bomb project. The participants agreed that the idea, though very costly, was feasible and Teller predicted that a super-bomb could be built within two years. But in 1946 national policy was not in favour of going ahead.

Everything changed in September 1949 when American aerial reconnaissance planes picked up traces of radioactivity in the atmosphere that could only be explained by the Russians having exploded an atomic bomb. This news came as a great surprise to the United States authorities, who had been estimating that it would be at least 1956 before Russia could possibly make a bomb, and Teller proposed that a super-bomb should be built as a counter-measure. The matter was considered at a meeting of the General Advisory Committee to the AEC, with Oppenheimer in the chair, on 19 October 1949, but, much to Teller's disgust all eight members turned down his idea and Oppenheimer likened the bomb to 'the plague of Thebes'.[11] They agreed that it *could* be made but argued that its manufacture would be too expensive. They also recorded that, in their judgement, there was no requirement for such a powerful bomb and that the moral position of the United States would be damaged if they escalated the stakes in the developing arms race.

President Truman had to balance that advice against the military view that the new bomb was necessary. Greatly influenced by the Russian bomb-making programme, he issued a decree on 31 January 1950, which read:

It is part of my responsibility as Commander-in-Chief of the Armed Forces to see that our country is able to defend itself against any possible aggressor.

Accordingly, I have directed the Atomic Energy Commission to continue its work on all forms of atomic weapons, including the 'hydrogen' or super-bomb. Like all other work in the field of atomic weapons, it is being and will be carried forward on a basis consistent with the overall objectives of our programme for peace and security.

The resulting increase in research and development led to the first test of a hydrogen bomb, code-named Mike, at Eniwetok atoll in the Marshall Islands in the South Pacific on 1 November 1952. It was not a bomb that could be carried in any aeroplane because it consisted of 66 tonnes of equipment, including a refrigeration plant to keep the deuterium-tritium mixture in the bomb below -253°C so that it remained liquefied, but it did demonstrate that the principle of making a fusion bomb could be put into practice. It went off with the power of over 10 million tons of TNT (10 megatons) – more than a thousand times more powerful than the Hiroshima bomb – and obliterated the island of Elugelab, replacing it by a crater 3.2km wide and 0.8km deep.

To make a portable bomb it was necessary to reduce the weight and this was eventually achieved by replacing the deuterium-tritium mixture by solid lithium deuteride, a compound between lithium-6 and deuterium. The first bomb made in this way was code-named Shrimp. It weighed 10,645kg and could be carried in the bomb-bay of a B-47 aeroplane. It was tested, as *Castle Bravo*, the first of a series of *Castle* tests, on 1 March 1954 in Bikini atoll in the Marshall Islands where it exploded with a power of 15 megatons – which was twice what had been expected. One observer on a ship 30 miles away wrote: 'It was pretty frightening. There was a huge fireball. The thing was glowing and it looked like a diseased brain up in the sky. It was a much more awesome sight than a puny little atomic bomb.'[12] The explosion left a crater almost 2,000m in diameter and 80m deep in the coral and white radioactive dust spread from it far and wide like a snowstorm. An American destroyer thought to be out of range in a safe area was drenched so heavily that the crew were sent below decks while the contamination was hosed away. It also engulfed the 236 people who lived on the islands of Rongelap, Ailinginae and Utirik, and a Japanese fishing boat called the *Fukuryu Maru* (or, in translation, 'The Lucky Dragon'), which was trawling for tuna well outside the test zone.

The local islanders, who had been moved to the outer island Kwajalain, felt sick, lost their appetite and experienced skin and head lesions. Those from Rongelap had to stay away for three years and when they did return they suffered an unusually high number of thyroid complaints. The twenty-three Japanese

The 'Mike' test at Eniwetok. The bomb is in position on Elugelab, the fourth island from the bottom. (Los Alamos National Laboratory)

fishermen aboard *Fukuryu Maru*, suffering from dizziness, itching skin, aching eyes and vomiting, set sail for their home port of Yaizu, but not knowing what had happened they did nothing to decontaminate their boat. Some of the crew had to spend six months in hospital and the radio operator, Aiticki Kuboyama, died on 23 September 1954. Lewis L. Strauss, the millionaire financier who was the new Chairman of the Atomic Energy Commission, suggested that their boat must have been within the delineated danger area and that it may well have been a Communist spy ship. After what they had already been through, the whole Japanese nation was horrified on all counts and Kuboyama was named as the 'first martyr of the H-bomb'.[13]

Further tests on devices called Runt, Koon, Yankee and Nectar confirmed that lithium deuteride was a satisfactory fuel for hydrogen bombs and that they could be made in a variety of sizes. The stock-pile of such bombs in the United States

After the blast, Elugelab has disappeared and the other islands are devastated. (Los Alamos National Laboratory)

began to escalate and the stakes in the forthcoming arms race were raised still higher. As a further refinement some work was done on designing a special enhanced radiation weapon (ERW), which came to be called a neutron bomb. This was a small hydrogen bomb with limited blast but very high neutron radiation. The idea was that the bomb would not greatly damage buildings but would kill people, in up to six days, within the range of its radiation. Nikita Khrushchev spoke of it as 'the bestial ethics of the most aggressive representatives of imperialism'[14] and its possible use raised such an outcry that the idea was dropped.

So the McMahon Act and the AEC set the course for the Americans well enough but there was much less success on the international scene. Article 11 of the United Nations Charter empowered the General Assembly to consider principles

A Mark-17 H-bomb weighing over four times as much as a Fat Man bomb. (Los Alamos National Laboratory)

for arms control and disarmament, and Article 26 required the Security Council to establish 'a system for the regulation of armaments', but until very recently these were hopes rather than realities. In 1947 various ideas were floated as to what the United Nations might do about controlling atomic bombs and atomic energy, with the formation of a United Nations Atomic Energy Commission or an International Atomic Development Authority in the forefront. All dangerous activities would be banned, there would be international ownership of the raw materials, and peaceful uses of atomic energy would be promoted internationally. But as has been the case for the most part ever since, it was not possible to get much agreement and no great progress was made. Lewis L. Strauss of the AEC wrote that 'it was the purpose of the AEC to maintain and increase the lead of the US, whereas the international agency, if established, would take over all aspects of national agencies' activities in the field that related to weapons'.[15] And the AEC's Chairman, David Lilienthal, was even blunter when he wrote: 'So long as we are in an atomic arms race, it is only sense to do everything we can to slow up other countries.'[16]

Such isolationist views were incorporated into the McMahon Act which forebade the exchange of nuclear information with foreign powers and this was interpreted so strictly that it even prevented the United States from responding to a request from the Norwegian Defence Research Establishment for a minute amount of radioactive iron for use in developing alloys for gas turbine engines. But it also had the much more important effect of demolishing the good Anglo-American relationship which had been built up during the war and it contributed greatly to the start of the arms race and the Cold War.

Any country that wanted to be involved in any sort of nuclear research was forced to strike out on its own. Most of those who chose to do so were at first mainly interested in building their own arsenals of nuclear weapons, but with the prospect of peaceful days ahead much attention was also given to the possibilities of using the heat generated in an atomic pile or nuclear reactor to propel a ship or to drive a power station to provide electricity. The peaceful use of atomic or nuclear energy came to be seen as a possible solution to the world's energy shortage. It was regarded as a gift from Heaven; Winston Churchill spoke of it as 'a perennial fountain of world prosperity';[17] and there was even some talk of domestic electricity being supplied by it without meters on the same basis as water.

In England the starting point of the nuclear programme was the decision announced in the House of Commons by Prime Minister Attlee on 29 October 1945 'to set up a research and experimental establishment covering all aspects of the use of atomic energy'.[18] It was called the Atomic Energy Research Establishment (AERE), and building began in April 1946 on the site of an air-force station at Harwell in Berkshire, the land for which had been bought in 1937 for £11,650. Few government purchases can have been more fruitful. Cockcroft was the first director at Harwell and many of the British scientists who had worked in the USA and Canada during the war were recruited on to the staff. The establishment was originally intended as an all-purpose research centre, and within two years a large cyclotron and two experimental nuclear reactors – GLEEP (Graphite Low Energy Experimental Pile) and the more powerful BEPO (British Experimental Pile O) – were built. The high chimney for BEPO was fitted with a heat exchanger which provided hot water for all the Harwell site – and this must have been the first peaceful, practical use of atomic energy.

The work at Harwell was expanded in January 1946 by the establishment of a new station at Risley, near Warrington in Lancashire. This was to organise the production of fissile material so that, in Mr Attlee's words, we 'could take advantage rapidly of the technical developments as they occur, and develop our programme for the use of atomic energy as circumstances may require'.[19] The station was directed by Sir Christopher (later Lord) Hinton. As a railway workshop apprentice he had won a scholarship to Cambridge, and he was the

The GLEEP reactor at Harwell. (UKEAE)

chief engineer at the Alkali Division of Imperial Chemical Industries from 1931 to 1940, and the Deputy Director of Explosive Filling Factories during the Second World War. But once the British government decided, albeit somewhat secretly, in January 1947 to back a full-scale programme of bomb manufacture it became necessary to expand the facilities still further. To that end a plant was built at Springfields near Preston to manufacture uranium; Windscale, nowadays known as Sellafield, on the coast of Cumbria, was established as the centre where plutonium would be made from the Springfields' uranium in two atomic piles; Aldermaston was chosen as the site for making the actual bombs; and a plant at Capenhurst in Cheshire was built to separate uranium–235 from uranium–238. The industrial side of the operations was directed by Hinton and the bomb-making side by Sir William (later Lord) Penney, who had been an observer when the atomic bomb was dropped on Nagasaki. Before the war he was the Professor of Mathematics at the Imperial College of Science in London, and during the war

The 'topping out' of the BEPO chimney at Harwell in 1948. It was finally demolished in 2000. (UKAEA)

he worked first on bomb blast research, then on the artificial Mulberry Harbours used in the Normandy landings, and finally at Los Alamos.

The control of the work on nuclear energy was originally vested in the Ministry of Supply, a huge government department run by civil servants but, mainly on the suggestion of Lord Cherwell, Churchill's wartime scientific adviser, a new organisation, the United Kingdom Atomic Energy Authority (UKAEA), was set up on 1 January 1954. Sir Edwin (later Lord) Plowden was the first chairman and he saw the workforce rise from a thousand in 1947 to two thousand in 1953 and six thousand in 1962. The production group involved in making fuel for nuclear reactors and in reprocessing it as necessary was reorganised in 1971 as British Nuclear Fuels Ltd. And the activities of UKAEA have declined still further in recent years with much of their former work having been taken over by

Aerial view of the Springfields site. (BNFL)

AEA Technology (AEAT), an international company operating in North America, the Middle East, Asia and thirty-one countries in Europe.

In France, General de Gaulle set up the Commissariat à l'Énergie Atomique (CEA) on 18 October 1945, under the direction of Joliot, with the intention that it would enable France to make its own nuclear weapons. But when de Gaulle was removed from power, Joliot took control and put all the emphasis on constructing a nuclear reactor to produce power for peaceful purposes in an effort to offset France's particular weakness in indigenous supplies of energy. Their first reactor, designed by Kowarski, came on stream in December 1948. When Joliot took the step of publicly announcing in 1950 that he would never take part in making nuclear weapons he was dismissed from his post and the French programme was stalled for some years until de Gaulle's return to power in 1958 when he ordered the go-ahead for making atom bombs.

In Russia there had been some interest in nuclear matters since 1910 when one of their mineralogists, Vladimir I. Vernadski, had reported that the discovery of radioactivity 'opened up new sources of atomic energy . . . exceeding by millions of times all the sources of energy that the human imagination has envisaged'.[20] The interest was heightened, too, by the discovery that they had good natural supplies of uranium. It was not surprising then, that Russian scientists studied Hahn's 1939 disclosure about the fission of uranium with great enthusiasm and that a Uranium Problem Commission

Lord Penney. (UKAEA)

was set up by the Soviet Academy of Sciences. By October 1941 Peter Kapitza, who had been the assistant director of magnetic research at the Cavendish Laboratory in Cambridge between 1924 and 1932 before he returned to Russia to become the Director of the Institute for Physical Problems, was writing that 'an atom bomb can easily destroy a large city with several millions of inhabitants'.[21] Yet, when it came to the point, he was not prepared to participate in making such a bomb and was dismissed from his post in August 1946 and was kept under house arrest for eight years. A contemporary physicist, Igor Kurchatov, was mainly responsible for Russian nuclear research but progress was spasmodic, largely because of the effects of the war with Germany. But when Stalin heard of the explosions of the atomic bombs at Hiroshima and Nagasaki he put his ruthless secret police chief, Leonid Beria, in charge of the programme and ordered him to catch up with the Americans.

So the main players had all thrown their hats into the ring and the mad rush began to make better and bigger bombs faster than the competitors. Today the United States, Russia, France, China and the United Kingdom are regarded as the major nuclear powers because they had all made and exploded nuclear weapons before 1 January 1967. Thereafter, Israel, India and Pakistan joined the fold, and South Africa would also be a member if President F.W. de Klerk had not abandoned their nuclear weapon programme in 1990. Ukraine, Belarus and Kazakhstan, formerly parts of the Soviet Union, did have nuclear weapons but they have now scrapped them or sent them back to Russia.

Recent estimates of the number of nuclear warheads in the world put the United States ahead with 7,519, Russia with 6,464, France with 450, China with about 300, the United Kingdom with 192 (all aboard Trident submarines), Israel between 75 and 125, India with between 45 and 95, and Pakistan between 30 and 50. Belgium, Germany, Greece, Holland, Italy and Turkey also house American nuclear weapons as members of the North Atlantic Treaty Organisation (NATO). North Korea, Iraq, Iran and Libya may also have made, or be on the verge of making, nuclear weapons.

CHAPTER 12

Atoms for Peace

President Eisenhower foretold the coming of a new era for nuclear energy in a speech to the United Nations General Assembly on 8 December 1953 when he said that 'experts would be employed to apply atomic energy to the needs of agriculture, medicine and other peaceful activities, and a special purpose would be to provide abundant electrical energy in the power-starved areas of the world'.[1] That hope has not been fully met but by 2002 there were 438 nuclear reactors operating in thirty-one different countries, as listed in Appendix III on page 224.

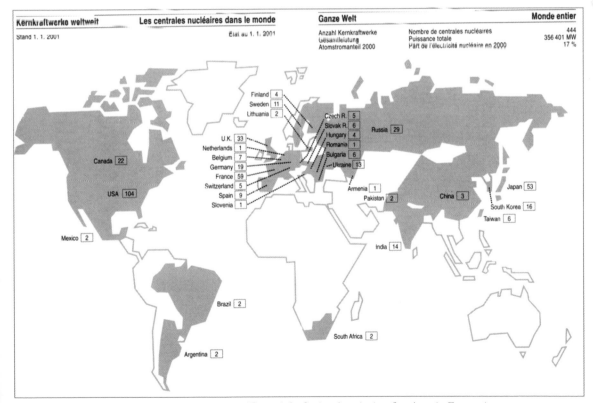

The world's nuclear power stations. (Copyright Swiss Association for Atomic Energy)

The opening of the Calder Hall nuclear power station by Queen Elizabeth II on 17 October 1956. (UKAEA)

The USA has 104, producing 20 per cent of its electricity; France has 59, producing 76 per cent; Japan has 54, producing 34 per cent; and the United Kingdom has 33, producing 22 per cent. Even a small number can make a large contribution, with just two reactors in Lithuania producing 74 per cent of that country's electricity, and one in Slovenia and one in Armenia producing 37 and 33 per cent respectively. In many countries it has been decided to build no new reactors and in Sweden it was also decided to close all their existing reactors but that has not yet been implemented. Nevertheless 35 new reactors are already under construction and 31 more are planned, with 12 in Japan, 4 in India, 8 in South Korea and 2 in Russia.

The new age of nuclear electricity dawned on 17 October 1956 when Her Majesty Queen Elizabeth II opened the Calder Hall Nuclear Power Station on the coast of Cumbria near Windscale. There had been a small-scale nuclear reactor producing electricity at Obninsk in the Soviet Union since 27 June 1954 and for some time a United States submarine had been driven by atomic power but the output of the first Calder Hall reactor was ten times higher than that at Obninsk and it was planned as the first of four to be constructed on the same site.

CP-1, built by Fermi and his associates at Chicago University between May and December 1942, had shown that it was possible to obtain a controlled amount of energy from a pile but it had never been designed to produce much and its maximum output was only that of two 100 watt light-bulbs. That first pile was dismantled in February 1943 and rebuilt in an improved form as CP-2 in the Argonne Forest at what is now the Argonne National Laboratory; it could produce 500 times more power than CP-1. Thereafter a pilot plant built at Oak Ridge paved the way for the construction of much larger reactors at Hanford on the banks of the Columbia River in the state of Washington. Three were completed by early 1945 and another six shortly after. At the time their main purpose was to provide the plutonium needed for making Fat Man bombs and all the vast amount of heat energy they produced went into heating up the Columbia River.

The Calder Hall reactor was based partly on those old designs, partly on studies carried out at the Montreal Laboratory in Canada, and partly on the two military reactors built at Windscale after the war. In the 1950s these had provided the plutonium to make the first British atom bomb, which was tested at the Monte Bello Islands off the north west corner of Australia on 3 October 1952. There was, too, a considerable input from the experience gained by operating the two experimental reactors, GLEEP and BEPO, at Harwell. The Calder Hall reactor was a dual-purpose reactor intended both to supply electricity and to produce plutonium, as was made clear in its code-name PIPPA, which could stand for Pressurised Pile Producing Power and Plutonium or for Pressurised Pile Producing Plutonium and Power. At the time it was politically convenient to play down the plutonium role because of its association with nuclear weapons but it was in fact of more importance than the power.

The fuel for the reactors was natural uranium, containing 0.7 per cent of uranium-235, which was made at Springfields from uranium ores imported from around the world. They were treated chemically to convert them into uranium tetrafluoride, UF_4, a green solid, which was then heated in a furnace with magnesium to a temperature over 600°. This formed molten uranium which ran to the bottom of the furnace from where it was tapped off and allowed to cool until it solidified. After remelting, it was cast into thin rods about a metre long; these were machined and then sealed in a casing of a magnesium alloy called Magnox. The reactors in which they were used thus came to be called Magnox reactors.

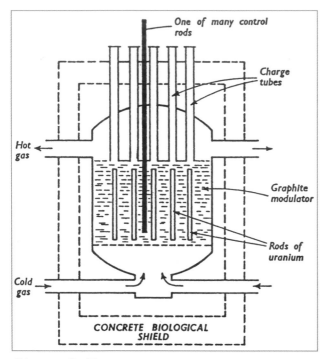

Diagram of a Magnox reactor.

The rods were embedded in graphite, which acted as a moderator to slow down the neutrons, and the overall amount of uranium in the reactor was greater than the critical size so that a chain reaction could develop. The extent of that reaction was controlled by incorporating control rods made of boron–steel, which is a good neutron–absorbing material. When they were partially withdrawn, the multiplication factor was greater than 1 so that a chain reaction took place and heat energy was produced. The amount of heat could be changed by adjusting the position of the rods and safety was achieved by having an automatic device which ensured that all the control rods moved into the reactor in any emergency.

The core of the reactor was enclosed within a cylindrical 50mm steel jacket through which carbon dioxide, at a pressure of 7 atmospheres, was passed to cool down the core, and the Magnox casing of each uranium rod was fitted with fins to assist the heat exchange. The cold gas which entered at the bottom emerged as hot gas at the top. This was then used, in heat exchangers, to boil water, the steam from which operated a steam turbine which in turn drove a dynamo to produce electricity. The whole was surrounded by an octagonal shield with 2m-thick concrete walls to prevent the escape of radiation. And to keep the concrete cool, air was blown through the space between it and a 15cm-thick wall of steel a few inches inside it.

The power station at Calder Hall eventually contained four Magnox reactors and a similar station was built at Chapelcross, across the border in Scotland. These plants were built quickly and successfully by British engineering firms under the auspices of the United Kingdom Atomic Energy Authority (UKAEA) and were run by the Central Electricity Generating Board, a new nationalised

Magnox reactor at Wylfa. (BNFL)

body. Shortly afterwards, two new twin-reactor stations were ordered to be built at Berkeley in Gloucestershire and Bradwell in Essex, and the scene seemed to be set for an ongoing programme which would provide cheap, readily accessible electricity from nuclear power stations which, it was thought at the time, would be lot more environmentally friendly than those dependent on coal, the stocks of which were in any case running down. It all seemed too good to be true and as the United Kingdom was the first in the field it was hoped that there would be a lucrative export market for Magnox reactors. A total of twenty-six Magnox reactors were constructed in the United Kingdom and that twenty of them are still operating must be counted as a success, but only two were sold overseas – one to Japan and one to Italy – and by the time the last one was built at Wylfa, on the island of Anglesey, in 1971 it was already clear that overseas buyers were not going to jump on to the British bandwagon because a different type of reactor being developed in the United States seemed to be a better proposition.

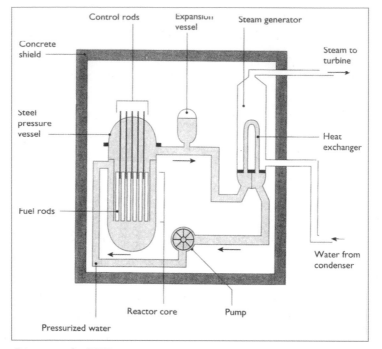

Diagram of a PWR reactor.

At the end of the war, there was not at first much interest in the United States for using nuclear reactors to generate electricity because there was no great shortage of coal or oil to run traditional power stations, but Captain Hyman G. Rickover of the US Navy realised that the power from a reactor might be used to propel a ship. It would, he argued, be particularly useful in propelling a submarine because it requires no air or oxygen so that a nuclear submarine could remain submerged for much longer than a conventional diesel-powered craft which has to surface periodically. In 1948 Rickover was put in charge of a newly created naval Nuclear Power Branch and in conjunction with the AEC and two private firms, Westinghouse and General Electric, two different types of reactor were investigated. One used liquid sodium as a coolant but this was rejected in favour of what was called a Pressurised Water Reactor (PWR). This used uranium oxide containing 3.2 per cent of uranium-235 – it was said to be enriched – as the fuel, and ordinary water as the moderator and the coolant; to distinguish it from heavy water it was referred to as light water. The core was contained in a thick-walled steel vessel because the water was under high pressure so that it would not boil and it emerged from the core of the reactor at a temperature of around 300°C. It was then passed into a heat exchanger where it boiled water in a separate circuit, and the steam thus generated was used to drive the turbines which both turned the submarine's propellers and supplied electricity. As both oxygen and purified water could be made on board from sea water the length of time for which a submarine could remain submerged was limited mainly by the amount of food that it could carry.

USS *Nautilus* was launched in 1954 and other countries soon followed with HMS *Dreadnought* being launched in Britain in 1962. There are today more than 250 ships in the world driven by nuclear power. Most of them are submarines in the navies of the United States, Britain, France, Russia and China, but there are also a few aircraft carriers and icebreakers. Nuclear-powered commercial cargo ships have also been operated by the United States, Japan and Germany but they were not economically successful, partially because many ports would not allow them to dock.

In 1957 the reactor from USS *Nautilus* was brought ashore and used to build the first nuclear power station in America at Shippingport, near Philadelphia. It began to generate electricity only fourteen months after Calder Hall was opened and by the time it was shut down in 1982 it had grown into the world's most successful design. There are today about 250 PWR reactors operating in the United States, France, Japan and Russia – more than 50 per cent of the total number of reactors in the world – but it was not until 1994 that one was built in the United Kingdom.

The next most popular design is the Boiling Water Reactor (BWR), with over ninety examples in operation in the United States, Japan and Sweden. It was developed in the United States and is similar to the PWR but much simpler because the water which acts as moderator and coolant is allowed to boil as it passes over the core and the steam produced is used to drive a turbine. It is consequently much cheaper to build than a PWR because there is no heat exchanger and the pressure at which the reactor operates is much lower.

In France the nationalised Électricité de France (EdF) decided that 'one cannot do other than follow the line taken by the British'[2] and that policy was adopted at first by the Commissariat à l'Énergie Atomique (CEA), which had been set up in 1945 and was under the direction of Joliot. Dual-purpose reactors were built to provide plutonium for military purposes and electricity for civil use, but progress was hindered by a constant battle between Joliot who favoured the civil use and General de Gaulle who favoured the military. Nevertheless, their first research reactor, Zoë (or EL-1), designed by Kowarski, was built at Fontenay-aux-Roses near Paris and came on stream in December 1948. It was followed by three reactors – G-1, G-2 and G-3 – built at Marcoule in 1956 and two larger ones at

Chinon in 1962. These reactors used natural uranium, a graphite moderator and gas cooling, as in British Magnox reactors, but by 1969, when Georges Pompidou took over the presidency from General de Gaulle, there had been a change in policy. This involved the formation of a new company, Framatome, in the steel town of Le Creusot, which began to manufacture PWR-type liquid-cooled reactors under licence from the American firm Westinghouse. The first was built at Fessenheim in 1968 and three more followed in the next two years, but there was a dramatic change after the Yom Kippur War between the Arabs and the Israelis in 1973. The war led to a rise in the price of a barrel of oil from 3 to 12 dollars over a period of three months and France, with very little oil or coal of her own, decided to abandon her heavy reliance on imported oil and planned to build forty new nuclear power stations between 1974 and 1981. By then, they were manufacturing PWR reactors of their own design and making enriched uranium at Tricaston on the Rhone in a plant jointly owned with Belgium, Italy and Spain. They were able to supply domestic electricity at a low price which only went up with inflation, and were exporting electricity to neighbouring countries, including the United Kingdom. Today, France has 59 reactors generating 76 per cent of their total output.

Canada followed a different route by choosing to be the only country to forgo the military option and to pursue a research programme based solely on power generation. Canada had contributed greatly to the Manhattan Project during the war through the work of the laboratory in Montreal, where an international group of scientists were directed first by Halban until 1944, and then by Cockcroft. The two nuclear reactors – ZEEP and NRX – which were still under construction at Chalk River, 200km north of Ottawa, when the war ended, were completed and provided a centre for an ongoing peacetime programme. Any plutonium that was produced was sold to the United States or Britain, and experience with those early reactors led to the design of the unique CANDU (CANadian Deuterium Uranium) reactors. They used natural uranium oxide, of which Canada is the largest world producer, as the fuel, with heavy water as the moderator and coolant. The heavy water was passed under pressure over the fuel which was contained in Zircaloy cans packed into a number of separate tubes. This heavy water was then used in a heat exchanger to boil ordinary water to raise steam to drive a turbine. The first CANDU reactor was built at Pickering, near Toronto, in 1971 and there are today fourteen in the country providing just over 12 per cent of the electricity demand.

The last Magnox reactor in Britain was completed in 1971 and brought to an end the first phase of the nuclear programme. By then Britain had generated more nuclear electricity than the rest of the world put together but the rest of the world had decided that cooling a reactor with a liquid was more effective than using a gas. It would have been possible to follow that lead and change from gas to liquid cooling, but such a policy was rejected and another gas-cooled design – the advanced gas-cooled reactor (AGR) – was chosen for the second phase of the UK nuclear power programme. It was even hailed by the Labour Minister of Power, Fred Lee, as the 'greatest breakthrough of all time'.[3] The reactor was not unlike the Magnox design but it was contained in a pressure vessel with pre-stressed concrete walls about 6m thick and it could be operated at a much higher temperature. That was achieved by using uranium oxide, which has a much higher melting point than uranium, as the fuel. It was in the form of small round pellets about 20mm by 5mm, which were packed into a thin cylindrical tube made of stainless steel. Because this steel is a good absorber of neutrons, the uranium oxide fuel had to be enriched, with the uranium-235 content being increased to about 3 per cent. This was done at Capenhurst, as described in Appendix IV on page 226. Graphite was used as the moderator and carbon dioxide as the coolant. The gas was used at twice the pressure than that in a Magnox reactor and its emergent temperature was 650°C instead of 400°C.

The first prototype AGR was built at Windscale in 1962 and five commercial twin-reactor stations were then built at Hinkley Point, Hunterston, Hartlepool, Dungeness and Torness, together with two similar stations at Heysham. There were, alas, considerable setbacks along the way with many design problems, a lot of accidents and some awful constructional delays. It had been expected that the average building time for each reactor would be about five years but it actually turned out to be fourteen years, and one of the three consortia in the country capable of building nuclear reactors, Atomic Power Constructions, was declared bankrupt in 1969 while building the station at Dungeness. So the start of the AGR programme was something of a disaster, and even though the reputation of the reactors improved as they were operated, the AGR programme was ended when the last station, at Torness, was completed in 1989.

By then the third nuclear programme, announced in 1974, was under way but PWR-type reactors were still not chosen by Tony Benn, the Labour Minister of State for Technology, even though they had many supporters. Instead it was planned to build six Steam Generating Heavy Water Reactors (SGHW) over the next four years. This was a British modification of the CANDU design and a small pilot plant had been running at Winfrith in Dorset since 1967. But the project was abandoned in 1978, and in January 1981 the CEGB, encouraged by Mrs Thatcher's Conservative government, at long last applied for permission to

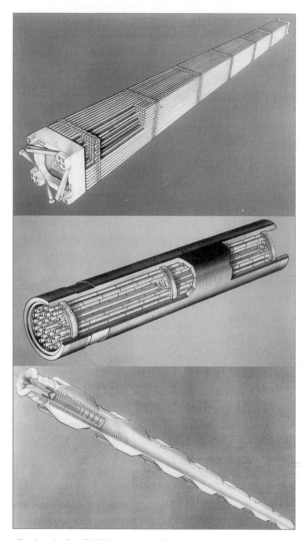

Fuel rods for PWR (top), AGR (centre) and Magnox reactors. (BNFL)

build a PWR–type reactor at Sizewell in Suffolk where an AGR reactor had been operating since 1966. A public enquiry under the chairmanship of Sir Frank Layfield began on 11 January and went on until 26 January 1987 at a cost of £10 million. There was strong opposition to the building of the reactor, voiced by, among others, Friends of the Earth and the National Union of Mineworkers, but permission to go ahead was eventually granted and work began on the £3 billion project on 4 June 1987, with the first electricity being fed into the national grid in February 1995. The reactor uses a fuel of enriched uranium oxide containing about 3.2 per cent of uranium–235 cast into pellets which are contained in zirconium alloy (zircaloy) tubes, and pressurised water as the moderator and coolant.

There had been discussions concerning building a new reactor every year in Britain in the decade beginning in 1982 but what came to be called Sizewell B turned out to be the last because an application to build a second PWR station at Hinkley Point was rejected following a public enquiry in 1988, which heard evidence from twenty-one nearby local authorities that the reactor was 'unsafe, uneconomic and unwanted'.[4] The opposing conclusions of these two public enquiries summarises the capricious nature of the decisions made over the years in Britain on nuclear matters and must have influenced an international team of consultants who, when asked to examine the reason why Britain was less competitive than other countries, concluded that 'the planning system must take much of the blame'.[5]

The 1990s saw the last new reactor to be built in Britain, and it also saw the demise of a long-term project on a completely different type of reactor called the liquid metal fast breeder reactor (LMFBR or simply FBR). All the reactors so far described are known as thermal reactors because they use moderators to provide slow neutrons to carry on the chain reaction within the reactor. In them, the number of uranium-235 atoms that are fissioned outweighs the number of uranium-238 atoms that are converted into fissionable plutonium by neutron absorption. Consequently, the overall number of fissionable atoms decreases, the reactor 'runs down', and it has to be refuelled when only 2–3 per cent of the uranium has in fact been used up. In a fast breeder reactor a mixture of enriched uranium oxide and plutonium is used as the fuel and liquid sodium or an alloy of sodium and potassium is used as the coolant. There is no moderator to slow down the neutrons, which is why it is known as a fast reactor. Some of the fast neutrons carry on a chain reaction by fissioning some of the uranium-235 and some of the plutonium atoms, while others are absorbed by uranium-238 atoms to form new plutonium atoms. The reactor is called a breeder because more plutonium is formed than is used up and this can, in due course, be separated from the used fuel for re-use. It is a clever idea but it has not been possible to bring it to fruition even after years of research in many countries.

After early experimental work at Harwell, where the two research reactors ZEPHYR and ZEUS were built in 1954 and 1955, a small FBR reactor was built at Dounreay in Scotland in 1959 and it operated until November 1981. A second, larger reactor on the same site, ordered in 1966, became operational in 1974, but as there were few signs that it could ever be commercially available in the short term government support was withdrawn in March 1994. Work on similar projects in France, Japan, Russia and the United States has also been curtailed.

The decisions to end the British FBR programme and to build no more thermal reactors closed a rather sad story of missed opportunities. One writer refers to the 'Byzantine complications which in retrospect can only excite astonishment and regret'.[6] And Lord Marshall, the former chairman of the Central Electricity Generating Board and the first chairman of the World Association of Nuclear Operators, pointed the finger when he said, on 30 November 1989, 'the broad story of nuclear power in this country is the most powerful argument in favour of privatisation that I have ever seen. Over the last forty years governments have interfered with this business so continuously, and

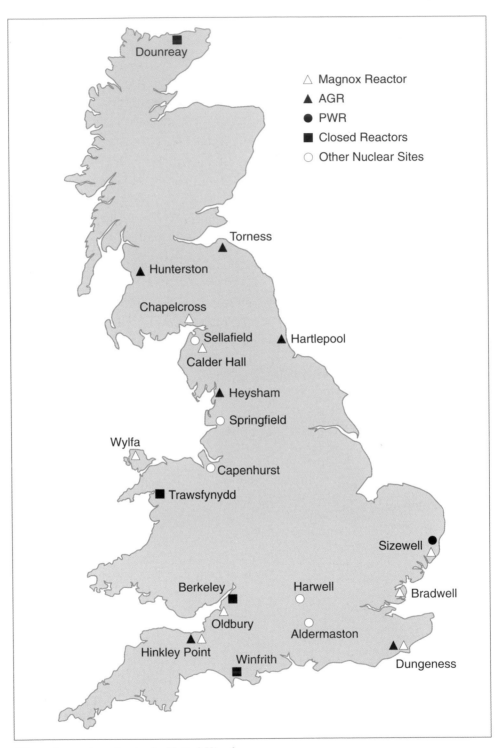

The major nuclear sites in the United Kingdom.

with such appalling effects, that I am thoroughly convinced that it must be best to do everything that can be done in the private sector.'[7]

There were, however, many other important factors. There was an uncertain economic climate with interest rates of 3 per cent in 1954 rising to double figures in the 1970s, and inflation which reached over 20 per cent in 1974. The price of a barrel of oil had fluctuated wildly between 3 and 35 dollars. Forecasts of future energy requirements have been notoriously unreliable. Labour and Conservative governments have had different views on many of the issues that had to be decided. There was the miners' strike of 1984–5; there was an apparently endless series of well-publicised nuclear accidents all over the world; and last but certainly not least there was an ever-increasing build-up in the strength of the anti-nuclear lobby.

The final outcome today is that there are thirty-three nuclear reactors operating in the UK at twelve different power stations. There are also plants concerned with fuel manufacture, waste disposal and decommissioning; a number of research and defence establishments including nuclear submarine bases; and some private companies manufacturing radioactive products. The total number of sites licensed under the Nuclear Installations Act of 1965 is therefore thirty-four.

CHAPTER 13
Living with Radiation

As it became clear at the start of the twentieth century that using both X-rays and radioactive substances was hazardous, the Röntgen Society, which had been founded in Britain on 2 April 1897, appointed a committee to investigate, and evidence soon mounted showing that the situation was potentially very serious. First, Clarence Dally, one of Thomas Edison's workers, died at the age of 39 from exposure to X-rays in 1904. Then Ernest Wilson, an X-ray photographer at the London Hospital,

The Martyrs' Memorial. This memorial was erected in the grounds of St George's Hospital in Hamburg by the German Röntgen Society to commemorate those who suffered from their early work with X-rays or radioactivity. (Deutsches Röntgen-Museum)

died in 1911, and Dr Ironside Bruce of the Charing Cross Hospital in 1921. But the full horrors of what could happen were highlighted by the death of Reginald Blackwell at the age of 44. He had begun work as an X-ray photographer at the London Hospital in 1899. He had to have a finger-nail removed in 1903, then three fingers were amputated; he was forced to retire in 1920 and in 1923 both his hands were amputated. The names of Wilson, Bruce and Blackwell, along with eleven others from Britain and many from other countries, are recorded on a Martyrs Memorial erected in the grounds of St George's Hospital in Hamburg by the German Röntgen Society. The names include that of

Madame Curie but, surprisingly, not Röntgen himself, perhaps because he kept his X-ray tubes in a metal box.

It is now known that X-rays, alpha-, beta- and gamma-rays, and a beam of neutrons all have these harmful effects because they have long since been recognised as what are called ionising radiations, which are unlike visible, ultra-violet or infra-red light. This means that they can knock electrons off atoms or molecules with which they impinge and change them in various ways. Ionising radiation can, for example, make steel harden and make copper brittle. It can also greatly influence the chemicals in the human body. An average adult is made up of about 60 billion cells and each day several million of them die but they are replaced naturally by new ones. Ionising radiation can, however, kill them or permanently change them. The effect is mainly determined by the doses of radiation and it may be short- or long-term. A high dose to the whole body can cause almost instant death or immediate sickness, skin burns or sterility. And any dose can cause delayed cancers, eye problems and skin damage, and possibly hereditary defects which will only appear in any offspring. If a foetus is irradiated, it may lead to stillbirth, gross malformation or mental retardation.

The suffering caused by radiation in the early days caused much alarm and the British X-ray and Radium Protection Committee was set up in 1921 to see what action was required to control the situation. The adoption of their recommendations for precautionary measures, which included the use of lead sheathing, the wearing of goggles and limitations on the dosage of rays and exposure times, was both timely and helpful. Progress was also made in setting international standards by the establishment in 1913 of the Röntgen Society's Committee on Measurement and Dosage. There have been many organisational changes over the years, but the main advisory bodies today are the International Commission on Radiological Protection (ICRP) with a secretariat in Stockholm, Sweden; the National Radiological Protection Board (NRPB) in Britain, with headquarters at Chilton, near Didcot; and the United Nations Scientific Committee on the Effects of Atomic Radiation (UNSCEAR), founded in 1955 and composed of scientists from twenty-one nations, which collects and disseminates detailed information on radiation.

Madame Curie's name was commemorated in the first ever unit of radio-activity, with 1 curie (1Ci) being adopted originally as the activity of 1 gram of radium. Later it was redefined as a rate of disintegration of 3.7×10^{10} atoms per second or the amount of radioactive substance that disintegrated at that rate. This has now been replaced by the Becquerel unit with 1 becquerel (1Bq) being equal to a disintegration rate of 1 atom per second. As it is a very small unit, multiples are commonly used with, for example, 1 megabecquerel (1MBq) being 1 million becquerels; 1 gigabecquerel (1GBq), 10 million becquerels; and 1 terabecquerel (1TBq), 100 million becquerels.

For individual isotopes the activity depends on the amount of material and on the relative atomic mass and the half-life. For example, 1 gram of uranium-238, with a relative atomic mass of 238 and a half-life of 4.5×10^9 years, has an activity of 12,350Bq. That means that 12,350 atoms disintegrate every second, but there are 2.5×10^{21} atoms to start with. Doubling the amount of material doubles the activity, but doubling the atomic mass or the half-life halves it. A loaf of bread may have an activity of 70Bq; 1kg of coffee, 1,000Bq; 1kg of Cornish granite, 1,200Bq; an average adult, 3,000Bq; and 1kg of superphosphate fertiliser, 5,000Bq.

A different unit is required to give a measure of the effect of radiation on the human body. When radiation impinges upon the body some of its energy is absorbed by the chemicals in the body and that amount of energy is called the absorbed dose. It is expressed in a unit known as the gray (Gy) where 1Gy is equal to an energy of 1 joule (4.2 calories) per kilogram; the unit is named after the English physicist Harold Gray (1906–65). As it is quite a large unit, submultiples are commonly used; a milligray (1mGy), for example, is one-thousandth of a gray.

The damage caused to the body by the absorption of radiation depends on the nature of the radiation with alpha-rays doing the most; X-rays, gamma-rays and beta-rays the least; and a beam of neutrons being in between. This is accounted for in what is called the equivalent dose. For X-rays, beta-rays and gamma-rays it is *equal* to the absorbed dose; for alpha-rays it is *twenty times* the absorbed dose; and for neutrons it varies between *five and twenty times* the absorbed dose depending on the energies of the neutrons concerned. In every case the unit for the equivalent dose is the sievert (Sv) named after Rolf Sievert, a Swedish physicist (1896–1966). Submultiples such as the millisievert (1mSv), which is one-thousandth of a sievert or the microsievert (1μSv), which is one-millionth of a sievert, are commonly used.

Different parts of the body respond differently to radiation so that each of the many tissues in the body is allotted a weighting factor to take into account their different susceptibilities. For example, the skin has a factor of 0.01; the thyroid, liver and oesophagus, 0.05; the lung, stomach and colon, 0.12; and the testes or ovaries, 0.20. All the factors taken together add up to 1. It then becomes possible to work out what is called the effective dose – or, commonly, simply the dose – as a single number. A person subjected to an equivalent dose of, say, 100 mSv to the lung, 50 mSv to the stomach and 20 mSv to the liver would have experienced an effective dose, or dose, of $(100 \times 0.12) + (50 \times 0.12) + (20 \times 0.05)$ – that is, 17mSv.

The risk involved would be equal to that of someone subjected to a dose of 17mSv distributed uniformly throughout the body, or in any other particular way.

Those figures refer only to individual doses, and in dealing with *groups* of people another definition is required. Adding up all the individual doses received by a group of people gives the collective effective dose (or simply the collective dose) in man sievert (man Sv). A group of 50,000 people subject to an individual dose of 2mSv, or a group of 25,000 subject to 4mSv, would both equate to a collective dose of 100,000 man mSv or 100 man Sv.

People have been subjected to ionising radiations from natural sources since time immemorial. Some come from cosmic rays, which originate in outer space; because they are partially absorbed as they pass through the earth's atmosphere, they are more intense at high altitude. The small dose of approximately 0.25mSv per year at ground level rises to 3 at a height of 5km, 60 at 10km and 90 at 15km. Other radiation originates from the radioactive substances in the ground such as uranium and thorium, together with radioactive potassium and rubidium ores. They produce gamma-rays and radon gas which escape into the atmosphere. Some of the radioactivity in the ground and the atmosphere passes naturally into food and drink, and into building materials such as wood or bricks, cement and mortar, which are made from earthy substances like clay and sand. And in more modern times these natural radiations have been added to, to some extent, by extra radiation from artificial, man-made sources.

In the United Kingdom 85.5 per cent of the absorbed radiation comes from natural sources, and 14.5 per cent from artificial sources. But there are wide variations depending on where you live, what your house is built of and what you do. The average annual figure for the whole country is 2.6mSv, which is the lowest rate in Europe. But it is 2.1mSv in London, 4.0 in Northamptonshire, 5.3 in Somerset and 7.8 in Cornwall. These differences are mainly due to geological differences. Where there is a lot of granite, for example, as in Cornwall, there is more uranium in the ground and more radon gas in the air. The radon can become dangerous if it is allowed to build up in a house; if this happens, its concentration must be lowered by fitting a fan below the floor level or by some other means. In some areas new building regulations have been introduced for new houses to prevent the entry of radon.

The 14.5 per cent of radiation from artificial sources comes mainly (14 per cent) from medical uses such as X-ray examinations and cancer treatments. The remaining 0.5 per cent comes from nuclear and coal-fired power stations; from everyday objects such as smoke alarms, luminous watches and signs, gas mantles, photocopiers and television sets; and from the radioactive fall-out of nuclear weapons tests and nuclear accidents (0.2 per cent).

There are also variations depending on an individual's occupation, with an estimated 250,000 workers getting higher than average doses because of what they do. Air crew might get 2mSv per year more; workers in the nuclear industry, 1mSv more; industrial radiographers, 0.8mSv more; and doctors, dentists and veterinary surgeons, 0.1mSv. There is at present a statutory limit for workers of 50mSv per year but it is hoped that this might soon be reduced to 20mSv. The annual dose limit for members of the public from artificially produced radiation, except from medical sources, is 1mSv.

Probable individual one-off doses, as compared with the average yearly dose of 2.6mSv, are exemplified by 0.01mSv from a flight to Madrid; 0.02mSv from a single chest X-ray; 0.065mSv from drinking one glass of mineral water every day for a year; 0.7mSv from an abdominal X-ray; 2mSv from a CT scan of the head; 7mSv from a lower bowel X-ray using a barium enema; and 10mSv from a CT scan of the pelvis.

Whenever there is risk of exposure to high levels of radiation it is necessary to take precautionary measures and a substantial body of legislation has built up in the UK since the passing of the British Radioactive Substances Act of 1948, which has led to the banning of some activities. It is, for example, no longer allowed to use radium compounds to make the figures or hands on a watch luminous, and pedoscopes, which use X-rays to test the fit of pair of shoes, are also banned. In other activities, such as the taking of X-ray images or working in a sensitive area of a nuclear plant, protective clothing might have to be worn; improved ventilation systems may have to be installed; steel, concrete or other shielding might be required; and both the dose of radiation and the exposure time might have to be controlled. The handling of radioactive materials might have to be carried out by remote control both on a small, laboratory scale and industrially. Some workers may need to wear personal monitoring devices, such as a small photographic plate or a holder containing some thermoluminescent material so that their exposure to radiation can be checked at the end of a day's work, and NRPB issues 450,000 such devices every year to about 5,000 customers. The radioactivity in the air in a room can also be monitored by automatic recorders.

There are also a number of very extensive monitoring programmes which continually measure radiation levels throughout the country. The various activities are coordinated by the government's Radioactivity Research and Environmental Monitoring Committee and the work is carried out by government departments, by local councils and by individual firms and organisations. The Department of the Environment, Transport and the Regions (DETR), for example, measures, among other things, the concentration of caesium-137 in the Irish and North Seas, the concentration of caesium-134 and caesium-137 in fish and shellfish, the

Handling radioactive materials by remote control. (Nycomed–Amersham)

concentration of strontium–90 and caesium–137 in milk, and the levels of radioactivity in various water supplies. Similar measurements are made by the Department of the Environment for Northern Ireland, the Scottish Environment Protection Agency, the Environment Agency, the Food Standards Agency and the National Radiological Protection Board. On a smaller, more local scale, about 150 local authorities collect data which is reported to the Local Authority Radiation and Radioactivity Monitoring Advice and Collation Centre (LARRMACC), which is based in Knutsford, Cheshire. Organisations which closely monitor conditions in the vicinity of their own operations include British Energy PLC, BNFL, UKAEA, Nycomed–Amersham and DERA Radiation Protection Services (DRPS), which watches over the submarine berths at Barrow-in-Furness in Cumbria, Davenport, near Plymouth, Gare Loch and Holy Loch in Argyll and Bute, and Rosyth in Fife. An enormous amount of detailed data is collected, collated and examined on a regular basis to ensure that legal requirements are met, that a reliable body of information about normal background levels is built up, that any unexpected changes are quickly detected, and to reassure the general public that their interests are being safeguarded.

It is difficult to be precise about the dangers arising from different doses of radiation. A single dose of 500mSv is likely to induce dangerous sickness and anything over 4,000mSv would probably be fatal. The safest dose would be zero

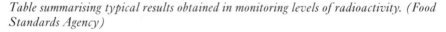

Table 6.7(a).   Radioactivity in food and the environment near Hunterston nuclear power station, 2000

Material	Location	No. of sampling observations	Mean radioactivity concentration (wet)[a], Bq kg⁻¹											
			^{54}Mn	^{60}Co	^{65}Zn	^{95}Nb	^{99}Tc	^{110m}Ag	^{137}Cs	^{144}Ce	^{155}Ce	^{238}Pu	^{239}Pu+^{240}Pu	^{241}Am
Aquatic samples														
Cod	Millport	2	<0.10	<0.10	<0.16	<0.34		<0.11	2.0	<0.26	<0.12			<0.10
Hake	Millport	2	<0.10	<0.10	<0.21	<2.4		<0.11	3.2	<0.38	<0.15			<0.11
Crabs[b]	Millport	2	<0.10	<0.10	<0.16	<0.17	9.1	<0.10	0.44	<0.32	<0.14	0.0040	0.025	0.040
Nephrops	Millport	2	<0.10	<0.10	<0.13	<0.12	5.7	<0.10	1.4	<0.20	<0.12			<0.10
Lobsters	Largs	1	<0.09	<0.08	<0.27	<1.1	280	<0.14	0.57	<0.46	<0.20			<0.32
Squat lobsters	Largs	4	<0.10	<0.10	<0.17	<0.23	<1.6	<0.10	0.55	<0.34	<0.17	0.0092	0.037	0.016
Oysters	Fairlie	1	<0.10	<0.10	<0.22	<1.7		0.22	0.39	<0.37	<0.13			<0.10
Winkles	Pipeline	2	0.41	0.48	<0.30	<0.29		<0.41	0.78	<0.56	<0.25	0.017	0.036	0.065
Scallops	Largs	4	<0.10	<0.10	<0.13	<0.33		<0.10	0.55	<0.27	<0.13	0.0093	0.037	0.014
Seaweed	N of pipeline	2	1.5	0.53	<0.19	<0.57		<0.10	1.3	<0.29	<0.12			<0.10
Seaweed	Pipeline	2	2.5	0.63	<0.18	<0.70		<0.11	1.6	<0.29	<0.13			<0.10
Seaweed	S of pipeline	2	2.7	0.53	<0.30	<1.1		<0.18	3.0	<0.40	<0.16			<0.22
Sediment	Pipeline	2	<0.23	<0.17	<0.29	<0.36		<0.27	18	<0.73	<0.40			<0.72
Sediment	Millport	2	<0.10	<0.10	<0.23	<1.6		<0.12	7.0	<0.47	<0.21			<0.32
Sediment	Ardneil Bay	2	<0.14	<0.11	<0.44	<10		<0.24	3.2	<0.83	<0.36			<0.60
Sediment	Gulls Walk	2	<0.11	<0.11	<0.28	<0.36		<0.13	9.2	<0.56	<0.31			<0.53
Seawater[c]	Pipeline	3	<0.10	<0.10	<0.15	<1.5		<0.10	<0.08	<0.30	<0.12			<0.10

Table summarising typical results obtained in monitoring levels of radioactivity. (Food Standards Agency)

but with so much natural radiation about that is impossible to achieve in normal everyday life. All the evidence suggests that any dose of radiation, however small, might be dangerous in that it might influence the body cell structure sufficiently to trigger off some long-term effect or initiate some hereditary defect. The best estimate of the risk of fatal cancer associated with the average annual dose of radiation of 2.6mSv is 1 in 7,700. Under normal circumstances, it is assumed that the risk is proportional to the dose so that the risk for an annual dose of 1mSv is 1 in 20,000. That compares with death risks of 1 in 300 from a heart attack; 1 in 400 from all causes at the age of 40; 1 in 7,000 for working in a coal mine; 1 in 16,000 for working on a building site; 1 in 100,000 for working in the chemical industry; and 1 in 170,000 for having a baby.

These average figures do not, however, give any idea of what might happen in an emergency. The estimated average annual dose in most of this country arising from the Chernobyl accident in 1986 was originally 0.02mSv and it has now declined to 0.001mSv. That implies a fatal risk of 1 in 20 million – which is of no interest to the many people killed at Chernobyl by the accident. People who have to live close to a nuclear power station or a radioactive waste site are more concerned about the potential harm if something should go wrong than about any average figures. People are prepared to accept the risk of 1 in 17,000 of dying in a road accident, or of 1 in 200 of dying from smoking ten cigarettes a day, because they have some control over the risks they take, but they certainly do not want some other unknown risk to be imposed on them.

In January 1988, after the Chernobyl accident, the British government published a National Response Plan to try to deal with the consequences of any further overseas nuclear accidents. This led to the establishment of the Radioactive Incident Monitoring Network (RIMNET), which aims to provide advance warning of any

A RIMNET gamma radiation monitor. (DETR)

future accidents. It is operated by the Environment Agency, and consists of a series of eighty-nine automatic radiation measuring instruments spread around the country. They continually record radiation levels and their readings are transmitted to a central headquarters where there is a sophisticated arrangement which allows any unusual readings to be identified and any necessary information to be disseminated. There is also an international agreement, organised by the International Atomic Energy Agency, that the United Kingdom will be warned of accidents overseas, and the British government has bilateral early notification agreements with the Dutch, Danish, French, Norwegian and Russian governments. The onset and consequences of any future accident cannot, however, be foreseen, and it must be hoped that eternal vigilance can prevent one. If given enough warning it might be possible to minimise its effects by evacuating the area or sheltering from the radiation within it. Taking iodate tablets to lessen the uptake of radioactive iodine into the thyroid gland and following advice about what to eat so as to avoid contaminated foodstuffs would also be helpful but for the most part there is little anyone can do.

Another more recent threat has arisen following the terrorist attacks in New York on 11 September 2001 because it has come to light that terrorist groups may

The distribution of RIMNET monitors around the country. (DETR)

be in possession of enough uranium or plutonium to make their own atomic bombs. It seems unlikely that they would have sufficient technical expertise at present to achieve that aim but they might well be able to create great problems by using a so-called 'dirty' bomb. This would consist of a normal explosive bomb containing some radioactive material which, on detonation, would spread far and wide and perhaps make large areas uninhabitable. It is not a happy thought.

CHAPTER 14

Modern Uses

There were many significant advances in the use of X-rays and of radioactive substances in the second half of the twentieth century. As far as X-rays were concerned, plain tomography developed into computerised tomography, which was invented in 1973 by the British engineer, Godfrey Newbould Hounsfield, and the South African physicist, Allan McLeod Cormack. In a computerised axial tomography (CAT) scanner, a thin beam of X-rays is rapidly rotated, at about one revolution per second, around a patient's head or body as the body is moved slowly through the scanner. Detectors pick up the transmitted X-rays, which are of varying intensity depending on the nature of the tissues through which they have passed, and a computer converts the signals into cross-sectional images. By viewing these images from different directions it is possible to build up a 3-dimensional 'picture' which allows any suspected irregularities to be analysed. The technique is also used in the archaeological examination of mummies.

It also became possible to obtain X-rays, from a linear accelerator or cyclotron, with energies up to 200 times greater than those from older X-ray tubes and they were much more effective in both diagnosis and treatment. Treating a brain tumour, for example, requires first the accurate identification of its size and position by a scan. Then the patient's head is held immobilised in a tailor-made plastic casing while beams of high-energy X-rays are directed on to the tumour for perhaps one minute. They are directed from varying angles so that the tumour receives a strong dose while the intervening, healthy tissues receive much less. The treatment is repeated at regular intervals for as long as necessary. It is not, in itself, painful but there are unpleasant side-effects in that the patient feels tired and perhaps sickly, and there will be some soreness of the skin on the head where the beams of X-rays entered and perhaps some loss of hair. The patient will also have to take drugs and to be examined regularly to avoid any recurrence of the growth.

Another important development derived from the realisation that X-rays could be replaced, in many cases, by the gamma radiation from naturally occurring

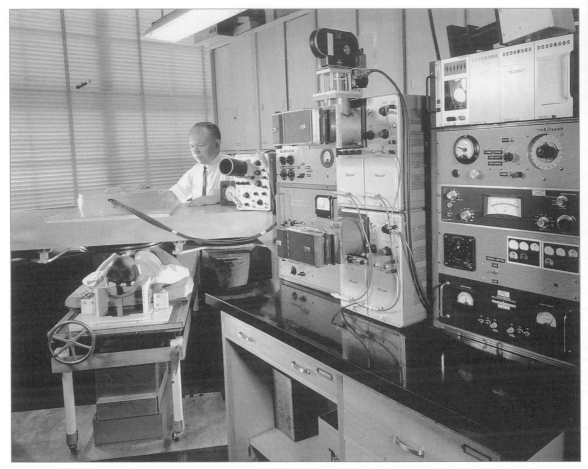

Hal Anger using a gamma-ray camera in 1963. (Ernest Orlando Lawrence Berkeley National Laboratory)

radioactive elements in what came to be called gamma-radiography. The gamma-rays are very much like X-rays but they have wave-lengths 100 to 1,000 times shorter, which means that they have more energy and are consequently more penetrating. And when artificially radioactive isotopes which emitted gamma-rays became widely available after the Second World War, it was possible to tailor-make an isotope to provide just the right sort of rays for almost any particular use. The isotopes were also cheaper, much smaller, and more portable and manoeuvrable than X-ray equipment. The welding in underground oil pipelines could be tested, for example, by placing a sample of iridium-192 inside the pipes adjacent to the weld so that any flaws could be detected on a photographic film wrapped round the outside of the pipe. The use of gamma-radiography also became more widespread and more efficient with Hal Anger's invention of a special gamma-ray camera, at the Lawrence Berkeley National Laboratory in the USA, in 1956. As this depends on the scintillations caused when gamma-rays impinge on a crystal of sodium iodide containing some thallium as an impurity, it is sometimes called a scintillation camera.

It was, however, the increasing availability of radioactive isotopes in the 1950s that provided the real breakthrough. They are now generally called radionuclides and their various uses in the diagnosis and treatment of diseases are referred to as nuclear medicine. Fermi and Seaborg had shown in the 1930s and 1940s that it was possible to make new isotopes by neutron bombardment and this method was greatly extended after the end of the Second World War as different countries embarked on their own research projects and built their own nuclear reactors. The new products came predominantly from within the reactor where there was a high concentration of internal neutrons. Some, particularly those in the middle of the periodic table, with relative atomic masses between 85 and 147, occurred as disintegration products from the original uranium in the reactor, but others were made from materials inserted into the reactors to undergo neutron bombardment for varying periods of time. In both cases the required isotope has to be isolated from other components by a chemical process which generally involves an ion-exchange column similar to that used in a domestic water softener. When a mixture of isotopes is absorbed on a resin within a column, each isotope is absorbed to a different extent and in due course each can be washed out of the bottom of the column by passing different solvents in at the top.

Other radionuclides are made by bombarding elements with high-energy protons ($^1_1$H), deuterons ($^2_1$H) or alpha-particles ($^4_2$He) provided by a particle accelerator such as a linear accelerator, a cyclotron or a synchroton. Typical examples are provided by cobalt-57 ($^{57}_{27}$Co), made from nickel-58 ($^{58}_{28}$Ni) and protons; sodium-22 ($^{22}_{21}$Na), from magnesium-24 ($^{24}_{12}$Mg) and deuterons; and iodine-123 ($^{123}_{53}$I) from antimony-121 ($^{121}_{51}$Sb) and alpha-particles.

In the United Kingdom manufacture of these new isotopes began at Harwell in September 1947 and the monthly shipments rose from around 100 in 1948 to 800 in 1951. By then some of the work had been transferred to the Radiochemical Centre at Amersham in Buckinghamshire, which has grown into today's international organisation Nycomed-Amersham. It started its life in a large empty house in Amersham which was bought for £2,000 in 1940 by the Thorium Company, when they were asked by the government to become the first British manufacturer of radium. At the time radium was required for making luminous

Extracting radioactive isotopes from the BEPO reactor at Harwell via a pneumatic hose.
(UKAEA)

paint but the imported supplies from Germany had dried up so a new source of supply had to be found quickly. The Thorium Company's business was making mantles for gas lights and they had no expertise in working with radium but in their newly acquired property they were soon making 1 gram of radium each month and that, together with imported radium from Canada, met the need. By the end of the war the company was also making other radioactive materials and when the government realised the importance of the company's work they bought it for £40,000 and established the Radiochemical Centre. The Conservative government privatised the organisation as Amersham International in the 1980s, and it is now part of the multinational Nycomed-Amersham which has annual

The Nycomed-Amersham site at Amersham. The original house from which it all grew stands in the middle foreground. (Nycomed Amersham)

sales of £1.3 billion and employs 8,500 people world-wide. Mighty oaks from little acorns grow.

In the early days radium had been the predominant element in radiotherapy, but in the 1960s and 1970s its use diminished as it was replaced by more effective radionuclides. Cobalt-60 and, much less commonly, caesium-137 were used in teletherapy; and cobalt-60, caesium-137, gold-198, iridium-192, iodine-125 and palladium-103 in brachytherapy. For the latter purpose the materials are produced in the form of needles, tubes, wires, pins, grains, seeds and pellets which were initially applied manually. That, however, exposed surgeons, nurses and others to possibly high doses of radiation so that today there are many more stringent regulations. These relate to the transport and storage of the radioactive materials, to the necessity for proper shielding in the rooms in which they are used, to the protection of nurses and visitors to the treated patients as they recover in the wards, and even to the actions to be taken if the patient should die with the implant still in place.

Considerable progress was made, too, in discovering what doses of radiation were necessary for different conditions and how best the dose could be applied,

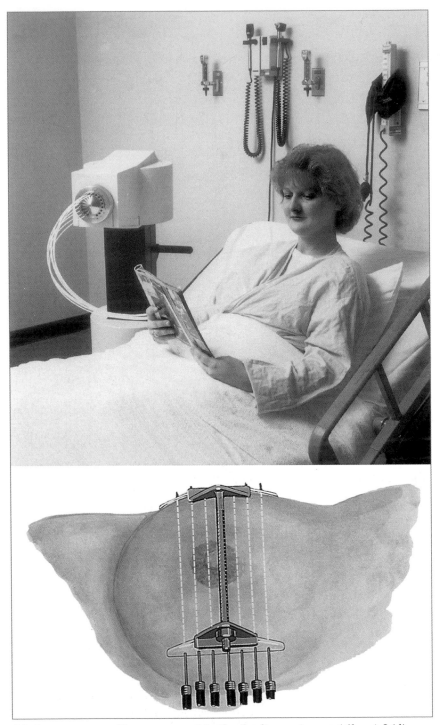

Modern treatment of breast cancer with after-loading equipment. (Above) Iridium-192 pellets are fed into the tubes by remote control from next door. (Below) Plastic tubes inserted in the breast. (Nucletron International BV)

and in the 1970s what came to be known as after-loading began to replace manual handling. In a typical modern treatment of breast cancer, for example, a number of parallel, thin plastic tubes are inserted through the breast of a patient so that small pellets of iridium-192 can be fed into them from a machine situated alongside the patient's bed but operated by a nurse in the room next door. The pellets are held in the correct position for any chosen period of time before being withdrawn and the treatment may be repeated later, with the pellets being positioned differently if necessary, before the tubes are finally removed. The whole process may, in fact, be controlled by a computerised programme designed specifically for a particular patient.

The other main aspect of nuclear medicine involves the use of radionuclides either as tracers in diagnosis or in direct therapy. In one of the first applications, carried out at the Massachusetts Institute of Technology and the Massachusetts General Hospital in 1936, iodine-128 was used to study the physiology of the thyroid gland, and this led to the first treatment of thyroid cancers in 1946. Today, technetium-99m is the most widely used radionuclide. It is a meta-stable isotope (hence the letter m) which decays, with a short half life of six hours, to technetium-99, which is not radioactive. It is chosen because, due to its short half-life, it does not irradiate the body for very long if it is used internally; it only emits gamma-rays so there are no complications caused by alpha- or beta-rays; and the gamma-rays are of the right energy to react well with a gamma-ray camera. Because of its short life, technetium-99m cannot be stored for long so it is obtained as required from another radioactive isotope, molybdenum-99, which is absorbed, as ammonium molybdate, on an ion-exchange column made

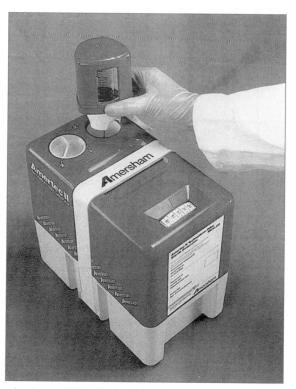

An Amertec^{TM}II Technetium generator. (Nycomed-Amersham)

of aluminium oxide in what is called a radionuclide generator; a typical example is marketed under the tradename Amertec II. The molybdenum-99 decays, with a half-life of 66.7 hours, into technetium-99m and that isotope can be washed off the column as required by a solution of sodium chloride in water, in the form of sodium pertechnetate, leaving unused molybdenum-99 behind to provide some more. The generator is commonly referred to as a 'cow' because the technetium-99m is effectively 'milked' from it. In a typical usage, a hospital will have new generators delivered each week and keep them for a fortnight before returning them for recharging. The newer generators are used for obtaining doses as required of about 4,000MBq per millilitre and the older one for doses around 1,000MBq per millilitre. In use, the technetium-99m may be combined with some other compound, stored in a sealed vial, to form a compound which, when administered internally, will be absorbed by some particular tissue in the body. The product is known as a radiopharmaceutical and detecting it in a body is known as nuclear imaging. It is widely used in medical diagnosis.

Technetium-99m combined with a phosphate, for example, gives a radiopharmaceutical product which is absorbed by bones. Other similar products are absorbed by tissues in the heart, gall bladder, brain, kidneys, lungs, thyroid, liver and spleen. Other examples are provided by the use of iron-59 in ferrous citrate to investigate the part played by iron in the formation of haemoglobin in blood; chromium-51 in sodium chromate to label red blood cells; gallium-67 in gallium citrate to pick up bone tumours and abscesses; thallium-201 for investigation of the kidneys; and indium -111 in indium oxide for labelling white blood cells. Krypton-81m and xenon-133, which are both gases, are used for studying the functioning of the lungs by direct inhalation.

Many radiopharmaceuticals, administered by ingestion, inhalation or injection, are also used directly in radiotherapy. Examples are provided by the use of iodine-131, as sodium iodide, for treating the thyroid when it is overproducing hormones or when there is a tumour; phosphorus-32, as sodium phosphate, for treating blood disorders and malignant tumours; yttrium-90, as yttrium silicate, for injection into arthritic joints; strontium-90, as strontium chloride, in prostate and breast cancers; and strontium-89, rhenium-186 or samarium-153 in various compounds in the relief of bone pain.

The internal emission of gamma-rays by radioisotopes absorbed in the body also enabled two new procedures to be adopted. The first is known as single photon emission tomography (SPET). The gamma-rays emitted from the labelled pharmaceutical absorbed in a particular tissue in the body are detected by cameras

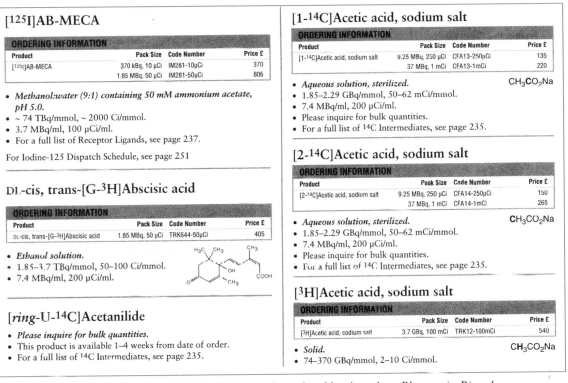

[125I]AB-MECA

ORDERING INFORMATION

Product	Pack Size	Code Number	Price £
[125I]AB-MECA	370 kBq, 10 μCi	IM281-10μCi	370
	1.85 MBq, 50 μCi	IM281-50μCi	805

- *Methanol:water (9:1) containing 50 mM ammonium acetate, pH 5.0.*
- ~ 74 TBq/mmol, ~ 2000 Ci/mmol.
- 3.7 MBq/ml, 100 μCi/ml.
- For a full list of Receptor Ligands, see page 237.

For Iodine-125 Dispatch Schedule, see page 251

DL-cis, trans-[G-3H]Abscisic acid

ORDERING INFORMATION

Product	Pack Size	Code Number	Price £
DL-cis, trans-[G-3H]Abscisic acid	1.85 MBq, 50 μCi	TRK644-50μCi	405

- *Ethanol solution.*
- 1.85–3.7 TBq/mmol, 50–100 Ci/mmol.
- 7.4 MBq/ml, 200 μCi/ml.

[ring-U-14C]Acetanilide

- *Please inquire for bulk quantities.*
- This product is available 1–4 weeks from date of order.
- For a full list of 14C Intermediates, see page 235.

[1-14C]Acetic acid, sodium salt

ORDERING INFORMATION

Product	Pack Size	Code Number	Price £
[1-14C]Acetic acid, sodium salt	9.25 MBq, 250 μCi	CFA13-250μCi	135
	37 MBq, 1 mCi	CFA13-1mCi	220

- *Aqueous solution, sterilized.* CH_3CO_2Na
- 1.85–2.29 GBq/mmol, 50–62 mCi/mmol.
- 7.4 MBq/ml, 200 μCi/ml.
- Please inquire for bulk quantities.
- For a full list of 14C Intermediates, see page 235.

[2-14C]Acetic acid, sodium salt

ORDERING INFORMATION

Product	Pack Size	Code Number	Price £
[2-14C]Acetic acid, sodium salt	9.25 MBq, 250 μCi	CFA14-250μCi	150
	37 MBq, 1 mCi	CFA14-1mCi	265

- *Aqueous solution, sterilized.* CH_3CO_2Na
- 1.85–2.29 GBq/mmol, 50–62 mCi/mmol.
- 7.4 MBq/ml, 200 μCi/ml.
- Please inquire for bulk quantities.
- For a full list of 14C Intermediates, see page 235.

[3H]Acetic acid, sodium salt

ORDERING INFORMATION

Product	Pack Size	Code Number	Price £
[3H]Acetic acid, sodium salt	3.7 GBq, 100 mCi	TRK12-100mCi	540

- *Solid.* CH_3CO_2Na
- 74–370 GBq/mmol, 2–10 Ci/mmol.

An extract from the A–Z list of radiochemicals marketed by Amersham Pharmacia Biotech. The complete list contains over 800 chemicals. (Amersham Pharmacia Biotech UK Ltd)

which take a series of images at successive angles around the patient, showing how the radioactive tracer is distributed within the patient. By using the camera in different planes and reconstructing the various images on a computer it is possible to build up a detailed image of the tissue being investigated.

In positron emission tomography (PET), which is particularly useful in the investigation of brain disorders such as dementia, strokes and epilepsy, schizophrenia, and Alzheimer's and Parkinson's diseases, other radioactive isotopes such as carbon-11, nitrogen-13, fluorine-18 and oxygen-15 are used. They are injected into the brain and emit positrons which when they collide with electrons yield two gamma-rays which move in opposite directions. By using a ring of cameras around the patient's head it is possible to locate the source of the radiation from within the brain.

Radioactive tracers are also widely used in the industrial and biological fields. In industry, radioactive tracers can be used to mark the joint in a pipe or a cable, or the efficiency of a mixing process can be followed by adding a tracer to one of the components before mixing and subsequently observing the level of radiation throughout the mixture. The wear inside an engine can be studied by labelling the various moving parts by attaching a tracer and measuring the resultant radioactivity in the circulating oil. The flow of almost any material – oil or gas along a pipe; molten glass through a furnace; gases in ventilation systems; leaking gases or liquids; concrete poured into a hole; silt in a river estuary; the flow of water in a cooling system; or underground movements of water – can be investigated by tracer techniques.

More recently the use of phosphorus-32 and sulphur-35 tracers in labelling long, complex helical-shaped DNA molecules has played a major part in the successful outcome of the human genome project in which the correct sequence of the genes in each of the chromosomes which make up our cells has been deciphered. The different DNA molecules are all made from the same four bases – adenine (A), cytosine (C), guanine (G) and thymine (T) – but they are arranged in different sequences within the DNA molecules of which some 30,000 different genes are composed. These then make up the 46 chromosomes which are found, as 23 pairs, in human cells. Each individual has a unique sequence of genes in his or her cells which determines his or her inherited characteristics.

The modern technique of radioimmunoassay has also grown out of the earlier tracer methods. It was developed by Rosalyn Yalow working in the Radioisotope Unit of the Veterans' Administration (VA) Hospital in the Bronx in New York and she shared the Nobel Prize for Physiology and Medicine in 1977 for her work with radioactive iodine on the thyroid gland and with radioactive insulin on diabetes. The method is now used very widely to measure minute amounts of biological substances, particularly hormones and proteins associated with antibodies and antigens, in the human body. It has been said that, in every-day terms, the method could find a ping-pong ball in the Atlantic Ocean!

The ability of gamma-rays to kill micro-organisms was first recognised in 1896, and patents were granted for such use as early as 1900 in the United States and the United Kingdom. At that time, however, the technology was not commercially viable because radium, which was required to provide the gamma-rays, was expensive and not readily available. That changed in the 1950s as artificial radioactive isotopes came to replace radium, and today gamma-rays are used to sterilise many items of medical equipment such as gloves, syringes, specimen containers and bandages. Because of possible health hazards, the work is closely regulated and in the United Kingdom it is carried out in six plants run by

Isotron plc, whose headquarters are in Swindon. They use sealed rods of cobalt-60, made by the Canadian firm MDS Nordion, to provide the gamma-rays. The half-life of the isotope is 5.3 years and the rods have a useful life of fifteen to twenty years, after which they are returned to the maker in part exchange for new ones. When in use, the rods are stored in a rack which can either be immersed in water, which absorbs the emitted gamma-rays, or raised out of the water into a radiation room with concrete walls 2m thick. The products to be sterilised are transported into and out of this room on a conveyor system and treated with the required dose of gamma-rays.

A similar process is also used to irradiate foodstuffs. It is sometimes referred to as 'cold pasteurisation' and it has the potential of reducing the risk of food borne diseases such as salmonella, campylobacter and listeria. It can also reduce spoilage of food, delay ripening in fruit, prevent sprouting in vegetables such as potatoes and onions, and kill any insects or parasites on the food. The treatment was tried first in the 1950s in a number of academic and government organisations in the United States, and the first commercial uses were in Germany in 1957, Russia in 1958 and Canada in 1960. It has not, however, been widely adopted. Even though it has so many obvious advantages, and decades of research by many organisations all over the world have found it to be safe and effective, the response of the general public to eating irradiated food is not favourable, though it does differ from country to country. Many seem to think that irradiating food must, necessarily, make it radioactive, while others are suspicious that radiation which can do such harm to humans must in some way damage food.

The matter is, however, kept under constant review by such bodies as the World Health Organisation and the International Consultative Group on Food Irradiation. In the United Kingdom the Advisory Committee on Novel Foods and Processes (ACNFP) reports to the Food Standards Agency, which in turn advises the government on what legislation is necessary. Current regulations allow for the treatment, under licence, of seven categories of food – fruit; vegetables; cereals; bulbs and tubers; herbs, spices and condiments; fish and shellfish; and poultry. However, only one licence, for the irradiation of some herbs and spices, has so far been granted to Isotron plc. Animal foodstuffs can, however, be irradiated.

Radioactive carbon-14 can be used for estimating the age of ancient materials in a method known as radiocarbon-dating, which was invented in 1947 by Willard Libby. He was Professor of Chemistry at the University of California in Berkeley from 1959 to 1976, worked for the Manhattan Project during the Second World

War, and was a member of the US Atomic Energy Commission from 1954 to 1959. In 1939 Serge Korff of New York University discovered that cosmic rays produced neutrons in their initial collisions with the upper atmosphere and that some of these neutrons then collided with nitrogen atoms to form radioactive carbon-14, which has a half-life of 5,720 years:

$$^{14}_{7}N + ^{1}_{0}n \longrightarrow ^{14}_{6}C + ^{1}_{1}H$$

The resulting carbon-14 forms radioactive carbon dioxide, $^{14}CO_2$, which passes into living plants and eventually animals. While the plants are alive there is a constant exchange in both the plants and the atmosphere between radioactive carbon-14 and non-radioactive carbon-12 atoms, because they are chemically alike, and this accounts for a radioactivity in living matter of around 15 disintegrations per minute per gram of carbon. But when the living matter dies the natural interchange ceases and the carbon-14 in the matter simply goes on disintegrating. Consequently, 5,720 years after its death the radioactivity would be halved so that it is possible to discover the time that has elapsed since the death of any specimen simply by measuring the actual radioactivity of the specimen. The method, for which Libby was awarded the 1960 Nobel Prize for Chemistry, has been used for dating bones, coffins, ancient manuscripts such as the Dead Sea Scrolls, the Turin Shroud and objects from archaeological sites such as Stonehenge in Wiltshire. Within the range of 600 to 10,000 years ages can be estimated with an accuracy of 1–200 years.

There are a number of other varied uses of radioactive isotopes. The beta- or gamma-rays emitted by an isotope such as strontium-90 can be used to measure or control the thickness of a material because the amount of radiation passing through it will decrease as it gets thicker. If a source of beta- or gamma-rays is placed on one side of the material and a detector on the other side, the scale reading will give a measure of the thickness. Typical uses are in controlling the thickness of paper, plastic sheeting or sheet metal; in checking the packing of tobacco in cigarettes; in measuring or monitoring the thickness of coating of one metal on another; and in checking the level to which a container is filled with a solid or a liquid. In some cases commercial, automatic machines are available.

One of the more surprising uses of isotopes is that of americium-241 oxide in smoke alarms. The alpha-rays which it emits pass through a container full of air and render it conducting but if smoke interferes to prevent the passage of the rays the air becomes non-conducting and this triggers off an alarm bell. Only a minute

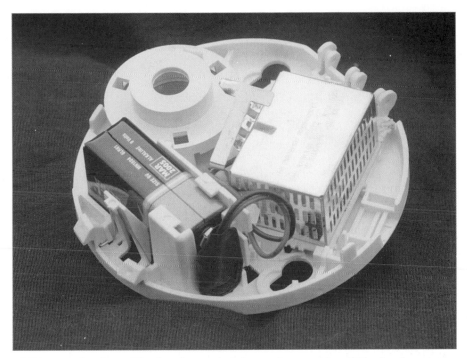

A Dicon smoke alarm. The chamber on the left contains americium–241; the alarm is to the right; and the battery is in the foreground. (Photograph by Colin Flood)

amount of the radioactive oxide, providing less than 35kBq, is needed and there is no health hazard because any alpha-rays that escape through the case of the detector are absorbed by a few centimetres of air. (It is of interest that the alarm bell in most smoke detectors is a modern-day application of the piezoelectric effect discovered by Pierre Curie and his brother in 1880.)

CHAPTER 15

Nuclear Accidents

The nuclear industry has been bedevilled by a series of accidents over the past fifty years and some of them have been so serious and had such a devastating effect on public opinion that governments have had to modify or even stop their building programmes. The geographical spread, and the passage of time, are well illustrated by the accidents which occurred in Canada in 1952, in Britain in 1957, in the United States in 1979, in the Ukraine in 1986 and in Japan in 1999.

The first serious nuclear reactor accident occurred in Canada on 12 December 1952 on the site of the NRX heavy water reactor on the Chalk River. This reactor, an early version of the later CANDU reactors, had come into service in 1947 and was used for research and for making plutonium, which was sold to the USA and Britain. It had natural uranium fuel rods clad with aluminium, used heavy water as a moderator and twelve boron carbide control rods pneumatically driven by compressed air, and it was cooled by water from the River Ottawa.

The accident began when, prior to an experiment to compare the performance of old with new uranium fuel, an operator in the basement opened three or four air valves which lifted three or four control rods out of the reactor. When the supervisor at the control panel saw the red lights flashing, which indicated what had happened, he went down to the basement and reset the valves. This caused the raised rods to fall enough to extinguish the alarm lights on the control panel but, unbeknown to anyone, they did not fall fully back into place. Simultaneously the supervisor telephoned his assistant in the control room to restore normality by pressing buttons 4 and 1. Unfortunately the message should have been to press buttons 4 and 3, and pressing button 1 had the effect of lifting four more control rods out. There was no immediate concern because the assistant thought that the original raised rods had been successfully lowered, but when, within twenty seconds, the power level had risen alarmingly he pushed the emergency button to insert all the control rods and close the reactor down. Twenty-five seconds later the power was still rising so the operators took the last-ditch emergency step of draining the heavy water away.

But it was too late. The heat released had already melted some of the uranium fuel and its aluminium cladding and the hot metals had reacted with some of the cooling water, and the steam coming from it, to form hydrogen. With air entering through burst pipes there was a hydrogen–oxygen explosion which severely damaged the reactor core and spread radioactivity far and wide, with much of it being carried into the basement by 4 million litres of cooling water that escaped. As more and more alarms sounded, the whole plant was evacuated except for some control staff who were left to try to prevent things from getting worse. It is something of a miracle that both during the accident, which was all over in about seventy seconds, and in the subsequent clean-up, no workers were exposed to particularly high radiation doses, and the reactor was rebuilt and back in service fourteen months later. It was able therefore to provide cover for its successor, the NRU, when it had to be repaired following an internal fire in 1958, and it went on operating successfully until 1987.

To provide plutonium for making a British atom bomb, it was decided in 1947 to build two atomic piles on the site of a disused ordnance factory at a place called Sellafield on the Cumbrian coast in north-east England. To avoid any confusion with Springfields its name was changed to Windscale Works after a clump of trees known as Windscale Nook on the banks of the River Calder. The site was, however, always called Sellafield by the locals and that is the chosen name today.

The piles contained rods of natural uranium, clad in aluminium, which were positioned in horizontal channels in an octagonal block of graphite 15m in diameter and nearly 8m long. When the pile was in operation, they were cooled by using eight large fans to blow air through cooling ducts in the graphite which passed into the atmosphere through a chimney, 125m high and 12m wide. The power at which the piles operated was regulated by moving twenty-four horizontal boron-steel control rods in or out of the core, and there were sixteen vertical rods which entered automatically to shut down the piles in any emergency. The whole pile was surrounded by a biological shield made of reinforced concrete, over 2m thick and lined on the inside with steel plates. On the front face there was a charge hoist, which could be moved in any direction to feed the fuel elements into the channels in the graphite. As necessary they were discharged by pushing them out through the back of the pile into a water duct from which they were transferred into a water storage pond to allow them to cool and to lose some of their residual radioactivity.

The Windscale Number 1 pile, completed in July 1950 at a cost of £3.7 million, was one of the first post-war piles to be built and its name is well remembered

The two military reactors which opened in 1950 and 1951 at Windscale. On the right is the prototype Advanced Gas-cooled Reactor which opened in 1962. (UKAEA)

because it caught fire early in October 1957. The fire was associated with the newly discovered Wigner effect, named after Eugene Wigner, a Hungarian-born physicist who was Professor of Mathematical Physics at Princeton University between 1938 and 1971. A close associate of Szilard and Fermi during the war years, he won the Nobel Prize for Physics in 1963. The Wigner effect

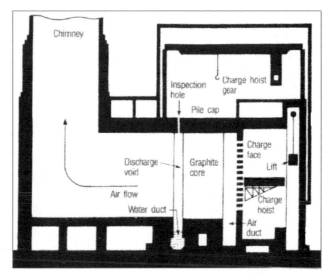

Plan of the Windscale military reactor. (UKAEA)

is caused by the impact of neutrons on graphite which causes a distortion in the crystal structure. This shows up as a slight deformation in the shape of the graphite and a change in its thermal and electrical conductivity. The distortion also sets up some strain in the graphite so that there is a build-up of energy within it, as in a compressed spring; this is known as Wigner energy. At regular intervals a process known as releasing the Wigner energy has to be carried out before the energy reaches too high a level and releases itself unexpectedly. This is, in effect, an annealing process, like that used for glass, which is carried out by carefully raising the power of the pile to increase the temperature of the graphite and then allowing it to cool slowly so that the displaced atoms can rearrange. The temperatures within the graphite and the uranium, during this process, were monitored on eighty-six thermocouples inserted at strategic points.

This operation had been carried out on the Number 1 pile eight times between August 1953 and November 1957, though not without some hitches, but when it was attempted for the ninth time, on Monday 7 October 1957, it all went horribly wrong. The procedure involved closing down the pile and then starting it up at a low power, with the cooling fans turned off, to heat up the graphite and the uranium. The fans were turned off at 11.45 a.m., some control rods were slowly withdrawn, and a careful watch was kept on the thermocouple readings. By 1.00 a.m. on Tuesday 8 October the overall graphite temperature varied between 50°C and 80°C but one thermocouple showed a measurement of 210°C, which indicated that Wigner release was taking place at that point. As it was expected that the energy release would now spread throughout the graphite, and all seemed to be going well, the pile was shut down. The graphite temperature readings, however, did not rise steadily as expected but actually began to fall so it was decided to re-start the pile and apply a second heating up process. To do this, the control rods began to be adjusted, at 11.05 a.m., with the aim of keeping the uranium temperature at 330°C, and the heating was continued until 7.25 p.m. One of the operators described the pile as 'very touchy', because the temperature fluctuated haphazardly around 330°C until in the afternoon of Wednesday 9 October it rose to as high as 415°C. At that stage, according to instructions, the operators switched on four fans to cool the pile down.

The temperature did initially fall but by midnight it was rising again. It was only at this stage that the operators really began to think that all was not well, and their concerns were heightened when, at 5.40 a.m. on Thursday 10 October, instruments in the reactor chimney indicated an abnormal rise in radioactivity. By 2.00 p.m., when excess radioactivity was detected in the air half a mile away, it was clear that the pile was in serious trouble, and at 3.45 it was realised that it was on fire. Visual examination through an inspection port on top of the core showed that flames were coming out of about 150 fuel channels and playing on to the inside of the concrete outer wall.

The staff on duty knew that trying to extinguish the fire with water would be hazardous because it might react with the hot metals or graphite to produce hydrogen which, when mixed with air, would give an explosive mixture. So their first reaction was to try to establish a fire-break by climbing on to the charge hoist and using heavy steel bars, including scaffolding poles, to push the fuel elements out of the channels immediately surrounding the burning zone. When they had done that, with some success, they tried to eject some of the burning elements. The men involved, wearing protective clothing and respirators, were dripping with sweat, and the steel bars came out red hot and partially molten, but their heroic efforts had to be abandoned because most of the elements within the reactor were severely deformed and could not be moved.

The fire was contained but it still raged and it was not extinguished when a tanker full of carbon dioxide gas, intended for cooling the nearby Calder Hall reactors, was pumped into it between 4.00 and 5.00 on Friday morning. The temperature was probably so high that the carbon dioxide was split into carbon and oxygen, and the latter simply hastened the burning. As a last resort it was decided to take the risk of using water to put the fire out and, with the cooperation of the local authorities and the Chief Constable of Cumberland, everything was prepared for a possible major emergency. There was no easy way of feeding water into the reactor so four hoses from the Windscale fire engine were connected to long scaffolding poles which, at 8.55, were pushed into it about 0.6m above the region of the fire and the water was turned on. The critical seconds passed with no explosion; the fire was under control by midday; it was out after a further drenching for another twenty-four hours; and by the afternoon of Saturday 12 October the pile was cold.

The situation was, however, still dangerous because some radioactivity had been released into the air through the chimney of the pile. It would have been much more were it not for the fact that filters had been installed in the top of the chimney, late in the day, at the insistence of Sir John Cockcroft. These filters had not been included in the original design. Many of his colleagues thought they were unnecessary and they were known locally as 'Cockcroft's Folly' but they almost certainly prevented a serious accident from becoming a catastrophe.

The major component of the radioactivity was iodine-131, with a short half-life of only eight days, and when this was found to be present in high doses in local cow's milk, over an area of 500 sq. km, about two million gallons of milk was ordered to be thrown away into the sea or local rivers. This ban on local milk, applied with commendable speed, lasted for up to forty-four days in some areas but no other restrictions were deemed to be necessary and the Medical Research Council Committee, which investigated the accident in 1957 and 1960, concluded that 'it is in the highest degree unlikely that any harm had been done to the health of anybody, whether a worker in the Windscale plant or a member of the general public'.[1] There have been many reappraisals since then and a television programme entitled 'Windscale: the Nuclear Laundry', which was broadcast in 1983 claimed that there might be a link between the Windscale accident and the number of local cases of cancer in the region since 1954. But in 1997 a thorough reassessment, on the 40th anniversary of the fire, by the National Radiological Protection Board found that 'the risks to the most exposed individuals and to the population as a whole were very small. It is unlikely that any effects could be seen in the population that could be attributed to the Windscale fire.'[2]

That may well be attributable more to good luck than to good management and it was clearly a close-run thing. There is still some mystery surrounding the cause of the fire and it is remarkable that a team of experienced operators did not seem to see anything very wrong for some forty-two hours during the Wigner release. Indeed, the Works General Manager H.G. Davey said that, until Thursday morning, it was 'one of the best releases we have had'.[3] The Committee of Enquiry, however, under the chairmanship of Sir William Penney reported, sixteen days after the accident, that 'the primary cause of the accident was the second nuclear heating' which was started at 11.05 on 8 October. It was, the committee concluded, 'started too soon and applied too rapidly'[4] so that between 11.20 and 11.35 the temperature was rising at 10°C per minute. This caused one of the fuel element casings to burst and the resulting burning of the exposed uranium, together with further release of Wigner energy, started the fire.

The Penney report praised the operators of the pile for their 'considerable devotion to duty'[5] after the fire but it seemed to blame them for allowing the fire to start, even though it admitted that they had probably been misled about the temperatures within the pile because the thermocouples were wrongly placed and there were not enough of them. Later enquiries, therefore, investigated other possible causes of the fire but no clear-cut answers were forthcoming and precise answers to the questions as to when, where and why the fire began will probably never be known. The evidence has long since been entombed because it was decided on 15 July 1958 not to try to repair the badly damaged pile, and after considerable clearing-up work had been done it was sealed in November by capping the chimney with specially treated timber planks and by filling in all the holes in the existing outer concrete shield. By then, after close examination of the costs, it had also been decided not to modify Pile Number 2 so it was written off and shared the same coffin-like fate as Number 1.

The secrecy surrounding the origins of the two Windscale piles was continued when Mr Macmillan's Conservative government decided not to publish the Penney report. He thought its contents would be misused by hostile critics and that public confidence in the ongoing programme of nuclear power station construction would be shattered even though their reactors were of a different design. He was also concerned that its publication might adversely affect his sensitive negotiations with President Eisenhower on improving nuclear collaboration to counter the threat posed by the launch of the first Russian space satellite, *Sputnik*, on 4 October.

The two ill-fated piles still encumber the Sellafield site. Work began on removing the top 30m sections (containing the filters) of the two chimneys in the mid-1980s, and a £54 million contract was signed in 1997 for the dismantling of the damaged core of Number 1 pile. But it is clear that removing the piles will take much longer, and be much more costly, than building them was more than forty years ago.

The China Syndrome, a Hollywood film starring Jane Fonda and Jack Lemmon, was released on 14 March 1979. It told the exciting tale of a nasty accident at a nuclear power plant and the subsequent attempt to cover-up the cause. The title of the film derived from the name given to the awesome (but wildly remote) possibility of the molten mass of a reactor core in a hypothetical American nuclear disaster boring its way right through the earth to China.

Truth may not be stranger than fiction but it can often match it, and only a fortnight later there was a real, and not very dissimilar, accident at the power station recently built by Babcock & Wilcox for Metropolitan Edison at Three Mile Island in the Shenandoah River near Harrisburg in Pennsylvania. The station had two PWR reactors, with Unit 1 (TMI-1) entering service in 1974 and Unit 2 (TMI-2) in 1978. The accident centred around a breakdown in the cooling system of TMI-2, which had two parts. The *primary* cooling circuit circulated water, under pressure, around the hot core of the reactor with cold water entering at the bottom. The water emerging from the top was at a temperature of 324°C and it passed through a heat exchanger in which it converted the separate water in a *secondary* circuit into steam which drove turbines to provide electricity.

The chain of events that triggered off the accident began at 4.00 a.m. on Wednesday 28 March when three workers were carrying out routine maintenance on the secondary circuit. Quite unexpectedly the two pumps circulating the water stopped running whereupon the reactor's safety mechanism responded, correctly, by immediately switching on three emergency pumps. Unfortunately, without any of the operators seeming to know, the valves in the water pipelines were shut so that there was no subsequent flow of water. It seemed likely that the valves had been left shut inadvertently two days earlier during a routine test. The lack of any water flow in the secondary circuit caused the water in the primary circuit to overheat with a consequent rise in pressure, which led to the automatic opening of a pressure-release valve and the automatic shut-down of the reactor. As expected, the hot reactor did not cool down immediately but the operators thought that everything was under control because the reactor had shut down. They had not noticed, however, that the pressure-release valve, which should have shut automatically thirteen seconds after it had opened, had not done so. The instrumentation indicated that a SHUT command had been sent but not that it had been effective.

With this valve still open, coolant was escaping unnoticed into a drainage tank – it was rather like running a car engine with the radiator cap off – and within minutes the control panel was flashing everywhere, indicating almost a hundred different faults. Some of the instruments were even going off-scale. This made it very difficult for the operators, taken completely by surprise, to know what to do and they made matters worse by taking some wrong decisions. Two high-pressure pumps in the emergency primary cooling circuit were triggered automatically to try to maintain the correct water level around the core, but the operators thought they were not needed so they switched one off and turned the other down; and when, at 5.00 a.m., the primary circuit cooling pumps began to vibrate because they were pumping steam as well as water they were also closed down.

It was not until 6.22 a.m. – nearly two and a half hours down the line – that it was realised where the main fault lay and a valve covering the open pressure-release valve was closed. By then nearly a million gallons of cooling water had escaped, mainly into a space under the reactor, and the cooling water level had fallen well below the upper level of the core. Consequently the temperature of the fuel rods had risen alarmingly and some of them, together with their zircaloy cladding, had begun to melt. Radioactive fission products had entered the escaping cooling water but, even worse, the hot zircaloy had reacted with the steam to form hydrogen which had collected as a bubble above the core. There was a dull explosion at about 1.50 p.m. on Friday 29 March, which was thought to have been caused by some hydrogen that had leaked through the open pressure-release valve, but all the experts now gathered at the plant could do was to wait to see if the main bubble of hydrogen would explode. The Governor of Pennsylvania recommended that children and pregnant women within an 8km area should be evacuated and many others left too. But fortunately, by the Sunday, it had been possible to disperse the hydrogen by periodically opening a vent valve, and to cool the reactor to some extent. The main dangers had passed but the reactor was not fully cold until 27 April, almost a month later, and it was many months after that before it was possible to enter the reactor building.

The long-drawn-out accident was caused in the main by the failure of the open pressure-release valve to close automatically but it seems odd, at least in retrospect, that it took so long for this to be noticed. It is, however, much easier to say that now than it was to do anything about it amid the general chaos and confusion at the time. Luckily, and more by glorious inaction than by any heroic deeds or bold decisions, what was very nearly an enormous disaster ended with no one killed or even injured. Moreover the extensive shielding in the reactor design meant that the escape of radioactivity was largely limited to that in the leaked coolant water, which remained on the site. Twelve epidemiological studies on the local population in the years after the event have shown no cause for concern. But the reactor had to be written off. It was cleaned up over a period of twelve years, at a cost of almost $1,000 million by evaporating the contaminated water and by removing 100 tonnes of damaged fuel and 50 tonnes of other material from the reactor. It was then sealed and put into long-term monitored storage in 1993 to await final decommissioning when the power station is eventually closed.

With hindsight, it can now be seen that the contemporary media coverage of the TMI-2 accident greatly exaggerated the dangers and caused unnecessary confusion and fear. But it meant that the accident did have a shattering impact on the public's perception of the safety of nuclear energy both in the United States and around the world. Since the accident the performance of TMI-1 has done something to redress the balance. It was closed down for refuelling during the accident to TMI-2, but after some modifications and changes in the operating procedures it was restarted in October 1985 and has performed excellently ever since. It was sold in 1999 to AmerGen, a joint venture between British Energy and PECO Energy.

In 1986 the large Chernobyl nuclear power station, built just outside the town of Pripyat, 110km north of Kiev and close to the boundary between the Ukraine and Belarus, provided about 10 per cent of the Ukraine's electricity. It consisted of four reactors, numbered 1 to 4, which had been commissioned in 1977, 1978, 1981 and 1983 respectively. Two more were under construction. They were all RBMK (Reaktor Bolshoy Moschnosty Kanalny)-1000 reactors fuelled by uranium oxide enriched with an additional 2 per cent of uranium-235 and they used graphite as the moderator and water as the coolant. A large block of graphite was perforated by zirconium-lined vertical channels to allow for the insertion of the fuel rods, encased in zirconium alloy metal tubes, and boron carbide control rods.

When operating, the reactor was cooled by pumping water up through each of the channels in the graphite around the fuel rod assemblies, and the steam that emerged from the top was used, after drying, to drive turbines and generate electricity. The cooling water came from a 22 sq. km pond alongside the River Pripyat, a tributary of the River Dnieper, and it was fed into the reactor by six pumps, with two in reserve. There was also an emergency cooling system consisting of water stored under pressure in tanks which could be fed into the core automatically in the event of any overheating. The reactor core was encased in a concrete shield with a steel cap over the top through which the control rods and the refuelling equipment for removing and replacing the fuel rods could move as required.

The whole power station was housed in three large buildings. The central one, 400m long, 50m wide and 32m high, contained eight pairs of turbines and generators. On each side there were buildings 153m long, 73m wide and 71m high divided by thick walls into three compartments to accommodate a reactor at both ends, and a central area which contained shared equipment and the base of a 150m-high chimney.

The area around Chernobyl. (Uranium Institute)

The RBMK design, which was unique to the Soviet Union, had an advantage over the American PWR design in that it could be refuelled without closing down. It had the disadvantage, however, of being notoriously difficult to control at low output levels because the particular arrangement of the water cooling system allowed pockets of steam to form. Because steam is both a less efficient coolant than water and, unlike water, has no moderating effect on neutrons, the reactor automatically produced more power when steam was formed. There was also a potentially dangerous time lapse of 40–50 seconds before the stand-by electricity supply from a diesel-operated generator could be connected in any emergency.

On 25 and 26 April 1986, just before the May Day holiday, the Number 4 reactor, which was connected to the No. 7 and No. 8 turbines, was due to be shut down for routine maintenance and the operators decided to take this opportunity to carry out an overnight experiment designed to improve the safety of the plant. The idea was to see whether the turbine would go on rotating and providing electricity after the reactor was shut down for the 40–50 seconds it took before the emergency supply came into play. The plan was to run down the reactor over a period of some hours by inserting the control rods, until it was operating at 25 per cent of its full capacity, and then disconnect it from the turbine. But it all went very much awry, predominantly as a result of wrong decisions made by the operators, some of which were entirely contrary to written instructions on how to run the reactor safely.

The plan was put into operation at 1.00 a.m. on 25 April and by 2 p.m. the reactor power had been reduced to 50 per cent. Shortly after, turbine no. 7 was shut down and the emergency cooling system for the reactor was cut off. There was then an unexpected delay when the director of the electricity grid in Kiev asked for turbine no. 8 to be kept running until 11.10 p.m. to meet the high local demand. Thereafter the planned run-down to 25 per cent was continued, even though it was known that there would be a shift change at midnight. The run-down was done by manual control with some of the automatic shut-down systems switched off and it resulted in a completely unexpected fall in the power of the reactor to just 6 or 7 per cent. To try to increase the power some of the control rods were raised from within the core. By 1.22 a.m. on 26 April the instruments in the control room were showing abnormal readings and it would have been sensible at this point to abandon the experiment. There were, for example, only seven control rods in position within the core when the minimum should have been thirty. But reason did not prevail. The operators pushed on with the experiment and, at 1.23 a.m., they cut the steam supply to the turbine.

Almost immediately the temperature inside the reactor soared by about 250°C every second and the reactor power had soon increased to a hundred times its design value. Imagine the feelings of the supervisor in the control room. He was astonished and horrified, but all he could do was press the emergency button as quickly as possible to drop *all* the control rods into the reactor. When he saw that they had not dropped in fully he cut the power supply to their operating mechanism so that they could fall under their own weight. But it was all too late and at 1.24 there were two enormous explosions. The first was probably caused by the build-up of steam when the red-hot fuel rods broke through their zirconium casing and came into contact with the cooling water. It lifted the 2,000 tonne shield off the top of the core, shattered the walls and the floor, and threw red-hot and burning fragments up into the sky. The second explosion probably came from reaction between the incoming air and the hydrogen formed from the red-hot graphite and the cooling water. The air also reacted with the hot graphite to form carbon monoxide gas which caught fire. What had been a nuclear reactor just minutes before was now a raging inferno; about a quarter of it had been

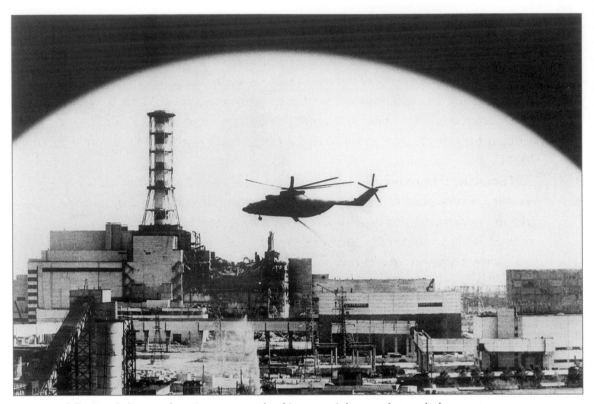

A Russian helicopter dropping neutron–absorbing materials on to the wrecked reactor at Chernobyl. (UKAEA)

hurled out into the air; the turbine building was ablaze and there were twenty-nine other fires; the roof and vast walls of the reactor building were destroyed; and the strong up-draft had carried highly radioactive debris 1km up into the sky before the winds began to distribute it all over Europe. There was, moreover, a possibility that what was left of the reactor might blow up like an atomic bomb.

There was no need to sound an alarm because the two bangs had been heard far away and it was not difficult to guess their source. The local power station firemen arrived on the scene at 1.30, and another crew from Pripyat came at 1.35. They had no special protective gear and they quickly saw that the dosimeter recording the level of radioactivity had gone off the top of the scale – but they fought the flames heroically and had many of them out or under control by 5.00. But the core of the reactor, particularly the graphite, went on burning and pouring water on to it was utterly ineffective as it was instantly vaporised. Even pumping water in at 250 tonnes an hour for half a day had little impact and simply threatened to flood nearby equipment. In the end the fire was only extinguished by dropping 5,000 tonnes of a mixture of boron carbide, lead, dolomite, clay and sand on to it from helicopters between 27 April and 10 May. The boron carbide was intended to absorb neutrons and prevent any possibility of a nuclear chain reaction building up; the lead absorbed heat, melted into open spaces and acted as a neutron shield; the hot dolomite gave off carbon dioxide which acted as a fire extinguisher; and the clay and sand acted as filters and extinguishers. Between 4 and 5 May the temperature of the fire had reached 2000°C.

Meanwhile, a new concrete foundation was constructed under the reactor to prevent contamination of ground water; a concrete wall was built 30m into the ground to prevent contaminated water from getting into the Pripyat River; cold nitrogen gas was pumped in under the core; and finally the reactor was entombed in a concrete and steel shell like a sarcophagus. It is 60m high, 60m in diameter and 6–18m thick and contains 160,000 cu. m of concrete. It has a filtered air ventilation system to keep it cool, and is pierced by a cylindrical steel pipe, 10cm in diameter and 18m long, which contains instruments to monitor the internal temperature and radiation levels. It is estimated that the sarcophagus contains about 200 tonnes of radioactive material and recent signs that some of the concrete may be cracking are a cause for concern.

The immediate death-toll of workers on the site was surprisingly low, with only two being killed. Fifteen others died from radiation burns within two days, and another fourteen within a few months. And

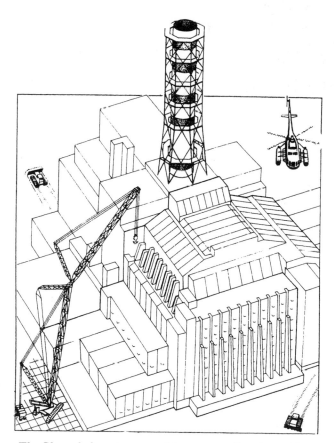

The Chernobyl reactor encased in concrete after the accident. (ASE)

the clean-up operation, carried out by some 200,000 helpers (who, in the translation of their Russian name, became known as liquidators), was so effective that some management teams had moved back on to part of the site by mid-July and the number 1 and 2 reactors were in service again in November 1986 and number 3, which had been damaged, in December 1987. But the radioactivity did not go away and it is probable that some 15,000 of the liquidators, including most of the firemen, died over the years as a result of their exposure to high levels of radiation.

It was lucky that the wind initially was from the south-east so that the cloud was not blown over the city of Kiev. Instead it moved, slowly but relentlessly, to the north-east, over the Ukraine, Belarus, Latvia and Lithuania. It was detected in Poland, Finland, Sweden and Denmark on 27 April; in Norway, East Germany, Austria, Hungary, Yugoslavia and Italy on 29 April; in West Germany, Switzerland and Turkey on 30 April; in France on 1 May; and in Greece, Belgium, the Netherlands and the United Kingdom on 2 May. The long-term damage caused by this radioactivity was spread rather haphazardly, with particular danger areas across the Soviet republics, and in Scandinavia, Britain, southern Germany and Greece, because it was in those places that heavy rain washed the radioactivity out of the clouds and on to the ground. The fall-out contained a deadly brew of about thirty radioactive isotopes but the main potential hazard was the possibility of iodine-131 and caesium-137 entering the food chain. Both these elements are absorbed by plants through their leaves and roots. At first, it was the iodine-131 which caused most concern because it quickly passed from grass into cow's milk and then threatened to damage the thyroid glands of anyone who drank it. Workers from the power plant and many of the inhabitants of Pripyat were given potassium iodate tablets as an antidote as early as 26 April, and many countries restricted the sale of milk and, in some cases, of green vegetables grown in the open. The half-life of iodine-131, however, is only eight days so its impact soon fades, and it was the caesium-137 isotope, with a half-life of 30.1 years, that caused more concern. When, for instance, it was found to be present in dangerous doses in sheep on farms in Scotland, north-west England and Wales the movement, sale and slaughter of almost 5 million animals on nearly 9,000 farms was restricted. And there are still some restrictions today on 386 farms with 230,000 sheep.

The level of radiation in the vicinity of the power station immediately after the accident was so high that the State Commission, which had taken control of the area, decided at 9 p.m. on 26 April to evacuate the local population. This was announced on the local radio at 2 p.m. on 27 April and a fleet of 1,100 buses collected from Kiev and other Ukrainian towns carried 45,000 people to safety in

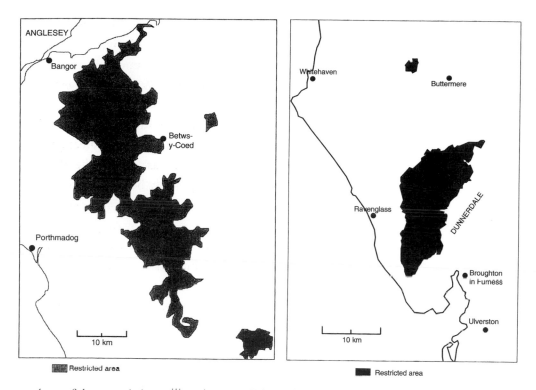

Areas of sheep restrictions still applying in Wales (left) and England (right) in 2000 as a result of the Chernobyl disaster. (DETR)

the south in a convoy which stretched for 20km. Tens of thousands of cattle were moved by rail. Moving other people from an area within 10km of the power station began on 29 April and the zone was extended to 30km early in May with evacuation going on into June. By then, 135,000 people had been moved, a vast house-building programme had been started, and it was hoped that no further evacuation would be necessary. But by February 1989, following further measurements of contamination by caesium-137, it was realised that the 30km zone would have to be extended. This meant, unfortunately, that some people had to be evacuated for a second time and some newly built houses had to be abandoned. The new arrangement involved a 10,000 sq. km 'zone of strict control' within which only imported food would be eaten until evacuation was completed, it was hoped, by 1990; a 21,000 sq. km 'zone of permanent control' which would, in due course, be evacuated; and a third zone in which all the food that was grown would be rigorously inspected. The overall effect of these measures was that normal daily life for some four million people was, to put it mildly, greatly disrupted.

Today there is an exclusion zone covering 2,600 sq. km, corresponding roughly to the original 30km limit. Patrolled by 800 militiamen, it is a completely desolate, uninhabited wasteland with rusting cars, fire engines, buses, bulldozers, ambulances and helicopters scattered about, together with wolves, boars, wild horses and all sorts of unusual plants. The old cooling ponds at the power station contain huge catfish some 2m long and Pripyat, where 48,000 people lived in 1986, is simply a ghost-town slowly falling to pieces and reverting to nature. The interiors of many of the private and public buildings are just as they were left fourteen years ago. And the rate of thyroid cancer among its former residents has risen to 250 cases per million people, compared with an average of 0.5 cases.

Who was to blame? A trial which opened on 7 July 1987 under Judge Raimond Brize, the deputy chairman of the Soviet Supreme Court, found that 'there was an atmosphere of lack of control and lack of responsibility at the power station'[6] and six engineers and managers were found guilty of varying degrees of negligence. They were sentenced to imprisonment in a labour camp for terms of between two and fifteen years. Many of those in the ministries of energy and the electrical companies, who had been involved in the project behind the scenes, were also removed from office or admonished for their part in the disaster.

It is the height of irony that such a nightmare should spring from an apparently straightforward experiment designed to improve safety. The scale and the international aspect of the disaster put an immediate brake on any plans for building future nuclear power stations. The two reactors under construction at Chernobyl were abandoned but the local demands for energy did not go away and the power station went on operating. There was a bust of Lenin outside and a sign in the entrance lobby which proclaimed 'Safety, Efficiency, Social Progress', and the six thousand staff lived in a new town called Slavutich built in 1986 outside the exclusion zone on land cleared of all its topsoil. Reactor Number 2 was shut down in 1991 following a fire, and Number 1 was closed in 1996 as part of a deal with other European countries, which provided the Ukrainian government with $3.1 billion of aid on condition that the whole Chernobyl power station was completely closed by the end of the year 2000. Some $1.5 billion of that aid went towards completing two replacement reactors at the Rovno and Khmelnitski power stations but the Ukrainian government held out for more before agreeing to close the last, Number 3, reactor on 14 December 2000. The vital switch, labelled BAZ, was pressed by the chief technician, Oleksandr Yelchishchev, and many of the 800 well-paid remaining workforce wept and wore black armbands as their lives were torn apart.

It was the end of an era which had had profound political impact. It took place when Mikhail Gorbachev's economic restructuring, *perestroika*, was only about two months old and it highlighted the absolute necessity for change. It was expressed both in deed and word by Valerii Legasov, the deputy director of the Kurchatov Atomic Energy Institute and a member of the State Commission. On the second anniversary of the accident he committed suicide after writing of Chernobyl as the 'apotheosis and peak of the economic mismanagement of our country over decades'.[7] A new dawn was very timely and there was plenty of room for *glasnost*.

The accident at Tokaimura in Japan on 30 September 1999 was of a different kind because it took place in a chemical plant and did not involve a nuclear reactor. The small plant, operated by the Japan Nuclear Fuel Conversion Co. since 1988, was making highly enriched uranium oxide, containing 18.8 per cent of uranium-235 for experimental use in the fast breeder reactor at Yoyo. This involved mixing a solution of uranyl nitrate with a solution of ammonia in a stainless steel tank with a capacity of 100 litres. Because the reaction produced heat the tank was surrounded by a water-cooled jacket.

It was well known that the volume of liquid in the tank must be limited to keep the amount of uranium below 2.4kg, at which level a critical point was reached when a self-sustaining chain reaction might begin. The particular procedure had not, however, been carried out for three years and the operating staff did not seem to have been clearly briefed. Consequently, at 10.35 a.m. on 30 September, when the volume in the tank reached 40 litres, corresponding to 16kg of uranium, the alarm signals sounded and it was found that the liquid in the tank was boiling vigorously. There was no explosion but there was an intense emission of gamma-radiation and neutrons, and a variety of fission products were released into the building.

It was a helter-skelter ride because the turmoil declined as voids in the boiling liquid formed and stopped the chain reaction only for it to restart as the voids disappeared. But it went on for twenty hours and only abated when the water in the cooling jacket was drained and replaced by boric acid solution which is a good absorber of neutrons. It transpired that the cooling water had been reflecting neutrons back into the tank, which reinforced the chain reaction.

The operator exposed to the highest dose of radiation died twelve weeks after the accident and one of his colleagues died four months later, while 119 others were subjected to a dose higher than the safe *annual* dose. Five hours into the accident, when low levels of iodine-131 were detected in the air around the plant,

161 people living within 350m were evacuated, and seven hours later residents within 10km were advised to stay indoors, but everything was back to normal within two days and the escaping radioactivity was mainly contained within the plant building. This was due to the efficient filters fitted to the extractor system and to the fact that the pressure inside the building was kept below the external pressure, thus ensuring that air leakage was inwards. So at least some precautions had been taken and had worked but the official enquiry concluded that the accident was caused by human error and serious breaches of safety regulations. The company conceded that it was at fault and now faces criminal charges.

There is a long list of other accidents of varying degrees of nastiness. To try to assess them sensibly a safety scale known as the International Nuclear Event Scale has been introduced by the International Atomic Energy Agency, a branch of the United Nations organisation with 130 member states and headquarters in Vienna, and the Nuclear Energy Agency of the Organisation for Economic Co-operation and Development, with 27 member states, based in Paris. This scale attempts to do for nuclear accidents what the Richter scale does for earthquakes. The main criteria are the breakdown in the safety arrangements and the on-site and off-site impact of the radioactive releases. Chernobyl is given the highest ranking at Scale 7, with Three Mile Island and Windscale at Scale 5. Scale 3 involves very little release of radioactivity with no off-site impact and lower scales are classified as incidents with few or no safety implications.

CHAPTER 16

Problem Areas

The inherent difficulty of disposing of the waste from nuclear power plants was recognised some years ago and Sir Harold Hartley, in his presidential address to the British Association in 1950, said that 'the removal and disposal of the radioactive products from the reactors will be a costly and puzzling task'. And so it has turned out to be.

When radioactive materials were first used, the disposal of the relatively small amounts of waste from hospitals, research units, defence organisations and industrial firms was not regarded as a great problem. None of it was very highly radioactive and would today be classified as very low level waste (VLLW) or low level waste (LLW). It was disposed of very haphazardly, either by burying in the ground, dumping at sea or as ordinary rubbish in land-fill sites. But the advent of nuclear power stations changed all that because they produce high level waste (HWL) and intermediate level waste (IWL) as well as a lot of VLLW and LLW. This arises because the uranium used as the fuel in a reactor undergoes a number of changes over the 3–5 years before it is removed from the reactor and replaced by new fuel. The heat and the constant bombardment by neutrons causes the fuel to become discoloured and possibly to swell, but more importantly much of the uranium, which is not itself dangerously radioactive, is converted into a cocktail of hundreds of different isotopes. It includes plutonium-239, -240, -241 and -242 and other trans-uranium elements such as neptunium-237 and americium-241, together with such isotopes as uranium-237, krypton-85, strontium-89 and -90, iodine-129 and -130, thorium-232, and caesium-135 and -137. Many of these have short half-lives so that their radioactivity decays markedly after storing for some months, but there is a real problem about how to handle those isotopes with long half-lives and high levels of radioactivity. Caesium-135, for example, has a half-life of 2.3 million years; iodine-129 one of 20 million years; and thorium-232 one of 14,000 million years.

The spent fuel (SF), which contains about 96 per cent uranium, 1 per cent plutonium and 3 per cent waste products, can either be regarded as high level waste and disposed of without any prior treatment or it can be reprocessed, and different countries have adopted different policies on this. The original thinking behind reprocessing, some fifty years ago, was based on the assumption that the use of nuclear energy would expand so rapidly that there might be a shortage of uranium so it seemed sensible to try to recycle it. Reprocessing would also cut down the amount of high level waste which had to be dealt with and would provide a steady supply of plutonium for making nuclear weapons for research purposes and for use in fast breeder reactors.

Today's scenario is, however, very different. The expansion in the use of nuclear energy has been limited, partially because of the number of accidents that have occurred and partially because the cost of building and running nuclear power stations has escalated. Uranium has also become much more freely available and it is now realised that it was only thought to be rare because, with no known use before the nuclear age, no one had bothered to look for it very seriously. Furthermore, with some measure of nuclear disarmament taking place and the collapse of the fast breeder programmes, there is far too much plutonium available in the world and no one quite knows what to do with it.

Consequently reprocessing is today somewhat controversial and it has never been practised in Canada, Sweden, Finland and Spain and is not fully supported by the United States. In 1976 President Ford decreed that the reprocessing and recycling of plutonium should not proceed unless there is sound reason to conclude that the world community can effectively overcome the associated risk of proliferation. President Carter went even further in 1977 when he spoke of nuclear energy as a 'last resort'.[1] Today, however, because of severe energy shortages in the United States, President Bush is at least talking about the possibility of increasing the amount of electricity generated by nuclear power stations, of beginning to reprocess spent fuel, and of higher spending on developing new technologies to deal with nuclear waste. Such actions would bring the United States more into line with other countries, such as France, Belgium, the United Kingdom, Russia, Germany and Japan, which all went ahead with their nuclear programmes and decided in favour of reprocessing. Indeed, all but Germany still have their own reprocessing plants. The one in France, at La Hague on the tip of the Cherbourg peninsula, is operated by COGEMA (Compagnie Générale des Matières Nucléaires) and reprocesses 1,600 tonnes of spent fuel annually. Similarly, there is a plant in the United Kingdom at Sellafield, run by BNFL.

Reprocessing has been carried out at Sellafield for almost fifty years and 40,000 tonnes of spent fuel have been treated successfully. It began when the B205 plant,

Aerial view of the Sellafield site.

completed in 1952, was used to reprocess the fuel from Magnox reactors, which begins its life as unenriched uranium clad in a magnesium alloy. The plant is expected to be required for at least another ten years until all the Magnox reactors have closed down. Thereafter the Thermal Oxide Reprocessing Plant (THORP), which was opened in 1994, will take over all the reprocessing work. It can treat Magnox spent fuel as well as that from AGR reactors (enriched uranium oxide clad with stainless steel) and from water-cooled reactors (enriched uranium oxide clad with a zirconium alloy). It cost £1.85 billion to build, can handle 900 tonnes of fuel annually and has an expected lifespan of twenty-five years. For the first years of its life it has met all the home demand even though about two-thirds of its capacity has been used to treat materials from European countries such as Germany, and from Japan.

The first stage of reprocessing is the removal of the fuel rods, in their cladding, from the reactor. This has to be done by remote control because standing alongside the rods even for a short time would be fatal. In on-load refuelling a few rods are removed and replaced with new ones while the reactor is still operating; in off-load refuelling the reactor is shut down to enable around a third of the rods to be replaced all at once. The spent fuel is stored in a nearby cooling pond for at least ninety days to lower its temperature and allow some of the radioactivity to decay. The fuel is then transported in massive steel flasks weighing up to 110 tonnes but carrying no more than 10 tonnes of fuel. The flasks, which are loaded on to specially designed trucks, trains, ships or planes, have been tested for strength by dropping them on to a solid surface and on to a steel spike, by heating in a fire to 800°C for thirty minutes and by having a 14 tonne train moving at 160 kilometres per hour driven into them. For long journeys arrangements have to be made for cooling the flasks, and all the various procedures are carried out according to rules laid down by the International Atomic Energy Agency (IAEA).

On arrival at Sellafield the spent fuel is again stored in a cooling pond and then subjected to a series of chemical operations. These begin by stripping the casing from the rods and dissolving the fuel in concentrated nitric acid in a tank with 2m-thick concrete walls to provide the necessary radiation shielding. The resulting solution is then passed into other tanks with all the material being handled by remote control and viewed via closed-circuit television cameras. At the end of the line the uranium and the plutonium have been separated out but the solution remaining still contains the 3 per cent of high-level waste.

The uranium presents no real problems because it is recycled at Springfields, and over 15,000 tonnes of uranium from the spent fuel of Magnox reactors has been re-used in AGR reactors. It is difficult, however, to know what to do with the plutonium and the high-level waste, both of which are very hazardous. The plutonium is particularly dangerous because it is very toxic, has a long half-life and can be used for making nuclear weapons – it only needs about 4kg (about the size of a grapefruit). There is, moreover, a fear in many quarters that if there is too much of it in store or in transit, it will be easier for terrorist organisations to get their hands on it.

The isotopic composition of the plutonium obtained by reprocessing depends on the type of spent fuel from which it has been made but a typical sample from a

Testing the strength of a nuclear fuel transport flask by running a train into it. (BNFL)

Magnox reactor would contain 68.5 per cent of plutonium-239, 25 per cent of plutonium-240, 5.3 per cent of plutonium-241 and 1.2 per cent of plutonium-242. It is referred to as civil plutonium to distinguish it from weapons-grade plutonium, which normally has a typical composition of 93 per cent of plutonium-239, 6.5 per cent of plutonium-240 and 0.5 per cent of plutonium-241. Because the easily fissionable isotopes are plutonium-239 and -241, it is easier to make weapons from weapons-grade plutonium but it is, nevertheless, also possible to make them from civil plutonium.

Much of the surplus plutonium is stored at Sellafield after being converted into plutonium oxide, and the stocks are monitored under international agreement by inspectors from the UN International Atomic Energy Agency. Since 1993, however, some plutonium has been used for making what is known as mixed oxide fuel (MOX), a mixture of about 5 to 8 per cent of plutonium dioxide with uranium dioxide, which can be used as a component of a reactor fuel in some cases. A mixture of one-third MOX with two-thirds natural uranium, for example, is a good fuel for some reactors and is being used increasingly in France, Germany, Japan, Belgium and Switzerland. There are, however, no reactors as yet which have been specifically designed to use MOX fuel and it is not used in the United States, United Kingdom, the Netherlands, Sweden or Canada.

MOX has been made in France by the Centre de Fabrication de Cadarache (CFCa) since 1962 and by MELOX in Marcoule since 1995, in Belgium by BN Dessel since 1984, and by BNFL at Sellafield since 1993. The original British plant made only about 7–8 tonnes each year, mainly for a Swiss client, but it was replaced by a new plant with an annual capacity of 120 tonnes, which was built at a cost of £460 million. Shortly after opening, however, it was shut down and mothballed in 1999, because there was a scandal when quality-control staff falsified some data on a shipment of MOX to Japan. That led to a long government investigation but it was decided in October 2001 that the plant could reopen. Both the Irish government and anti-nuclear groups such as Greenpeace and Friends of the Earth were so dismayed by this decision that they took legal action to try to get it overturned, but with no success. Joe Jacob, the Irish minister with responsibility for nuclear safety, said that the decision 'defied logic in the current climate of international terrorist threats'.[2] And Charles Secrett, the Director of Friends of the Earth, said: 'It beggars belief that the government can give the go-ahead to a process involving the use and transport of plutonium that could be used to make weapons. Producing MOX at Sellafield will make the world a less safe place.'[3]

In full production the five MOX plants would use up about 20 tons of plutonium annually and thus reduce the amount kept in store. But it does not lower the total amount of plutonium in circulation, because as the plutonium in the MOX in a reactor fuel is used up new plutonium is made from the uranium-238 which is present. And some claim that it would be relatively easy for determined terrorists to steal MOX fuel, particularly when in transit, and extract the plutonium from it to make weapons. There is then something of a plutonium problem because the present amount in store in this country – about 50 tonnes – is likely to double by 2010 and this will represent about two-thirds of the world's stock of civil plutonium. The only current use for it is to make more MOX fuel which may or may not be required. Is it to be regarded as a valuable resource or as a waste product? There is, at present, no home demand for it and by international agreement it can only be sold to countries which have provided the plutonium from which it is made, in the form of spent fuel, in the first place. BNFL claims that 'the plutonium would represent a valuable source of energy' and that 'the potential market for MOX exceeds the amount of plutonium that will be available'[4] but a House of Lords Committee on the Management of Nuclear Waste, which reported in 1999, recommended that 'the Government develops, as soon as practicable, a clear policy on the long-term management of the United Kingdom's plutonium stock. Our view is that this should consist of maintaining a minimum strategic stock of civil plutonium and declaring the remainder to be waste. Surplus defence-related plutonium should be declared to be waste and plans made for its long-term management.'[5] That's all very well but it simply adds the difficulty of plutonium disposal to an already existing waste management problem which has still to be resolved.

The carefully kept inventory of radioactive waste in store in Great Britain, last recorded in 1998, shows 7,980 cu. m of LLW; 70,950 of ILW and 1,800 of HLW. The total radioactivity is about 50 million TBq, with 90 per cent of it in the HLW, 10 per cent in the ILW and only about one-millionth of the whole in the LLW. That is a legacy from the past that will not go away and the figures will rise annually in the future. What can be done with all this stuff?

A start was made in 1959, when a site at Drigg, 6km south of Sellafield, was opened for storing low level waste. It now covers 110 hectares and is managed by BNFL. The waste was originally tipped into shallow trenches cut into the natural boulder clay and then covered by stones and soil, but in 1988 a series of reinforced concrete vaults were constructed to contain the waste. To make the maximum use of the available space, the waste is nowadays compacted under high pressure in 1 cu. m steel boxes and the squashed boxes, known as pucks, are cemented together in a container before disposal. About a million cubic metres of low level waste has already been disposed of at Drigg and it is estimated that it can expand until about the year 2050 when an alternative site will be required.

About 65 per cent of the intermediate level waste is stored at Sellafield. Some 80 per cent of it is in the raw state but a treatment process known as conditioning was begun in 1990. During conditioning, the waste is encased in cement in 500 litre steel drums before storage, and the backlog of raw waste is being treated in the same way as quickly as possible. The remainder of the ILW, most of which awaits conditioning, is held in store at the nine Magnox power station sites, at Harwell, at Aldermaston and in an old shaft at Dounreay which was abandoned in 1998 and is now being excavated and cleaned up at an estimated cost of £355 million.

A good deal of ILW also arises from the nuclear-powered British submarine fleet which has been built up since the launch of the first vessel, HMS *Dreadnought*, which was in service between 1962 and 1982. Since then, as the

Aerial view of Drigg. (BNFL)

submarines are withdrawn from service, their spent fuel is stored in ponds at Sellafield, awaiting possible reprocessing, while the de-fuelled vessels, still with highly radioactive reactor compartments, are stored, afloat, at Davenport and Rosyth. There are eleven of them at the moment but this will rise to about twenty in 2020 and perhaps fifty in 2050. So this presents formidable problems, particularly if it proves impossible to reprocess the spent fuel and it has to be reclassified as high level waste.

It is that waste which poses the greatest problems. There is not a great deal of it – it would make a pile about 2m high if spread evenly over a 100m running track –

but it is the nastiest waste produced in any industrial process. It will remain dangerously radioactive for tens of thousands of years and produces so much heat that it may require external cooling for as long as fifty years. Until the early 1980s the solution containing the waste was reduced in volume by evaporation under vacuum to maintain a low temperature. It was then stored in double-walled stainless steel tanks, fitted with cooling coils to prevent over-heating and surrounded by thick concrete walls. Some of the older tanks have had this liquid waste stored in them, quite safely, for more than thirty years. It was always recognised, however, that leakage of material would be more difficult from a solid than from a solution, so in the late 1970s a start was made at Sellafield to convert the solution into a glass-like solid by a process of vitrification which originated in France. The solution is first calcined to convert it into a solid powder and this is then heated with boro-silicate glass at 1150°C. This so-called conditioned waste is then sealed in cylindrical double-walled, stainless steel containers, about 1m long and 0.3m in diameter, which are stored in blocks of concrete at Sellafield. The stores have a design life of about fifty years but could probably be used for twice that time if necessary. They are not, however, a long-term solution to the problem, and if no other answer is forthcoming BNFL is planning to build a new safe storage facility at Sellafield where the waste would be 'retrievable and monitorable'.

Many possible solutions, including ejection of the waste into outer space or deposition within Antarctic ice sheets or in rock under a deep ocean, have been suggested, but the 'front runner' is burial in a secure land site where there is no possibility of contamination of underground water. This was first suggested by a panel of experts appointed under the Radioactive Substances Act of 1948 and the UKAEA began work in 1954 to investigate the various options to implement such a policy. The British Geological Survey was commissioned to carry out a survey to identify possible disposal sites but none of them was seriously investigated, mainly because of local opposition from residents close to the sites.

Burial in a stable geological formation was also recommended by a Royal Commission on Environmental Pollution, chaired by Lord Flowers, which published its Sixth Report in 1976 on *Nuclear Power and the Environment*. The stark conclusion that 'there should be no commitment to a large programme of nuclear fission until it has been demonstrated beyond reasonable doubt that a method exists to ensure safe containment of long-lived, highly radioactive waste for the indefinite future' emphasised the seriousness of the position and led to another geological survey being undertaken. Once again, as soon any possible site for disposal of HLW was identified the local population rose up in arms and both NIMBY (Not In My Back Yard) and OMDB (Over My Dead Body) syndromes

Vitrified product store at Sellafield. (BNFL)

had a field day, as did the anti-nuclear environmental bodies. Whatever case the experts and the scientists made for any particular site was soon swamped by the strong perception among the local population that radioactive waste, however little there might be of it, was highly dangerous and potentially lethal. It was suicidal for any local MP to support any proposal that his constituency should become what was commonly referred to as a nuclear dumping ground.

On the recommendation of the Royal Commission, a Radioactive Waste Management Advisory Committee (RWMAC), consisting of a chairman and twenty independent members, was set up in 1978 to advise the government. The responsibility for taking some action was passed in 1982 to a new organisation named Nirex (Nuclear Industry Radioactive Waste Management Executive) with headquarters at Harwell. The outcome was that the government decided that all radioactive waste, except VLLW, should be buried in very deep repositories and Nirex set about trying to implement this policy. In 1988 they started to examine some 500 possible sites and within a year they had cut that number down, first to twelve and then to two. These two, which seemed to be geologically satisfactory if not ideal, were at Sellafield and at Dounreay, and one of the factors in their selection was that, although local opinion was not universally in favour, the opposition to building in areas where there were already nuclear installations was less than in other parts of the country. Sellafield was the final choice, probably because it was the main source of waste so that transport costs would be lower than at Dounreay.

In June 1994 Nirex, under the impression that it had government support, submitted an application to Cumbria County Council for permission to build an underground laboratory deep down in the rocks at Longlands Farm at Gosforth, close to Sellafield. It was known as the Rock Characterisation Facility (RCF) and was intended only as a provisional, experimental site on which various tests could be carried out under realistic conditions. The application was rejected by the council in December; an appeal against that decision was rejected after a year-long public enquiry in 1996, and on 17 March 1997 John Gummer, the Environment Minister, supported that decision.

Nirex was praised for its scientific work but heavily criticised for the way in which it had approached the task and presented the evidence. Much of what it did, or the way in which it did it, made it appear to be a very secretive and arrogant organisation. But, in its defence, it is not easy to behave 'normally' when most of the world seems to be against you. Perhaps its mission was impossible. Be that as it may, it is estimated that the cost of the public enquiry was £20 million and that of the whole exercise around £450 million. No further sites are at present being examined, but the Department of the Environment issued a consultation paper on 'Managing Radioactive Waste Safely' in September 2001. It outlines the existing situation both in the United Kingdom and other countries, and sets out a proposed programme of action. This has five stages, involving consultation, research and debate, with, it is hoped, a final decision and any new legislation coming in the year 2007.

The site of Longlands Farm in the foreground, with test drillings taking place in the adjacent fields. The Sellafield site is in the background. (Nirex)

It is difficult to see how any solution other than that of burial in rocks well below the Earth's surface can be reached. All the best geological advice points clearly in that direction and it is supported by some overseas experience. In the United States there is a deep burial site known as WIPP (Waste Isolation Pilot Plant) at Carlsbad in the remote Chihuahuan Desert in south-east New Mexico. It consists of fifty-six rooms dug out of a 600m-thick formation of salt, 650m underground, which is thought to have been stable for 200 million years, and it was opened on 26 March 1999 after a study that lasted twenty years. It is expected that it will receive 37,000 shipments of waste from the existing twenty-three waste sites in the US over the next thirty-five years, and extensive work is being carried out to investigate the possibility of opening a further site, in 2010, at Yucca Mountain in Nevada. In Sweden spent fuel is stored at Forsmark in rock

60m below the Baltic Sea, and the Finnish government has recently decided to develop underground storage at Olkiluoto. In other countries, however, the work can only be described as exploratory, as in Britain. Possible long-shot answers to the problem come from proposals to develop a 'European' solution, to locate an international repository in the Australian outback, and a report that Russia is ready to offer storage for foreign nuclear waste. Any country that would take in the world's dirty linen would certainly find plenty of customers prepared to pay almost any fee.

It is, however, much more likely that a solution will have to be found much nearer to home and the House of Lords Select Committee report on the 'Management of Nuclear Waste' in 1999 recommended 'that the government acts without delay. The programme for repository development is a long one and cannot be rushed. Delay in starting the programme entails risks and additional costs which an early start to policy development would avoid.'[6] So the time must come when discussion stops and decision takes over but past history does not make a solution any easier because public confidence has been so dented. There is, moreover, no immediate time limit by which any decision has to be made because the temporary arrangements for waste storage at Sellafield are working well and can probably survive for another hundred years. But in that time the amount of waste will increase dramatically, and on a purely ethical basis should anyone go on and on creating more and more dangerous waste without knowing what to do with it and leaving our descendants to find an answer? For organisations such as Greenpeace and Friends of the Earth a vital part of any waste management policy is to stop the reprocessing of spent fuel and to close all existing nuclear power stations.

They will in due course have to be closed because although their fuel rods can be replaced over and over again a reactor eventually comes to the end of its life and has to be decommissioned. Early reactors were designed with an expected life of around thirty years but many have been shut down well before that while others have lasted longer, and a modern reactor would be expected to last for between forty and sixty years. At the end of that time almost every part of a reactor is radioactive to some extent and the operators are confronted with a formidable problem when it comes to dismantling it and disposing of all the material. A relatively small reactor, for example, can weigh 300,000 tonnes, is supported on 500,000 tonnes of foundations and may have concrete walls 6m thick. One option would be to entomb the whole reactor in concrete, as was done at Chernobyl, but that stems from desperation and the International Atomic Energy Agency is recommending a stage-by-stage approach to decommissioning which allows each case to be treated on its merits. In this country the work is carried out under the supervision of the Nuclear Installations Inspectorate.

Stage 1 involves removing all the fuel and coolant, which accounts for at least 99 per cent of all the radioactivity. The remaining structure is then sealed and kept on a secure care and maintenance basis for as long as necessary, which may be many years. In Stage 2 the buildings outside the reactor and its shield are dismantled and removed, together with any equipment they contain, and in Stage 3 the whole site is cleared for reuse as a greenfield site. This procedure is referred to as the Safestore strategy in this country or as Safstor in the United States. It is extremely flexible, particularly as far as the time scale is involved. If required, all three stages can be implemented together as soon as a reactor is shut down; this is called the Decon option in the United States. Alternatively different storage times, suitable for each country and each project, can be adopted. The time for total decommissioning is fixed at five to ten years in Japan, where land is at a premium, and sixty years in the United States. In the United Kingdom a time of 135 years is planned in some cases. The actual time scale chosen for any single reactor depends on a number of technical and economic factors. In particular, deferring decommissioning work allows radioactive decay to take place so that the site becomes more and more accessible to humans, which decreases the need to use remote control systems for demolition. Computerised systems have been worked out to estimate the likely dose of radiation at any site at any time.

Meanwhile experience in the new technology is building up and both BNFL and the UKAEA are well established in the field. World-wide, over 80 nuclear reactors, over 250 research reactors and a number of submarine reactors have already been decommissioned successfully at a reasonable cost and on an acceptable time scale. Typical examples include the light water reactor at Shippingport in the United States, which operated between 1957 and 1982; the gas-cooled reactor at Fort St Vrain in the United States; the two Magnox reactors at Berkeley in Gloucestershire, which were shut down in 1989 after twenty-six years in service; and the Harwell experimental reactors GLEEP, DIDO and PLUTO which closed in 1990. It took two years to remove the fuel from Shippingport and a further five years to clear the site completely. Fort St Vrain was completely decommissioned in eight years. At Berkeley a three-year period for defuelling is being followed by an estimated storage period of thirty years; thereafter, the buildings will be contained and stored for around a hundred years. And at Harwell Stage 2 decommissioning has been completed so that the reactors are in safe storage.

Further ongoing work in the United Kingdom includes the decommissioning of Windscale Pile 1, which was damaged by fire in 1957; Stage 2 work on the prototype AGR reactor at Windscale, which was closed in 1982; the clearing out of an old shaft at Dounreay into which waste was tipped for twenty years before an explosion in 1977 drew attention to its shortcomings; decommissioning of the steam-generating heavy water reactor at Winfrith, which was shut down in 1990; the dismantling of the first, 61m-tall reprocessing plant built at Sellafield in the 1950s; and decommissioning of the first plant at Capenhurst which enriched uranium by a gaseous diffusion method before it was replaced by a centrifugal process.

In dealing with many of these situations, BNFL has been able to develop ways and means of removing low levels of radioactivity from such materials as steel and aluminium so that they can be reused. BNFL is also exploiting the expertise it has built up by expanding overseas. BNFL Inc, an American group company based in Fairfax, Virginia, and strengthened by the purchase of the Westinghouse Electric Company in 1999, has an order book worth $9 billion for decommissioning work, which includes an old gaseous diffusion plant built at Oak Ridge in the 1940s and shut down in 1985, and a former nuclear weapons site at Rocky Flats in Colorado. And with many reactors due to close within the next twenty years, decommissioning is an expanding market.

The involvement of both BNFL and UKAEA in the work has, however, been completely changed by a government decision, made in November 2001, to establish a Liabilities Management Authority (LMA). This new body, which will employ about 200 people, will supervise the estimated £42 billion of work which needs to be done by subcontracting the work, on a competitive basis, to companies that might include both BNFL and UKAEA. The decision is linked to a possible partial privatisation of BNFL in the year 2004/5.

Reprocessing, waste disposal and decommissioning are essentially technical problems but those associated with the public perception of radiation and nuclear matters are of no less significance and may, indeed, be harder to overcome – first, because there are so many long-established, well-funded and well-organised anti-nuclear pressure groups, and secondly because the general public's assessment of 'expert advice' is at such a low ebb.

The pressure groups, naturally enough, feel very strongly about the issues they represent, express their views very aggressively, and regard their activities as something of a war against the nuclear industry. They began, like Higinbotham's Association of Atomic Scientists, among workers in the nuclear field but they

The decommissioning of the Windscale AGR began in the late 1990s. Here, a crane is lifting out one of the four heat exchangers. (UKAEA)

soon spread more widely. Albert Einstein had always been against the bomb and two days before he died in 1955 he signed a statement drafted by Bertrand Russell, the Welsh philosopher and mathematician who was involved in a number of controversial issues during his 98-year-long life. What became known as the Russell-Einstein Manifesto called for all nations to unite in an attempt to solve the problems brought about by nuclear bombs and this led to the establishment of the Pugwash Conferences on Science and World Affairs. The first, of many, was sponsored by Cyrus S. Eaton, a millionaire industrialist who had founded

Professor Rotblat. (Pugwash)

the Republic Steel Corporation, and it was held on his estate at Pugwash in Nova Scotia, Canada, where he had been born. The conference was organised by Professor Joseph Rotblat, a physicist who was educated at the Free University of Poland and the University of Warsaw before winning a fellowship at Liverpool University. He worked at Los Alamos for a short period in 1944, but he left and returned to Britain when he learnt that the Germans were not going ahead with making their own bomb. He then turned his attention to medical physics and became a professor at St Bartholomew's Hospital Medical School in 1950, but he maintained a close link with Pugwash, acting as its secretary-general from 1957 to 1973 and as president from 1988 to 1997. It is a measure of his commitment that Otto Frisch could write 'he has done as much for peace as anybody I have ever encountered'[7] and he and Pugwash were jointly awarded the Nobel Prize for Peace in 1995. That prize was also awarded, in 1962, to the American Linus Pauling, who had already won the Chemistry Prize in 1953, and in 1985 to the International Physicians for the Prevention of Nuclear War organisation, founded in 1980 by the American Dr Bernard Lown and the Soviet Dr Yevgeny I. Chazov.

In 1958 Bertrand Russell, who was a founder member of Pugwash and presided over the first conference, was appointed President of the Campaign for Nuclear Disarmament (CND) in Britain, which grew from a number of smaller organisations such as the Direct Action Committee (DAC). In 1969, Friends of the Earth was founded in the United States by David Brower, who, as executive director of the Sierra Club since 1952, had already campaigned against excessive deforestation, the use of animal furs, the killing of porpoises by tuna fishermen and the building of two major dams in the Grand Canyon. He launched Friends of the Earth in Britain in 1971, and Greenpeace was founded in the same year in British Columbia to oppose the nuclear testing taking place at Amchitka Island in Alaska.

In 1970 the Natural Resources Defense Council was started by a group of lawyers from Harvard and Yale; in 1973 Ralph Nader brought a number of anti-nuclear groups together in the United States in his Critical Mass organisation; in 1977 WISE – the World Information Service on Energy – was founded in Denmark; in 1982 came the Nuclear Age Peace Foundation with headquarters in Santa Barbara in California; and in 1995 Abolition 2000, which shares the same headquarters, prepared an 11-point statement which has been supported by over two thousand organisations in over ninety countries. And there are many, many more of the same ilk.

Each organisation has its own individual point of view and method of proclaiming it, and many of them nowadays campaign on many fronts, but there is general agreement that nuclear power and all that goes with it should be abandoned. It is hazardous, they argue, because all parts of the nuclear fuel cycle, from uranium mining, through reactor building and operation to reprocessing, decommissioning and waste disposal, create dangerous radiation. It is not safe, as shown by the long list of nuclear accidents, which can have disastrous consequences and are quite unlike any other accidents. It is not cheap and can be replaced by other, sustainable sources of energy. In short it is not clean, it is not safe and it is not wanted.

The struggle to uphold such views has been fierce and at times violent. An early indication of what was to come was signalled in 1975 in Germany, where the Green environmental party has always been strong, when a long-term occupation of the building site prevented the construction of a new nuclear power station at Wyhl in the south-western corner of the country. There were also riots at the Grohnde station near Hamburg in November 1976 and at Brokdorf near Hannover in March 1977, and it required a massive police presence to contain a demonstration at Kalkar in September 1977. Ongoing protests culminated in a massive attempt to prevent the return of 85 tonnes of high level waste to Germany from the reprocessing plant at La Hague in France in March 2001. The waste, in six containers, was transported by train via Karlsruhe to Dannenberg and then by road to Gorleben, where it was buried in an old salt mine, but it needed 15,000 police using water-cannon and other heavy-handed methods to clear the way through 10,000 protestors, some of whom tied themselves to the railway line and on to bridges.

Similar demonstrations, beginning in 1975, stopped the building of a power station at Kaisergaust, east of Basel in Switzerland; at Creys-Malville in France, in July 1976, there was a pitched battle between riot police and protestors, in which one demonstrator was killed; in Spain in 1981 more than 250,000 people demonstrated against the power station at Lemoniz in the Basque country and two chief engineers were murdered by the militant separatist organisation ETA; in Japan in 1984 thousands turned out to demonstrate against the building of a power station at Ohi-cho, north of Osaka, but did not achieve their aim; and in 1985 the Greenpeace ship *Rainbow Warrior*, which was due to sail to Mururoa Atoll to protest against French nuclear testing, was sunk by two bombs placed on it by French agents while it was berthed in Auckland Harbour in New Zealand.

Activity in the United Kingdom was comparatively peaceful, as in the annual Easter weekend marches by CND supporters from London to Aldermaston, which began in 1958. In February 1961 some 4,000 protestors besieged the Ministry of Defence in Whitehall, and later in the year 1,300 demonstrators were arrested in Trafalgar Square and 350 more at Holy Loch in Scotland where the US *Poseidon* nuclear submarines were based. In 1980, when the Americans were allowed to store Cruise missiles at the Greenham Common Air Base in Berkshire, a group of women protestors set up a camp on the perimeter which they occupied for nineteen years. Some of the ill-feeling engendered over the years came out when the rejection of the Nirex planning application in 1997 was hailed by Charles Secrett, the Director of Friends of the Earth, with the words: 'This decision makes sense for public safety, the environment and the taxpayer. This is the first time that the nuclear industry has lost a public enquiry in the UK and shows that Friends of the Earth's 25-year campaign against the industry is approaching the final victory. The environmental movement has given the nuclear industry a bloody nose from which it will not recover.'[8]

Most members of the public do not feel as strongly as that, but over the years there has been an alarming decline in their readiness to accept what any expert says on almost any issue. A recent poll showed only 44 per cent of the British public have a 'great deal' or a 'fair amount' of confidence in what government

The CND march to Aldermaston in March 1958. (CND)

scientists say, whereas the figure for scientists speaking on behalf of environmental groups is 83 per cent. There is, then, some sense of disillusionment around; a general increase in the awareness and importance of environmental issues; a breakdown of trust between the public and the experts; and numerous headaches for governments. The situation is highlighted, where radiation is concerned, by the element of fear which creeps in when you can't see it, hear it, smell it or feel it, yet you know it can kill you. It may be much more difficult to change such public perceptions than to solve any number of technical problems.

CHAPTER 17

What Next?

In the thirty-five years between the opening of the power station at Calder Hall in 1960 and that at Sizewell B in 1995, the amount of electricity generated in the United Kingdom by nuclear energy rose from 0 to 27 per cent. Since 1995, however, no new nuclear stations have been built so that, on the present programme of station closures, the 27 per cent figure will decline to around 5 by 2025 and to 0 by 2040. If some of the reactors last longer than expected, that time scale will be extended somewhat, but all the time the demand for electricity will be increasing annually unless there is an economic depression. The increase in demand may well be 25 per cent in the next twenty years for the United Kingdom and western Europe, and for the world as a whole 40 per cent by 2020, 200 per cent by 2050 and 500 per cent by 2100.

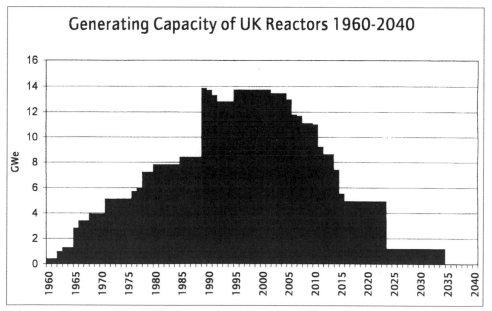

The generating capacity of UK Nuclear Reactors, 1960–2040. (BNFL)

Such assessments involve many imponderables and looking into the future has something of picking the winner of a horse race about it. Past experience, too, shows how wrong predictions can be and so-called experts have consistently misjudged, for example, the price and the availability of oil. So it is necessary to take all forward-looking estimates with a pinch of salt. Nevertheless, some early decisions will have to be taken as to how the gap in electricity generation which might develop can best be filled, and the recent power cuts and black-outs in California highlight the problems that might arise.

The traditional fuels for power stations have been the fossil-fuels such as coal, crude oil and natural gas, which formed over a period of many years from the fossilised remains of plants that lived millions of years ago. Globally, they still account for 85 per cent of the energy used. In the United Kingdom coal dominated until 1994 and still contributes almost 30 per cent, though much of it is now imported from the USA, Columbia and South Africa. As coal declined it was replaced by oil and natural gas, with the latter eventually becoming the preferred option, both because it was cheapest and because it produced less carbon dioxide than coal or oil. This led to what became known as a 'dash for gas', and in an effort to maintain a good balance the government placed a moratorium on the building of new gas-fired power stations between 1998 and 2000. It does, however, still produce just over 40 per cent of the country's electricity.

All three fossil-fuels suffer from the same two disadvantages. First, they are not clean fuels because burning them has a deleterious effect on the environment caused by the production of carbon dioxide, which is the main cause of the greenhouse effect, and sulphur dioxide, which causes acid rain. To use them, then, would run counter to the government's policy of meeting the requirements of the Kyoto Protocol, agreed in December 1997, by achieving a 20 per cent cut in carbon dioxide emissions by the year 2010. Secondly, because the fuels cannot be quickly replaced once they are consumed, they are becoming increasingly scarce so that they are classified as non-renewable. In due course they will run out, but it is estimated that, on the existing rate of use, the global reserves will last 40 years for oil, 100 for gas and 200 for coal.

The problems associated with using fossil-fuels have been recognised for some time and there has been an ongoing, if somewhat half-hearted, search to find renewable energy sources which might replace them. This has involved an investigation of both old and new technologies and the possible use of wind power, water power, solar power, biomass, fuel cells and geothermal energy. It is easy enough to see what enormous supplies of energy lie in some of these resources, even though those which rely on the weather would be unreliable, but it is another

The UK's first offshore wind farm was built off the Northumberland coast at Blyth and opened in December 2000. The blades are 66m in diameter and operate at wind speeds between 4 and 25 metres per second, producing 2 megawatts of electricity. (AMEC Border Wind)

matter to harness the energy at an economic cost. It is tantalising, too, that the use of most of this energy would be very environmentally friendly, so if any of it can be brought into practical use, at an economic cost, it will be an ideal solution.

But it is a big IF. Had the same amount of money been put into developing renewable sources, fifty years ago, as the £1,200 million originally used to support nuclear power, the situation would be very different, but that is not what happened so present-day efforts to redress the balance are distinctly belated. Nevertheless, the British government's policy 'to ensure secure, diverse and sustainable supplies of energy at competitive prices' strongly supports the development of renewable energy sources. To help in that, the Electricity Act of 1989 empowers the Secretary of State to require, by order, that public electricity suppliers in England and Wales generate a specified amount of electricity from non-fossil fuels. The costs of complying with what is called the Non-Fossil Obligation (Noffo) can be covered by increased charges to customers, and an annual subsidy is paid.

Moreover, the World Bank, the Global Environmental Facility and the International Finance Corporation are backing schemes to promote the greater use of renewable energy in developing countries; the European Commission is investing 165 billion ECU; Shell International Renewables, a new subsidiary company, has a five-year, US$500 million development programme; and the World Energy Council estimates a total investment of between £150 and £400 billion between 2000 and 2010. All that might sound generous but the money available has to be spread over a number of different technologies and substituting the old with the new is always difficult.

Nor is it easy to decide where the best opportunities for research lie, particularly as they vary from country to country. The four most fruitful areas would seem to be wind energy, solar energy, biomass and fuel cells. The energy available from the wind-turbine generators at present sited on land could increase enormously as it becomes possible to site them off-shore. Photovoltaic cells, in which light energy falling on to crystalline silicon is converted directly into electricity, are mainly used at present in special situations such as calculators, watches, burglar alarms, parking meters and spacecraft, but a few larger scale schemes in which they are used for heating buildings have been started. They might become much more common as the price of the cells drops, and the European Commission plans to have 1 million roofs covered by PV cells by 2010. There is also plenty of scope for an increase in the use of so-called biomass, made up of organic non-fossil material such as wood, dung, straw and agricultural or domestic waste. At present biomass contributes about 14 per

The solar power installation on the roof of the Zetec-SE engine plant at the Ford factory in Bridgend. There are twenty-six solar units, each 9m long and 4–5m wide, and containing 1,540 photovoltaic cells. The panels cover 25,000 sq. m of the roof space and provide electricity for all the lighting requirements of the building below. (Ford Motor Company Ltd)

cent of global energy with most of it being used in developing countries. Africa, for example, uses 60 per cent whereas in Europe it is only 3 per cent. Both figures should rise, particularly if genetic modification of plants increases the amount of biomass already grown and enables it to flourish on hitherto unfertile land. And fuel cells provide exciting possibilities. In a hydrogen cell, for example, hydrogen and oxygen are combined to form water in such a way that the energy released is produced as electricity. Shell Hydrogen, formed in 1999, is one of a number of companies actively engaged in this field with an immediate aim of making a viable motor car driven by hydrogen fuel cells. Because the only product formed in the cells is water, their use is very environmentally friendly.

In the United Kingdom it was originally hoped to increase the amount of electricity obtained from renewable sources of energy from the 1997 level of 2 per cent to 5 per cent by 2003 and 10 per cent by 2010. By August 2001, however, it had become clear that the 2003 target was not achievable, mainly because of the difficulty in getting local planning permission for new wind farms, so it was lowered to 3 per cent. The 2010 figure was held, optimistically, at 10 per cent, and the government announced an additional £100 million investment in May 2001. The European Commission is also proposing to double its contribution from renewables to 12 per cent by 2010, and there are even greater possibilities globally, particularly in countries where land is more readily available. New hydroelectric schemes, for example, are under construction in China and the former Soviet Union. Overall, then, it is not unreasonable to assume that, if all goes well, something like 40 per cent of the world's energy could come from renewable sources by the year 2050.

But if, in the end, none of the new renewables proves to be widely successful, and if fossil-fuels are ruled out of future use on environmental grounds, then consideration will have to be given to a return to nuclear energy. A House of Commons Trade and Industry Committee foresaw that possibility in 1998 when it recommended that 'a formal presumption be made now, for the purpose of long-term planning, that nuclear plant may be required in the course of the next two decades'.[1] That viewpoint was endorsed in 1999 when a joint Royal Society and Royal Academy of Engineering committee pointed out that it took at least eight years to build a new nuclear power station and recommended that 'the timetable for such considerations should allow a decision to be taken early enough to enable nuclear [power] to play its full, long-term role in national energy policy. This is likely to mean early in the next administration if a damaging decline in the role of nuclear [power] is to be avoided.'[2]

To plan the way forward, in Britain, the Prime Minister, Mr Blair, asked the Cabinet Office Performance and Innovation Unit (PIU), in June 2001, to review energy policy in the UK, and this has been done by a 45-strong team under the sponsorship of Brian Wilson MP. A total of 558 submissions from a wide variety of firms, organisations and individuals was considered and a 218-page-long report was issued in February 2002. The report is not a statement of government policy – that will come later in 2002 in the form of a White Paper – but it does, nevertheless, point the likely way ahead.

The report emphasises the importance of meeting the Kyoto agreements and suggests that this can best be done by making a serious attempt to increase the use of renewable energy, particularly wind energy, and a target of 20 per cent of electricity coming from renewable sources by 2020 is laid down. If this can be achieved it will fill much of the energy gap that will build up as nuclear power stations close down, and it will herald the dawn of a new age. To kick-start the process, it is proposed to build the world's largest wind farm near Stornoway on the Hebridean island of Lewis. It will house 300 wind turbines and generate about 600 MW of electricity, which is about half that of a large nuclear power station. Details of location, building, operation, maintenance and cost are being investigated, mainly by AMEC and British Energy. Money is also being provided, on a large scale, for research and development of all types of renewable energy. This is justified on the grounds that 'they are nascent industries needing support if they are to fulfil their potential'.[3] The nuclear option will be kept open, but 'there is no current case for further government support and the decision whether to bring forward proposals for new nuclear build is a matter for the private sector'.[4] To that end, British Energy and BNFL have recently set up a joint research group to look into the possibilities of using Westinghouse AP 1000 or CANDU reactors in any future programme.

Other proposals in the report include new targets to improve the efficiency of energy usage by 20 per cent between 2002 and 2010, and a further 20 per cent in the following decade; frequent reviews to monitor progress with a particularly thorough one in 2007; improvements in planning procedures; increased reliance on importing energy from countries such as Russia, Norway and the Middle East; and the establishment of a new Sustainable Energy Policy Unit to improve liaison between different departments.

The present report claims that 'this review will be the start of a debate rather than its conclusion'[5] but it admits that 'a change in direction will be difficult to achieve and . . . would require considerable clarity of purpose in all parts of government'.[6] That will certainly be required when it comes to converting the general ideas discussed in the present report into hard and fast government policy in the forthcoming White Paper, because there are still many difficult questions to be answered.

APPENDIX I
The Uranium (above) and Actinium (below) Decay Series

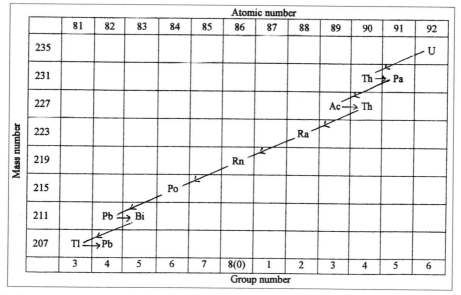

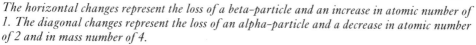

The horizontal changes represent the loss of a beta-particle and an increase in atomic number of 1. The diagonal changes represent the loss of an alpha-particle and a decrease in atomic number of 2 and in mass number of 4.

APPENDIX II
Einstein's Letter to President Roosevelt

Albert Einstein
Old Grove Rd.
Nassau Point
Peconic, Long Island

August 2nd, 1939

F.D. Roosevelt,
President of the United States,
White House
Washington, D.C.

Sir:

Some recent work by E.Fermi and L. Szilard, which has been communicated to me in manuscript, leads me to expect that the element uranium may be turned into a new and important source of energy in the immediate future. Certain aspects of the situation which has arisen seem to call for watchfulness and, if necessary, quick action on the part of the Administration. I believe therefore that it is my duty to bring to your attention the following facts and recommendations:

In the course of the last four months it has been made probable - through the work of Joliot in France as well as Fermi and Szilard in America - that it may become possible to set up a nuclear chain reaction in a large mass of uranium, by which vast amounts of power and large quantities of new radium-like elements would be generated. Now it appears almost certain that this could be achieved in the immediate future.

This new phenomenon would also lead to the construction of bombs, and it is conceivable - though much less certain - that extremely powerful bombs of a new type may thus be constructed. A single bomb of this type, carried by boat and exploded in a port, might very well destroy the whole port together with some of the surrounding territory. However, such bombs might very well prove to be too heavy for transportation by air.

The United States has only very poor ores of uranium in moderate quantities. There is some good ore in Canada and the former Czechoslovakia while the most important source of uranium is Belgian Congo.

In view of this situation you may think it desirable to have some permanent contact maintained between the Administration and the group of physicists working on chain reactions in America. One possible way of achieving this might be for you to entrust with this task a person who has your confidence and who could perhaps serve in an inofficial capacity. His task might comprise the following:

a) to approach Government Departments, keep them informed of the further development, and put forward recommendations for Government action giving particular attention to the problem of securing a supply of uranium ore for the United States;

b) to speed up the experimental work,which is at present being carried on within the limits of the budgets of University laboratories, by providing funds, if such funds be required, through his contacts with private persons who are willing to make contributions for this cause, and perhaps also by obtaining the co-operation of industrial laboratories which have the necessary equipment.

I understand that Germany has actually stopped the sale of uranium from the Czechoslovakian mines which she has taken over. That she should have taken such early action might perhaps be understood on the ground that the son of the German Under-Secretary of State, von Weizsäcker, is attached to the Kaiser-Wilhelm-Institut in Berlin where some of the American work on uranium is now being repeated.

Yours very truly,

A. Einstein

(Albert Einstein)

This photograph of Einstein's letter is taken from the President's Secretary's Files (PSF) Safe Files: State Department, 1939. (Franklin D. Roosevelt Digital Archives)

APPENDIX III
World Nuclear Reactors

This table shows the number of reactors in different countries in 2001, together with their electricity production in TWh (Terawatt-hours or billion kilowatt hours) and as a percentage of their total electricity production.

Country	Nuclear Electricity Produced		Number of Reactors		
	% of total	TWh	Operating	Building	Planned
France	76	395	59	0	0
Lithuania	74	8.4	2	0	0
Belgium	57	45	7	0	0
Bulgaria	45	18	6	0	0
Slovak Rep.	53	16	6	2	0
Sweden	39	55	11	0	0
Ukraine	47	72	13	2	0
South Korea	41	104	16	4	8
Hungary	42	15	4	0	0
Slovenia	37	4.5	1	0	0
Armenia	33	1.8	1	0	0
Switzerland	36	24	5	0	0
Japan	34	305	54	3	12
Finland	32	21	4	0	1
Germany	31	160	19	0	0
Spain	31	56.5	9	0	0
United Kingdom	22	78	33	0	0
Taiwan	24	37	6	1	0
Czech Republic	19	14	5	1	0
USA	20	754	104	0	0
Russia	15	120	30	3	2
Canada	12	69	14	6	0

Country	Nuclear Electricity Produced		Number of Reactors		
	% of total	TWh	Operating	Building	Planned
Romania	11	5.1	1	1	0
Argentina	7.3	5.7	2	1	0
South Africa	6.7	13	2	0	0
Mexico	3.9	7.9	2	0	0
Netherlands	4	3.7	1	0	0
India	3.1	14	14	2	4
China	1.2	16	3	8	2
Brazil	1.5	5.6	2	0	0
Pakistan	1.7	1.1	2	0	0
Iran	0	0	0	1	0
North Korea	0	0	0	0	2

APPENDIX IV
Enriching Uranium

Normal uranium contains 0.7 per cent of the uranium-235 isotope, and increasing this value is known as enriching the uranium. This has been done, commercially, at Capenhurst, near Chester, since 1951 on what was a Royal Ordnance factory site during the Second World War. The original method involved gaseous diffusion and depended on the fact that when a gas containing a mixture of two isotopes is allowed to pass through a porous partition, the lighter isotope passes through more rapidly than the heavier one. A single-stage diffusion through one partition gives only a very partial separation but more complete separation can be achieved by using several stages in a cascade arrangement. The lighter gas passing through a porous partition is taken on to the next stage, while the heavier gas which has not diffused is returned to an earlier stage for recirculation.

There are not many gaseous compounds of uranium but uranium hexafluoride, UF_6, which is a white solid at room temperature, turns into a gas when it is warmed slightly. It was made at Springfields from uranium ores and then transported to Capenhurst in strong containers for enrichment by gaseous diffusion. When the uranium-235 hexafluoride content had reached the required level of around 3 per cent, the product was returned to Springfields for reconversion into enriched uranium fuel. The operations were carried out originally by UKAEA and from 1971 by BNFL.

At that time an agreement had been reached between the British, Dutch and German governments to collaborate on a different method of isotope separation which involved a gas centrifuge. In

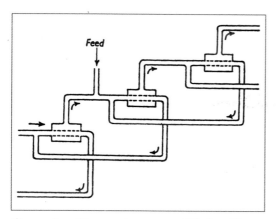

Separation of isotopes by gaseous diffusion. The dotted lines represent porous partitions. The lighter fraction, which passes more quickly through a partition, is passed to the right. The heavier fraction is returned, for recycling, to the left. Pumps are used to maintain circulation, and several thousand stages may be required to give a good separation.

this method the mixture of lighter and heavier gases in uranium hexafluoride is rotated in a high-speed centrifuge and this causes the heavier gas molecules to move to the outer wall. Consequently the gas close to the wall is depleted in uranium-235 while that close to the rotor axis is enriched. By controlling the temperature along the length of the centrifuge, it is possible to induce a flow of gas such that the depleted gas rises and enriched gas falls. This enables the depleted gas to be drawn off from the top and the enriched gas from the bottom of the centrifuge. The enrichment achieved in a single centrifuge is not very high so a number of them have to be arranged in cascade as in gaseous diffusion. When a suitable degree of enrichment has been obtained, the uranium hexafluoride is returned to Springfields for conversion to enriched uranium.

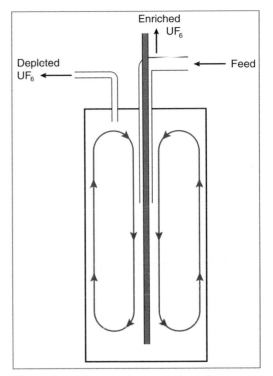

Separation of isotopes in a centrifuge. The diagram shows a single unit. In practice, a number of such units are operated in parallel, and linked in series in a cascade.

The first gas centrifuge plant at Capenhurst began operating in 1976 and ran until 1991, with the older gaseous diffusion plant being shut down in 1982. Since then three newer gas centrifuge plants have been brought into use, and there are similar plants at Gronau in north-west Germany and at Almelo in the Netherlands. They are owned by Urenco Ltd, a joint British-German-Dutch organisation of which Urenco (Capenhurst) is a fully owned subsidiary with BNFL holding the major share.

Notes

Chapter 1

1. E. Farber, *Great Chemists*, p. 278.
2. Thomas Thompson, *The History of Chemistry*, vol. 2 (1831), pp. 197–8.
3. Mary Elvira Weekes, 'Discovery of the Elements' (*Journal of Chemical Education*, 1945), p. 133.
4. Walter J. Moore, *Physical Chemistry*, p. 423.
5. Helge Kragh, *Quantum Generations: A History of Physics in the Twentieth Century*, p. 27.
6. *Science*, vol. 31, no. 786, 21 January 1910, p. 103.
7. H.A. Boorse, L. Motz and J.H. Weaver, *The Atomic Scientists. A Biographical History*, p. 95.

Chapter 2

1. David L. Anderson, *The Discovery of the Electron* (D. Van Nostrand Company, 1964), p. 56.
2. R.C. Weber, *Nobel Prize Winners in Physics* (Bristol Institute of Physics, *c*. 1980), p. 7.
3. G.W.C. Kaye, *X-rays: An Introduction to the Study of Röntgen Rays* (Longmans Green, London, 1914), p. 218.
4. Weber, *Nobel Prize Winners in Physics*, p. 9.
5. H. Poincaré, 'Les rayons cathodiques et les rayons Röntgen' (*Revue Générale des sciences pures et appliqués*, 1896, 7, 52–9).
6. Boorse, Motz and Weaver, *The Atomic Scientists*, p. 107.
7. A.K. Solomon, *Why Smash Atoms?*, p. 23.
8. J.J. Thomson, *Recollections and Reflections*, p. 98.
9. *G.P. Thomson papers, A1 f16* (manuscript autobiography, Trinity College Library).
10. F.W. Aston, 'Obituary of Thomson' (*The Times*, 4 September 1940).
11. W.L. Bragg, *Nature*, 14 September 1940, vol. 146, p. 354.
12. Ibid, p. 355.
13. Boorse, Motz and Weaver, *The Atomic Scientists*, p. 109.

Chapter 3

1. *Journal of Chemical Education*, February 1930, vol. 7, no. 2, p. 225.
2. Moore, *Physical Chemistry*, p. 431.
3. Weekes, 'Discovery of the Elements', p. 486.
4. Eve Curie, *Madame Curie*, p. 69.
5. Ibid, p. 82.
6. Ibid, pp. 120–1.
7. A.S. Russell, *Madame Curie Memorial Lecture* (Before the Chemical Society, Royal Institution, 28 February 1935).
8. *Journal of Chemical Education*, July 1988, vol. 65, no. 7, p. 561.
9. Jack Meadows (ed.), *Marie Curie. Her Life, Work and Times* (Equinox, Oxford, 1987), p. 200.
10. Eve Curie, *Madame Curie*, p. 162.
11. Alfred Romer, *The Science of Radioactivity, 1896–1913* (Dover Publications, New York, 1964), p. 105.
12. Eve Curie, *Madame Curie*, p. 165.

13. Ibid, p. 170.
14. Farber, *Great Chemists*, p. 1274.
15. Mme Curie, *Pierre Curie* (Macmillan Co., New York, 1926), pp. 24–6.
16. Eve Curie, *Madame Curie*, p. 218.
17. Ibid, p. 212.
18. Ibid, p. 187.
19. Ibid, p. 205.
20. Ibid, p. 219.
21. Ibid.
22. Ibid, p. 253.
23. Ibid, p. 374.
24. J.G. Crowther, *Six Great Scientists* (Hamish Hamilton, 1955), p. 220.

Chapter 4

1. Boorse, Motz and Weaver, *The Atomic Scientists*, p. 120.
2. *Nature*, October 1937, p. 746.
3. Sir Henry Tizard, *The Rutherford Memorial Lecture* (Chemical Society Meeting, 29 March 1935), p. 181.
4. P.B. Moon, *Ernest Rutherford and the Atom*, p. 23.
5. A.S. Eve, *Rutherford*, p. 57.
6. Moore, *Physical Chemistry*, p. 438.
7. W. Crookes, 'Radioactivity of Uranium' (*Chemical News*, vol. 81, 1 June 1900), pp. 253–5.
8. E. Rutherford, 'The Cause and Nature of Radioactivity' (*Philosophical Magazine*, 6th Series, vol. iv, 1902), p. 395.
9. Sir Henry Tizard, *The Rutherford Memorial Lecture* (Chemical Society Meeting in the Royal Institute, 29 March 1939), p. 183.
10. Ibid. p. 183.
11. William R. Shea, *Otto Hahn and the Rise of Nuclear Physics*, p. 4.
12. Moore, *Physical Chemistry*, p. 437.
13. Abraham Pais, *Inward Bound: Of Matter and Forces in the Physical World* (Clarendon Press, Oxford, 1986), p. 62.

14. Moore, *Physical Chemistry*, p. 438.

Chapter 5

1. Boorse, Motz and Weaver, *The Atomic Scientists*, p. 177.
2. Rutherford's Presidential Address to British Association Meeting in Winnipeg, 1909.
3. Eve, *Rutherford*, p. 384.
4. Isaac Newton, *Optics* (Bk III, *Works*, 1782, iv), p. 260.
5. J.J. Thomson, Lecture on the Structure of the Atom, at the Royal Institution, 10 March 1905), p. 1.
6. E.A. Davis and I.J. Falconer, *J.J. Thomson and the Discovery of the Electron*, p. 195.
7. Moore, *Physical Chemistry*, p. 444.
8. E.J. Holmyard, *Makers of Chemistry* (Oxford University Press, Oxford, 1931), p. 273.
9. Boorse, Motz and Weaver, *The Atomic Scientists*, p. 188.
10. C.P. Snow, *The Physicists* (Little, Brown, 1981), p. 38.

Chapter 6

1. F. Soddy, *Nobel Lecture on the Origin of the Concept of Isotopes*, 1921.
2. George B. Kauffman, *Frederick Soddy (1877–1956). Early Pioneer in Radiochemistry*, p. 168.
3. Ibid, p. 164.
4. F. Soddy, *Science and Life* (Aberdeen Address, London, 1926), p. 6.
5. F. Soddy, *The British Journal for the History of Science*, vol. 12, no. 42, 1979, p. 261.
6. *Nature*, 23 November 1957, p. 1087.

Chapter 7

1. Boorse, Motz and Weaver, *The Atomic Scientists*, p. 104.
2. Roger H. Stuewer, *Rutherford's Satellite Model of the Nucleus* (Studies in the

History and Philosophy of Science, 1986, 16), p. 322.

3. Gordon Squires, *Selected Apparatus in the Cavendish Laboratory* (Cavendish Laboratory, 1988), p. 8.

4. Roy Porter (ed.), *Hutchinson Dictionary of Scientific Biography* (Helicon Publishing Ltd, 1994), p. 728.

5. Alwyn McKay, *The Making of the Atomic Age*, p. 17.

6. Gerald Holton, *The Scientific Imagination. Case Studies*, p. 165.

7. Ibid, p. 170.

8. Ibid, p. 155.

9. Eve, *Rutherford*, p. 342.

10. *Nature*, 30 October 1937, p. 751.

Chapter 8

1. Lawrence Badash, *Radioactivity in America*, pp. 148-9.

2. James Hutton, 'Theory of the Earth' (*Transactions of the Royal Society of Edinburgh, vol. I, 1788*), p. 304.

3. Arthur Holmes, *Radioactivity and Geological Time* (United States National Research Council, Bulletin 80, 1931), p. 454.

Chapter 9

1. F. Soddy, *Atomic Transmutation* (New World, 1953), p. 95.

2. George B. Kauffman, *Frederick Soddy (1877–1956)*, p. 182.

3. Eve, *Rutherford*, p. 102.

4. Ibid.

5. Soddy, *Atomic Transmutation*, p. 95.

6. McKay, *The Making of the Atomic Age*, p. 31.

7. Otto Frisch, 'Lise Meitner: Nuclear Pioneer' (*New Scientist*, 9 November 1978), p. 426.

8. McKay, *The Making of the Atomic Age*, p. 26.

9. R. Jungk, *Brighter Than A Thousand Suns*, p. 71.

10. McKay, *The Making of the Atomic Age*, p. 29.

11. Margaret Gowing, *Britain and Atomic Energy 1939–1945*, p. 444.

12. David Wilson, *Rutherford* (MIT Press, 1983), p. 55.

13. Otto Frisch, *What Little I Remember*, p. 126.

14. Gowing, *Britain and Atomic Energy 1939–1945*, p. 392.

15. Ronald M. Clark, *The Greatest Power on Earth* (Harper & Row, 1965), p. 214.

16. Ibid, p. 218.

17. Ronald W. Clark, *Tizard*, p. 298.

18. Gowing, *Britain and Atomic Energy 1939–1945*, p. 407.

19. Winston S. Churchill, *The Second World War, Vol. III, The Grand Alliance* (Cassell & Co. Ltd), p. 730.

20. Gowing, *Britain and Atomic Energy 1939–1945*, p. 111.

21. Ibid, p. 39.

Chapter 10

1. Richard Rhodes, *The Making of the Atomic Bomb*, p. 317.

2. Ibid, p. 226.

3. Mark Oliphant, 'The Beginning: Chadwick and the Neutron' (*Bulletin of Atomic Science, 1982*), p. 17.

4. Third NAS Report by the Academy Committee on Uranium, 6 November 1941. Bush-Conant File, f.18, p. 3.

5. S.R. Weart and G.W. Szilard (eds), *Selected Recollections and Correspondence of L. Szilard* (Cambridge, MIT Press, 1972), p. 146.

6. P. Goodchild, *J. Robert Oppenheimer*, p. 56.

7. Nuel Pharr Davis, *Lawrence and Oppenheimer* (Simon & Schuster, 1968), p. 163.

8. McKay, *The Making of the Atomic Age*, p. 92.
9. Goodchild, *J. Robert Oppenheimer*, p. 69.
10. McKay, *The Making of the Atomic Age*, p. 93.
11. Ibid, p. 167.
12. Hans G. Greatzer and David L. Anderson, *The Discovery of Nuclear Fission* (Van Nostrand Reinhold, 1971), pp. 108–9.
13. Goodchild, *J. Robert Oppenheimer*, p. 162.
14. Leslie R. Groves, *Now It Can Be Told*, p. 398.

Chapter 11

1. McKay, *The Making of the Atomic Age*, p. 118.
2. Harry S. Truman, *Year of Decision* (Doubleday, 1955), p. 421.
3. Richard Rhodes, *The Making of the Atomic Bomb*, p. 735.
4. Groves, *Now It Can Be Told*, p. 415.
5. Frisch, *What Little I Remember*, p. 176.
6. Rudolf E. Peicrls, *Atomic Histories*, p. 203.
7. Alfred F. Hurley and Robert C. Ehrhart, *Air Power and Warfare* (Office of Air Force History, 1979), pp. 200–1.
8. Richard Rhodes, *Dark Sun*, p. 205.
9. McKay, *The Making of the Atomic Age*, p. 119.
10. Jungk, *Brighter Than A Thousand Suns*, p. 202.
11. Richard Rhodes, *The Making of the Atomic Bomb*, p. 777.
12. Richard Rhodes, *Dark Sun*, p. 541.
13. Jungk, *Brighter Than A Thousand Suns*, p. 280.
14. Nikita Krushchev, Speech to the Rumanian Party Congress, 1961.
15. Lewis L. Strauss, *Men and Decisions* (New York, Doubleday, 1961), p. 258.
16. David E. Lilienthal, *The Journals of David E. Lilienthal* (Harper & Row, 1964), p. 190.
17. Lorna Arnold, *Windscale 1957*, p. xxi.
18. *Harwell*, pp. 9–10.
19. Ibid, p. 10.
20. David Holloway, *Stalin and the Bomb* (Yale University Press, 1994), p. 29.
21. Jungk, *Brighter Than A Thousand Suns*, p. 237.

Chapter 12

1. Dwight D. Eisenhower, Speech to the 470th Plenary Meeting of the United Nations General Assembly, 8 December 1953.
2. Terence Price, *Political Electricity*, p. 49.
3. Fred Lee, Sunday Times Nuclear Power supplement, 5 February 1995, p. 3.
4. Price, *Political Electricity*, p. 314.
5. Leading article, *The Times*, 16 September 2000.
6. Price, *Political Electricity*, p. 134.
7. Lord Marshall, Address to the World Association of Nuclear Operators, 30 November 1989.

Chapter 15

1. Arnold, *Windscale 1957*, p. 141.
2. National Radiological Protection Board, Information Sheet, 10 October 1997.
3. Arnold, *Windscale 1957*, p. 44.
4. *The Penney Report on the Accident at Windscale on 10 October 1957*, ch. III, pp. 32, 33.
5. Ibid, ch. VII, p. 100.
6. Richard F. Mould, *Chernobyl*, p. 162.
7. Price, *Political Electricity*, p. 288.

Chapter 16

1. Price, *Political Electricity*, p. 53.
2. *The Times*, 4 October 2001, p. 16.

3. Ibid, p. 16.
4. *Third Report on the Management of Nuclear Waste, 1998–9*, Select Committee on Science and Technology, p. 63.
5 Ibid, p. 66.
6. Ibid, p. 69.
7. Frisch, *What Little I Remember*, p. 139.
8. Friends of the Earth Press Release, 23 August 2000.

Chapter 17

1. *Nuclear Energy and the Future Climate* (The Royal Society and the Royal Academy of Engineering, June 1999), p. vii.
2. Ibid, p. 49.
3. *The Energy Review*, p. 124.
4. Ibid, p. 11.
5. Ibid, p. 160.
6. Ibid.

Bibliography

Andrade, E.N. da C., *An Approach to Modern Physics* (G. Bell & Sons Ltd, 1956)

Arnold, Lorna, *Windscale, 1957. Anatomy of a Nuclear Accident* (Gill & Macmillan, 1992)

Badash, Lawrence, *Radioactivity in America. Growth and Decay of a Science* (John Hopkins University Library, 1979)

Blowers, Andrew, et al., *International Politics of Nuclear Waste* (MacMillan)

Bomford, C.K., Sherriff, S.B. and Kunkler, I.H. (eds), *Walter and Miller's Textbook of Radiotherapy. Radiation Physics, Therapy and Oncology* (Churchill Livingstone, 1993)

Boorse, Henry A., Motz, Lloyd and Weaver, J.H., *The Atomic Scientists. A Biographical History* (John Wiley & Sons Inc., 1989)

Brown, G.I., *Introduction to Physical Chemistry* (Longmans, 1964)

Brown, G.I., *The Big Bang. A History of Explosives* (Sutton Publishing, 1998)

Burchfield, Joe D., *Lord Kelvin and the Age of the Earth* (Macmillan, 1975)

Campbell, John, *Rutherford: Scientist Supreme* (AAS Publications, New Zealand, 1999)

Carter, April, *Peace Movements* (Longman, 1992)

Choppin, Gregory, *Nuclei and Radioactivity* (W.A. Benjamin Inc., 1964)

Clark, Ronald W., *Tizard* (Methuen & Co., 1965)

Clark, Ronald W., *The Birth of the Bomb* (Phoenix House, 1961)

Curie, Eve, *Madame Curie* (William Heinemann Ltd, 1942)

Davis, E.A. and Falconer, I.J., *J.J. Thomson and the Discovery of the Electron* (Taylor & Francis, 1997)

Evans, Iver B.N., *Man of Power, The Life Story of Baron Rutherford of Nelson* (Scientific Book Club)

Eve, A.S., *Rutherford* (Macmillan, 1939)

Feather, Norman, *Lord Rutherford* (Priory Press, 1940)

Frisch, Otto, *What Little I Remember* (Cambridge University Press, 1979)

Goodchild, P., *J. Robert Oppenheimer* (BBC Publications, London, 1980)

Gowing, Margaret, *Britain and Atomic Energy, 1939–1945* (Macmillan & Co. Ltd, 1964)

Gowing, Margaret, *Independence and Deterrence; Britain and Atomic Energy, 1945–52*, vol. 1: Policy making; vol. 2: Policy Execution (Macmillan & Co. Ltd, 1974)

Groves, Leslie R., *Now It Can Be Told* (Da Capo Press, 1983)

Harris, J.E. (ed.), *Radioactive Waste* (Interdisciplinary Science Reviews, The Institute of Materials, September 1998)

Harwell. The British Atomic Energy Research Establishment (HMSO, London, 1952)

Haynes, Victor and Bojcun, Marko, *The Chernobyl Disaster* (Hogarth Press, 1988)

Holton, Gerald, *The Scientific Imagination: Case Studies* (Cambridge University Press, 1978)

House of Lords Select Committee on Science and Technology, *Management of Nuclear Waste* (London, The Stationery Office, 1999)

Hughes, Donald J., *The Neutron Story* (Heinemann, 1960)

Jay, Kenneth, *Calder Hall. The Story of Britain's First Atomic Power Station* (Methuen & Co., 1956)

Jungk, Robert, *Brighter Than A Thousand Suns* (Penguin, 1960)

Kauffman, George B., *Frederick Soddy (1877–1956). Early Pioneer in Radiochemistry* (D. Reidel Publishing Company, 1986)

Kragh, Helge, *Quantum Generations: A History of Physics in the Twentieth Century* (Princeton University Press, 1999)

Lapp, Ralph E., *The Voyage of The Lucky Dragon* (Penguin Books, 1958)

Libby, Leona M., *The Uranium People* (Crane Russack & Charles Scribner's Sons, New York, 1979)

McKay, Alwyn, *The Making of the Atomic Age* (Oxford University Press, 1984)

Managing Radioactive Waste Safely (DEFRA, September 2001)

Moon, P.B., *Ernest Rutherford and the Atom* (Priory Press Ltd, 1974)

Moore, Walter J., *Physical Chemistry* (Longmans, 1962)

Mosey, David, *Reactor Accidents* (Nuclear Engineering International Special Publications and Butterworth Scientific Ltd, 1990)

Mould, Richard F., *A Century of X-Rays And Radioactivity in Medicine* (Institute of Physics Publishing, 1993)

Mould, Richard F., *Chernobyl, The Real Story* (Pergamon Press, 1988)

Nias, A.H.W., *An Introduction to Radiobiology* (John Wiley & Sons, 1998)

Nuclear Energy; The Future Climate (The Royal Society and the Royal Academy of Engineering, June 1999)

O'Riordan, M.C. (ed.), *Radiation Protection Dosimetry. Becquerel's Legacy; A Century of Radioactivity* (Nuclear Technology Publishing)

Pasachoff, Naomi, *Marie Curie and the Science of Radioactivity* (Oxford University Press, 1996)

Patterson, Walter C., *Nuclear Power* (Penguin Books, 1976)

Peierls, Rudolf E., *Atomic Histories* (American Institute of Physics, 1997)

Price, Terence, *Political Electricity. What future for nuclear energy?* (Oxford University Press, 1990)

Rhodes, Richard, *The Making of the Atomic Bomb* (Simon & Schuster, 1986)

Rhodes, Richard, *Dark Sun. The Making of the Hydrogen Bomb* (Simon & Schuster, 1995)

Romer, Alfred, *The Science of Radioactivity, 1896–1913* (Dover Publications, New York, 1964)

Rowland, John, *The Conquerors. The Atom* (Max Parrish & Co., 1965)

Rutherford, E., *Radioactive Substances and New Radiations* (Cambridge University Press, 1913)

Rutherford, Sir Ernest, Chadwick, James and Ellis C.D., *Radiations from Radioactive Substances* (Cambridge University Press, 1951)

Schonland, Sir Basil, *The Atomists* (Clarendon Press, Oxford, 1968)

Seaborg, Glenn T. and Valens, Evans G., *Elements of the Universe* (Methuen & Co., 1959)

Senior, John E., *Marie and Pierre Curie* (Sutton Publishing, 1998)

Sharp, P.F., Gemmell, H.G. and Smith, F.W. (EDS), *Practical Nuclear Medicine* (Oford University Press, 1998)

Shea, William R. (ed.), *Otto Hahn and the Rise of Nuclear Physics* (D. Reidel Publishing Company, 1983)

Solomon, A.K., *Why Smash Atoms?* (Penguin Books, 1940)

Strathern, Paul, *Curie and Radioactivity* (Arrow, 1998)

Streissguth, Thomas (ed.), *Nuclear and Toxic Waste (At Issue)* (Greenhaven Press, 2001)

The Energy Review. A Cabinet Office Performance and Innovation Unit Report, February 2002

The Royal Society, *Management of Separated Plutonium* (The Royal Society, February 1998)

Thomas A.M.K. (ed.), *The Invisible Light. 100 Years of Medical Radiology* (Blackwell Science, 1995)

Thomson, G.P., *J.J. Thomson and the Cavendish Laboratory in his Day* (Nelson, London, 1964)

Thomson, J.J., *Recollections and Reflections* (Bell, London, 1936)

Trenn, Thaddens J., *The Self-Splitting Atom. The History of the Rutherford-Soddy Collaboration* (Taylor & Francis, 1977)

United Nations Environment Programme, *Radiation: Doses, Effects, Risks* (Blackwell, 1985)

Van der Zwaan, B.C.C. (ed.), *Nuclear Energy. Promise or Peril?* (World Scientific Publishing Co., 1999)

Walker, J. Samuel, *Prompt and Utter Destruction. Truman and the Use of Atomic Bombs Against Japan* (University of North Carolina Press, 1997)

Williams J.R. and Thwaites D.I. (eds), *Radiotherapy physics in practice* (Oxford University Press, 2000)

Wilson, David, *Rutherford* (Hodder & Stoughton, 1983)

World Energy Council, *Energy for Tomorrow's World — Acting Now* (Atalink Projects Ltd, 2000)

SELECTED WEBSITES

Note: Many of these sites, particularly those marked with an asterisk, give good lists of linked sites.

1 Nuclear Place, http://www.1nuclearplace.com

*Abolition2000, http://www.abolition2000.org

ADAC Laboratories, http://www.adaclabs.com

AEA Technology (AEAT), http://www.aeat.co.uk

AMEC Group Ltd, http://www.amec.com

American Institute of Physics, http://www.aip.org/history

American Nuclear Society, http://www.ans.org

Arms Control Association, http://www.armscontrol.org

BP Solar, http://www.bpsolar.com

British Energy, htttp://www.british-energy.com

British Institute of Radiology, http://www.bir.org.uk

British Nuclear Energy Society, http://www.bnes.com

*British Nuclear Fuels Ltd (BNFL), http://www.bnfl.co.uk

British Nuclear Industry Forum, http://www.bnif.co.uk

British Nuclear Medicine Society, http://www.bnms.org.uk

British Wind Energy Association, http://www.britishwindenergy.co.uk

Campaign for Nuclear Disarmament in UK, http://www.cnduk.org

Center for Defense Information, http://www.cdi.org

*Centre for Renewable Energy and Sustainable Technology (CREST), http://www.crest.org

Department for Environment, Food and Rural Affairs, http://www.defra.gov.uk

Department of Trade and Industry,   http://www.dti.gov.uk

Dicon Safety Products (UK) Ltd,   http://www.diconsafety.co.uk

*Energy on the Internet. The University of Sheffield,   http://www.shef.ac.uk/uni/projects/emp

Foratom, http://www.foratom.org

Friends of the Earth,   http://www.foe.co.uk

Future Energy Solutions,   http://www.etsu.com

Greenpeace, http://www.greenpeace.org

HM Inspectorate of Nuclear Installations reports,   http://www.hse.gov.uk

Institut Curie,   http://www.curie.fr

International Atomic Energy Agency,   http://www.iaea.org

International Consultative Group on Food Irradiation (ICGFI),   www.iaea.org/icgfi

*International Physicians for the Prevention of Nuclear War,   http://www.ippnw.org

Isotron plc,   http://www.isotron.co.uk

Lord Rutherford,   http://www.rutherford.org.nz

MDS Nordion,   http://www.mds.nordion.com

National Cancer Institute,   http://www.cancernet.nci.nih.gov

*National Energy Foundation,   http://www.natenergy.org.uk

National Radiological Protection Board,   http://www.nrpb.org.uk

*Nicks xray2000 website,   http://www.xray2000.f9.co.uk

Nirex,   http://www.nirex.co.uk

Nuclear Energy Institute,   http://www.nei.org

Nuclear Industries Directorate,   http://www.dti.gov.uk/nid

Nycomed-Amersham,   http://www.nycomed-amersham.com

*OECD Nuclear Energy Agency,   http://www.nea.fr

Penn State University, Department of Radiology,   http://www.xray.hmc.psu.edu

Piezo Systems, Inc.,   http://www.piezo.com

The PIU Energy Review,   http://www.piu.gov.uk

*Rad Pro Ltd,   http://www.radpro.co.uk

Radioactive Waste Management Advisory Committee,   http://www.defra.gov.uk

Radwaste, http://www.radwaste.org

Royal Dutch Shell,   http://www.shell.com

Science Museum,   http://www.sciencemuseum.org.uk

Trade Partners UK,   http://www.tradepartners.gov.uk/energy

UK Electricity Association,   http://www.electricity.org.uk

* United Kingdom Atomic Energy Authority (UKAEA),   htttp://www.ukaea.org.uk

Uranium Information Centre, Australia,   http://www.uic.com.au

Urenco Ltd,   http://www.urenco.com

US Nuclear Regulatory Commission,   http://www.nrc.gov

World Coal Institute,   http://www.wci-coal.com

World Energy Council,   http://www.worldenergy.org

World Health Organisation,   htttp://www.who.int

*World Nuclear Association, London,   http://www.world-nuclear.org

World Nuclear Transport Institute,   http://www.wnti.co.uk

Index

Abbe, Robert 88
Abelson, P.H. 80, 110, 117
Aberystwyth University 44
Abolition 2000 210
Absorbed dose 154
Academy of Sciences 32
Accidents 174–92
Actinium 45
    Series 49, 221
Adenine 170
Advanced gas-cooled reactor
    147
Advisory committee 110
AEA Technology (AEAT)
    136
AEC 126, 132, 144
AERE 133
After-loading 167
Age of earth 93–5
AGR 147
Akers, W.A. 108, 114
Alamagordo 121
Aldermaston 134, 199, 211
Ailinginae 129
Alpha-particle 42, 61, 62
Alpha-rays 1, 41, 42
Alzheimer's disease 169
Amchitka Island 210
AMEC 215, 219
AmerGen 183
Americium 82
Americium-241 172, 193
Amersham 163

Amersham International
    164
Amertec II 168
Ammonium molybdate 167
Anacostia 117
Anderson, Carl D. 76
Anderson, Sir John 109
Anger, Hal 162
Anode 4
Argonne National Laboratory
    141
Association of Atomic
    Scientists 126, 207
Aston, F.W. 66–8, 110
Atom bombs 119–20, 129
Atomic Energy Research
    Establishment 133
Atomic mass, relative 3, 52,
    56
Atomic number 56
Atomic pile 111–14
Atomic Power Constructions
    147
Attlee, Clement 133
Ausonium 80
Autunite 26
Ayrton, Hertha 35

Babcock and Wilcox 181
Barium meal 86
Barium platinocyanide 9
Barium titanate 20
Battersby, J.C. 86

Beams, Jesse W. 117
Becquerel, A-C 3, 10
    A-E 3, 10
    A-H 3, 10, 88
    J 12
Becquerel, the 153
Belarus 183
Belgian Congo 88, 101
Bémant, Gustave 28
Ben Nevis 71
Benn, Tony 147
BEPO 133, 141
Beria, Leonid 137
Berkeley 80, 143, 206
Berkelium 82
Berlin University 1, 29, 49,
    100
Beryllium 59
Berzelius, J.J. 26, 52
Besnier, Dr 88
Beta-rays 1, 4, 42, 62
Bhagavad-Gita 121
Bikini Atoll 129
Biomass 216
Birkbeck College 98
Birmingham University 66,
    103
Blackett, Patrick 71, 76, 107
Blackwell, Reginald 152
BN Dessel 198
BNFL 135, 219
BNFL Inc. 207
Bohemia 2, 87

Bohr, Aage 58
    Niels 58, 97, 99, 101
Bohrium 83
Boiling Water Reactor 145
Bombardment experiments 54
Bonn University 4
Boot, H.A.H. 103
Boron steel 142
Brachytherapy 89, 165
Bradbury, Norris 126
Bradwell 143
Branly, E. 34
Breast cancer 167
Briggs Committee 111
Briggs, Lyman J. 110
British Association 6, 193
British Energy 183, 219
British Experimental Pile O
    133, 141
British Geological Survey 201
British Nuclear Fuels Ltd 135
British Radioactive Substances
    Act 156
Brize, Judge Raimond 190
Brokdorf 210
Bronchography 86
Brower, David 210
Bruce, Dr Ironside 152
Bush, President George Sr 194
Bush, Vannevar 111
BWR 145

Cadmium 112
Caesium-135 193
    -137 165, 188, 193
Calcium sulphide 90
Calder Hall 140, 213
Calder river 175
California Institute of
    Technology 76, 116
California University 80, 82
Californium 82
Cambridge University 17

Campaign for Nuclear
    Disarmament 209, 211
Campbell Swinton, A.A. 86
Canada 88, 146
Canal rays 65
Canberra University 104
CANDU reactor 146, 174, 219
Canon, W.B. 86
Canterbury College 39
Capenhurst 134, 147
Carbon-11 169
    -14 171
Carlsbad 204
Carnegie Institute 111
Carnotite 26, 88
Carter, President 194
Castle Bravo 129
CAT 161
Cathode 4
Cathode rays 1, 6
Cavendish, Henry 17
Cavendish Laboratory 17, 54,
    64, 69
Cavity magnetron 103
CEA 136, 145
Central Chemical Products
    Co. 87
Central Electricity Generating
    Board 142, 149
Central School of Arts and
    Manufactures 2
Centre de Fabrication de
    Cadarache 198
Centrifugal method 117, 227
CFCa 198
Chadwick, James 59
Chain reaction 99
Chalcolite 26
Chalk river 146, 174
Chapelcross 142
Chazov, Dr Yevgeny I. 209
Chemical News 5
Chernobyl 158, 183–91

Cherwell, Lord 108, 135
Chester College of Science 5
Chicago pile, No. 1 112
Chicago University 82, 128
Chihuahuan desert 204
China Syndrome 180
Chinkolobwe mine 88
Chinon 146
Chromium-51 168
Chromosomes 170
Churchill College 73
Churchill, Winston 123
Clerk Maxwell, James 17
Clinch river 115
Cloud Chamber 70–1
Clusius, Klaus 105
CND 209, 211
Cobalt-57 163
    -60 165, 171
Cockcroft, John 73, 107, 133,
    146
Collective dose 155
Collective effective dose 155
Collège Sévigné 75
Columbia river 115, 141
Columbia University 110, 111,
    127
COMEGA 194
Commissariat à l'Énergie
    Atomique 136, 145
Compton, A.H. 111
Computerised Axial
    Tomography 161
Computerised tomography
    161
Conant, James B. 111
Control rods 112
Coolidge, W.D. 86
Copenhagen University 58
Corbino, Orso Mario 78
Cormack, A. McC. 161
Corpuscles 53
Cosmic rays 155, 172

Cosmotron 75
Cow 168
CP-1 112, 141
    -2 141
Creys–Malville 211
Critical assembly group 118
Critical mass 106
Critical mass organisation 210
Critical size 106, 118
Crookes, Sir William 4, 45
Crookes tubes 6
Cruise missiles 211
Cumbria County Council 203
Curie, Eve 32
    Irène 25, 37, 75, 78
    Marie 19–38
    Paul Jacques 19
    Pierre 19–33, 172
Curie, the 153
Curictherapy 89
Curium 82
Cyclotron 75, 103, 133
Cytosine 170

Daghlian, Harry 118
Dally, Clarence 152
Dalton, John 2, 52
Danlos, Dr 88
Dannenberg 210
Darmstadt 82
Daughter 48
Davenport 157, 200
Davey, H.G. 179
Dead Sea Scrolls 172
Debierne, André 28, 34, 44,
    87
Decay product 48
Decay series 63, 221
Decommissioning 205–7
Decon option 206
de Gaulle, General 136, 146
Degrais, Paul 89
de Klerk, F.W. 138

de Lisle, Armet 89
Department of the
    Environment 156, 203
Department of the
    Environment for
    Northern Ireland 157
DETR 156
Deuterium 68
Deuterium oxide 68
DIDO 206
Direct Action Committee
    209
Directorate of Tube Alloys
    108
'Dirty' bomb 160
Discharge tube 3, 4
Disintegration series 49, 63,
    221
Dluski, Casimir 22
DNA molecules 170
Dnieper river 184
Dorn, F.E. 45
Dounreay 149, 199
Dreadnought, HMS 145, 199
Dresden 124
Drigg 199
Dr Lee's professor 64
Dubna 82
Dubnium 83
Duke of Devonshire 17
Dungarvon 73
Dungeness 147
Dunning, John R. 110
du Pont de Nemours 114

Eastbourne College 44
Eaton, Cyrus S. 209
École de Physique et de
    Chimie 19
École Lavoisier 76
École Polytechnique 10
EdF 145
Edison, Thomas 152

Effective dose 154
Einstein, Albert 38, 97, 101,
    207
    Letter to Roosevelt 222
Einsteinium 82
Eisenhower, President 139,
    180
Eldorado Gold Mine 101
Électricité de France 145
Electrodes 4
Electron 15
    Charge on 15
Electroscope 41
Electrotherapeutics 87
EL-1 145
Elugelab 129
e/m ratio 13
Energy Review 218–19
Enhanced radiation weapon
    131
Eniwetok Atoll 129
Enriched uranium 144, 146,
    148, 226
Environment Agency 157, 159
Equivalent dose 154
ERW 131
ETA 211
European Commission 216,
    218
Excited radioactivity 45
External beam radiotherapy 89

Farnborough 66
Farrell, General T.F. 121
Fast breeder reactor 149
Fat man 119
FBR 149
Federation of Atomic
    Scientists 126
Fermi, Enrico 78–80
    Laura 80
Fermium 82
Fessenheim 146

Fischer, Emil 49
Fission of uranium 96–109
Fluorescence 3
Fluorine-18 169
Flowers, Lord 201
Fonda, Jane 180
Fontenay-aux-Roses 145
Food Standards Agency 157
Ford, President 194
Forestier 86
Forsmark 204
Fort de Chantillon 76
Fort St Vrain 206
Fossil fuels 214
Fowler, R.H. 84
Fractional crystallisation 30–1
Framatome 146
French Atomic Energy
    Commission 76
Freund, Leopold 87
Friends of the Earth 148, 198,
    205, 210
Frisch, Otto 97, 104, 118, 125,
    209
Fuel cells 216
Fukurya Maru 129
Fusion of atoms 129

G-1, G-2, G-3 145
Gallium-67 168
Gamma-radiography 161–2
Gamma-ray camera 163
Gamma-rays 1, 41
Gamow, George 73
Gas centrifuge 226
Gaseous diffusion 117
Gaseous thermal diffusion 117
Geiger, Hans 51, 54, 61
Geiger-Müller Counter 62
Geissler, H. 3
Geissler tube 3, 4
General Electric Co. 86, 144
Genome project 170

George Washington
    University 127
Gesellschaft für
    Schwerioforschung 82
Gimingham, Charles H. 6
Glasgow Royal Infirmary 87
Glasgow University 65
Glasnost 190
GLEEP 133, 141, 206
Global Environmental Facility
    216
Goldstein, Eugen 6, 65
Gold-198 165
Gonville and Caius College 60
Gorbachev, Mikhail 190
Gorleben 210
Gosforth 203
Grand Canyon 210
Graphite 102
Graphite Low Energy
    Experimental Pile 133,
    141, 206
Gray, Harold 154
Gray, the 154
Great Bear Lake 88, 101
Greenham Common 211
Greenpeace 198, 205, 210, 211
Grey, Sir Edward 35
Grohnde 210
Groves, Leslie. R. 114, 125
GSI 82
Guanine 170
Gummer, John 203

Hahn, Otto 48, 80, 97, 126
Half-life 45
Hanford 115, 119, 141
Harborne 66
Harding, President 36
Harrisburg 181
Hartlepool 147
Hartley, Sir Harold 193
Harvard 111

Harwell 104, 133, 163, 199
Heavy hydrogen 68
Heavy water 68, 102
Hedley, W.S. 87
Heisenberg, Werner 102–3,
    126
Helium atom 57, 60, 68
Helium nuclei 61
Herschel, William 2
Hertz, Heinrich 6, 53
Hesperium 80
Hessium 83
Hevesy, George 92
Heysham 147
Higinbotham, Willie 126, 207
High Level Waste (HLW) 193
Hill, A.V. 111
Hinkley Point 147, 148
Hinton, Christopher 133
Hiroshima 96, 123
Hittorf, Wilhelm 4
Hofmann, A.W. 5
Holmes, Arthur 95
Holy Loch 157, 211
Hôpital St Louis 88
Hounsfield, G.N. 161
Hunterston 147
Hutton, James 93
Hydrogen atom 57, 60
Hydrogen bomb 126, 129
Hydrogen-3 68

IAEA 192, 196
ICRP 153
Ilford Co. 8
Imperial Chemical Industries
    108
Imperial College of Science
    94, 134
Implosion method 121
Indium-111 168
Induced radioactivity 45
Institut du Radium 35

Intermediate Level Waste (ILW) 193
International Atomic Energy Agency 192, 196
International Commission on Radiological Protection 153
International Consultative Group on Food Irradiation 171
International Finance Corporation 216
International Nuclear Event Scale 192
International Physicians for the Prevention of Nuclear War 209
Iodine-123 163
-125 165
-128 167
-129 193
-130 193
-131 168, 179, 188, 191
Ion-exchange columns 163, 167
Ionising radiations 153
Iridium-192 162, 165
Iron-59 168
Ishpeming 82
Isotopes 63
non-radioactive 67
of chlorine 67
of hydrogen 67
of neon 65–6
of oxygen 68
of phosphorus 76
of tin 67
of uranium 68
radioactive 65
separation of 66, 106, 226–7
Isotron plc 171
IUPAC 82

Jacob, Joe 198
Jáchymov 1, 28, 87
Japan Nuclear Electric Conversion Co. 191
Joachimsthal 1
Joachimsthalers 2
Joliot-Curie, F. and I. 37, 75–6, 99, 136
'Jolly-Curios' 76
Joly, John 94

Kaisergaust 211
Kaiser-Wilhelm Institute 97
Kalkar 210
Kalle & Company 48
Kanalstrahlen 65
Kapitza, Peter 73, 137
Karlsruhe 210
Karlsruhe Technical College 53
Kay, William 51
Kelvin, Lord 48, 93
Khrushchev, Nikita 131
Kiev 183
Klaproth, M.H. 1
Kobe 124
Koon 130
Korff, Serge 171
Kowarski, Lew 103, 137, 145
Krypton-81m 168
-85 193
Kuboyama, Aiticki 130
Kungälv 98
Kunz, George F. 90
Kurchatov, Igor 82, 137
Kurchatovium 82
Kyoto Protocol 214, 218

Labelling 91
La Hague 194, 210
Langevin, Paul 34–5
Langworthy, Professor 51
Lawrence, Ernest 75, 80, 117

Lawrence Radiation Laboratory 82
Lawrencium 82
Layfield, Sir Frank 148
Lead chromate 92
Lead-210 92
Le Creusot 146
Lee, Fred 147
Legasov, Valerie 190
Le May, Curtis 125
Lemmon, Jack 180
Lemoniz 211
Lennep 10
Lewis 219
Liabilities Management Authority 207
Libby, Willard 171
Lilienthal, David 126, 132
Lindemann, Professor 108
Liquid Metal Fast Breeder Reactor 149
Liquid sodium 144, 149
Liquid thermal diffusion 117
Lithium atoms 57, 60
Lithium deuteride 129
Little Boy 119, 123
Little Curies 35–6
Liverpool University 60
LMA 207
LMFBR 149
Lodge, Oliver 54
London Hospital 85, 152
Longlands Farm 203
Los Alamos 115
Low Level Waste (LLW) 193
Lown, Dr Bernard 209
Lucky Dragon 129
Luminous paint 90, 156
Lycée Lakanal 76
Lyon Jones, Professor 60

MacDonald Sir W. 43
Macintyre, Dr John 87

Magdalen College, Oxford 107
Magnesium-24 163
Magnox 141
Magnox reactors 141, 142
Malvern College 66
Management of Nuclear Waste
    Committee 198
Manchester College of
    Technology 73
Manchester Grammar School
    59
Manchester University 49, 70,
    73
Manhattan Project 114
Mantles 164
Marckwald, W. 29
Marconi, G. 40, 78
Marcoule 145, 198
Marsden, Ernest 54
Marshall, G.C. 112
Marshall Islands 129
Marshall, Lord 149
Martyrs' Memorial 152
Mason College 66
Massachusetts Institute of
    Technology 111, 114,
    167
Mass spectrograph 66
Mass spectrometer 67
MAUD Committee 107–8, 112
Max Planck Institute 92
May-Johnson, Bill 126
McGill, James 43
McGill University 43, 51
McMahon Act 126, 131
McMillan, E. 80, 110
Macmillan, Harold 180
MDS Nordion 170
Meitner, Lise 80, 97
Meitnerium 83
Melox 198
Mendeleev, D.I. 55
Mendeleevium 82

Merton College 44
Methodist College, Belfast 73
Metropolitan Edison 181
Mike 129
Millikan, R. 15
Minnesota University 110
Mitterrand, President
    François 38
Mixed Fuel Oxide 197
Moderation of neutrons 79,
    102
Moderators 102
Molybdenum-99 167
Monte Bello Islands 141
Montreal Laboratory 141, 146
Moon, P.B. 107
Moore, Henry 114
Morton, William 86
MOX 197
Mulberry Harbour 135
Müller, W. 61
Multiplication factor 99
Münster Academy 4
Münster University 26
Mururoa Atoll 211

Nader, Ralph 210
Nagaoka, Hantaro 54
Nagasaki 96, 123
Nagoya 124
National Bureau of Standards
    110
National Radiological
    Protection Board 153,
    157, 177
National Response Plan 159
Natural History Museum,
    Paris 3
Natural Resources Defense
    Council 210
Nautilus, USS 145
NDRC 111
Nectar 130

Neddermeyer, Seth 121
Nelson 39
Nelson College 39
Neon isotopes 65–6
Neptunium 80, 193
Neutron 59
    bombardment 79
    secondary 99
Neutron bomb 131
Nevada 204
New Mexico 115, 121, 204
Newton, Isaac 53
Newton, Mary 40
New Zealand University 39
Nicholson, John W. 54
Nickel-58 163
Nier, Alfred 110
NIMBY 201
Nirex 201
Niton 45
Nitrogen-13 169
Nobelium 82
Noble gases 45, 48
Nogent-sur-Marne 87
Non-fossil Obligation 216
Norwegian Hydro-Electric Co.
    102
NRPB 153, 156
NRX 146, 174
Nuclear Age Peace Foundation
    210
Nuclear Energy sculpture 114
Nuclear Installations Act
    151
Nuclear Installations
    Inspectorate 206
Nuclear medicine 163
Nuclear Power Branch 144
Nuclear reactors 150
Nycomed-Amersham 163

Oak Ridge 115, 141
Obninsk 140

Office of Scientific Research and Development 111
Ohi–cho 211
Okinawa 123
Old Chemistry Department 64
Oliphant, Mark 103–4, 112
Olkiluoto 205
OMDB 201
Omega Canyon 118
Oolen 88
Oppenheimer, Robert 116, 125
Osaka 124, 211
Owens College 17, 70
Owens, R.B. 45
Oxygen-15 169

Palladium-103 165
Paneth, Professor 65, 92
Panthéon, the 38
Parkinson's disease 169
Particle accelerators 73
Paul Scherrer Institute 82
Pauling, Linus 209
PECO Energy 183
Pedoscope 91, 156
Peierls, Rudolf 104, 125
Peligot, E. M. 2
Penney, William 134, 179
Penney report 179
Periodic table 55
Perrin, Jean 54
PET 169
Phosphate fertiliser 92
Phosphorescence 3
Phosphorus, isotopes of 76
Phosphorus-32 92, 168, 170
Photovoltaic cells 216
Pickering 146
Piezoelectric effect 26
Piezoelectricity 20
PIPPA 141
Pisa University 78

Pitchblende 1, 2, 26, 28, 88
PIU 218
Plain tomography 87, 161
Pleochroic haloes 94
Plowden, Edmund 135
Plücker, Julius 4
PLUTO 206
Plutonium 80, 119, 193
  civil 197
  isotopes of 81
  weapons 197
Plutonium oxide 197
Poincaré, Henri 11
Polonium 29
Pompidou, Georges 146
Port Richmond 115
Poseidon 211
Positive rays 65–6
Positron 76, 169
Positron emission tomography 169
Potassium uranium sulphate 3
Potsdam 123
Pressurised water reactor 144, 148
Prince Albert 5
Princeton 99, 177
Pripyat 183
  river 184
Problem areas 193–213
Promethium-147 91
Proton 57
Pugwash conferences 209
Pupin Laboratories 111
PWR 144, 148

Quartz 19
Queen Elizabeth II 140
Queen Marys 119

Radcliffe Observatory 5
Radiant matter 7
Radiation exposures 154–6

Radiation, hazards 152–60
  monitoring 156–60
  uses of 85–96, 161–73
Radioactive decay 45, 48
Radioactive disintegration 48
Radioactive isotopes 163
Radioactive Substances Act 201
Radioactive Waste Management Advisory Committee 203
Radioactivity 25
  artifical 75
  excited 45
  induced 45
Radiocarbon dating 171–2
Radiochemical Centre 164
Radiometric dating 95
Radioimmunoassay 170
Radionuclides 163
  generator 168
Radiopharmaceuticals 168
Radiotellurium 29
Radiotherapy 89, 165
Radiothorium 48
Radio waves 40
Radium 30
  in radiotherapy 89, 165
  pure metal 34
  relative atomic mass of 33–4
Radium bomb 89
Radium chloride 31
Radium emanation 45
Radium Institute 35, 76
Radium Therapy 89
Radon 45, 155
Rainbow Warrior 211
Ramsay, Sir William 48
Randall, James 103
Ray, Maud 107
Rayleigh, Lord 17, 94

RBMK reactors 183
Reale Scuola Normale
    Superior, Pisa 78
Red Eagle, Order of 1
Rehns, Dr 88
Relative atomic mass 3, 52,
    56
Renewable energy 214, 219
Reprocessing 194–6
Rhenium-186 168
Rickover, Hyman G. 144
Riedel, Josef 87
Rimnet 159
Risk assessment 158
Risley 133
Rjukan 102
Rochelle salt 19
Rock characterisation facility
    203
Rollins, William 88
Rome University 78
Rongelap 129
Röntgen Society 86, 152, 153
Röntgen, Bertha 85
    W.C. 8–10
Roosevelt, President 110
Rosyth 157, 200
Rotblat, Professor Joseph
    209
Royal Aircraft Establishment
    66
Royal College of Chemistry 5
Royal Society 6, 218
Royds, Thomas 62
Ruhleben 59
Runt 130
Russell, Bertrand 207
Russell-Einstein Manifesto
    209
Rutherford, Eileen 51
Rutherford, Ernest 39–50, 69
Rutherfordium 82
RWMAC 203

Safstore 206
Salmon, Dr 88
Salmonella 171
Samarium-153 168
Sancellemoz 37
Santa Fe 115
Scattering experiments 54
Sceaux 24, 33, 37
Scintillation camera 163
Schenectady 86
Schmidt, G.C. 26
Schuster, Sir A. 51
Scottish Environment
    Protection Agency
    157
Seaborg, Glen T. 81
Seaborgium 83
Secondary neutrons 99
Secrett, Charles 198, 211
Segrè, Emilio 120
Sellafield 134, 175, 194
SGHW 147
Shell Hydrogen 217
Shell International
    Renewables 216
Shenandoah river 181
Shippingport 145, 206
Shrimp 129
Sickard 86
Sierra Club 210
Sievert, Rolf 154
Sievert, the 154
Silicon crystals 216
Simon, Professor F. 117
Single Photon Emission
    Tomography 168
Sizewell 148, 213
Sklodowska girls 20–1
Slavutich 190
Slotin, Louis 118
Smoke alarms 172
Society for Heavy Ion
    Research 82

Society for Psychical Research
    6
Soddy, F. 44, 63–5, 96
Sodium iodide 163
Sodium, liquid 144, 149
Sodium-22 163
Solar energy 216
Sorbonne 21, 33
South African War 86
Soviet Atomic Energy
    Institute 82
Spent fuel 193
SPET 168
Spinthariscope 61
Springfields 134, 141
Sputnik 180
Stagg Field stadium 112
Stalin, Joseph 78
Staten Island 115
St Bartholomew's Hospital 209
St George's Hospital,
    Hamburg 152
St Petersburg University 55
St Thomas's Hospital 86
Steam Generating Heavy
    Water Reactors 147
Sterilisation 170
Stimson, Henry 112
Stone and Webster 114
Stonehenge 172
Stornoway 219
Strassmann, Fritz 80, 98
Strauss, Lewis L. 130, 132
Strontium-89 168, 193
    -90 172, 193
Strutt, R.J. 94
Suction pumps 3
Sudanese campaign 86
Suffolk, Earl of 103
Sulphur-35 170
Super bomb 127, 128
Synchroton 75
Szilard, Leo 99–101, 125

Technetium-99m 167
Teletherapy 89, 165
Teller, Edward 101, 126
Tennessee Valley Authority
    126
Thallium 5
Thallium-201 168
Thatcher, Mrs 147
Theory of the Earth 93
Thermal diffusion 105
Thermal oxide reprocessing
    plant 195
Thermoluminescent material
    156
Thickness measurement 172
Thomson, G.P. 17, 66, 107
Thomson, J.J. 53, 65, 70
Thomson, William 93
Thorium 26, 45, 46
    -A, B and C 49
    emanation 45
    series 49, 63
    -232 193
    -X 46
Thorium Company 163
Thoron 45
Thorp 195
Three Mile Island 181
Thymine 170
Tizard, Sir Henry 48, 107
TMI-1 and -2 181, 183
Todmorden 73
Tokaimura 191
Tomography 86, 161
Torness 147
Toronto University 44
Tourmaline 19
Tracers 91, 169
Trans-uranium elements 80
Tricaston 146
Trident 138
Trinity College, Cambridge
    17, 68, 103

Trinity College, Dublin 73
Trinity test 121
Tritium 68
Truman, President 123, 125,
    128
Tube Alloys 108
Turin Shroud 172

UKAEA 135, 142
Ukraine 183
Union Minière 88, 101, 115
United Kingdom Atomic
    Energy Authority 135
United Nations General
    Assembly 131, 139
Unnilennium 83
Unnilhexium 83
Unniloctium 83
Unnilpentium 83
Unnilquadrium 83
Unnilseptium 83
Ununbium 83
Ununhexium 83
Ununnilium 83
Ununoctium 83
Ununquadium 83
Unununium 83
UNSCEAR 153
Uranium 2
    atom 57, 60
    isotopes 68
    series 49, 221
    -X 45
Uranium hexafluoride 117, 226
Uranium hydride 118
Uranium oxide 2, 147
Uranium Problem
    Commission 137
Uranium tetrafluoride 141
Uranus 2
Urenco Limited 227
US Atomic Energy
    Commission 82, 126, 172

Utirik 129

van der Graaff 75
VE-Day 122
Vemork 102
Vernadski, Vladimir I. 137
Very low level waste (VLLW)
    193
Veterans' Administration
    Hospital 170
Villard, Paul 45
Virginia University 117
Vitrification 201
von Halban, Hans 103
von Helmholtz, Hermann 93
von Weizsäcker, Carl 102–3,
    126
von Welsbach, Baron 87

Wallace, Henry 112
Walton, Ernest 73
Waste disposal 193–205
Waste Isolation Pilot Plant
    (WIPP) 204
Watson, William 4
Wells, H.G. 96, 101
Wernigerode 1
Westinghouse 144, 219
Westminster School 107
Whyl 210
Wickham, Dr 88
Wien, Wilhelm 65
Wigner effect 177
Wigner energy 177
Wigner, Eugene 177
Wilson, Brian 218
Wilson, C.T.R. 70
Wilson, Ernest 152
Wind energy 216, 220
Windscale 134, 147, 175
Windsor Castle 103
Wind Turbine Generator 216,
    219

Winfrith 147
WIPP 204
WISE 210
World Association of Nuclear
    Operators 151
World Bank 216
World Energy Council 216
World Health Organisation
    171
World Peace Council 78
World Nuclear Reactors 224–5
Wormwood Scrubs 103

Würzburg University 10
Wylfa 143

Xenon-133 168
X-rays 1, 152
X-ray photography 85–6

Yalow, Rosalyn 170
Yankee 130
Yaizu 130
Yucca Mountain 204
Yelchischev, Oleksandr 190

Yom Kippur War 146
Yoyo 191
Yyttrium-90 168

ZEEP 146
ZEPHYR 149
ZEUS 149
Zeidses des Plantes, Bernard
    87
Zinc sulphide 54, 61, 90
Zircaloy 146
Zoë 145